ALSO BY DAMON LEE FOWLER

Dining at Monticello: In Good Taste and Abundance (editor)

Damon Lee Fowler's New Southern Kitchen:
Traditional Flavors for Contemporary Cooks

Fried Chicken:
The World's Best Recipes from Memphis to Milan, Buffalo to Bangkok

Beans, Greens, and Sweet Georgia Peaches:
The Southern Way of Cooking Fruits and Vegetables

Classical Southern Cooking:
A Celebration of the Cuisine of the Old South

DAMON LEE FOWLER

Photographs by Ann Stratton

DAMON LEE FOWLER'S NEW SOUTHERN BAKING

Classic Flavors for Today's Cook

SIMON & SCHUSTER
New York London Toronto Sydney

SIMON & SCHUSTER
Rockefeller Center
1230 Avenue of the Americas
New York, NY 10020

Copyright © 2005 by Damon Lee Fowler
Photography copyright © 2005 by Ann Stratton

Additional credits:
Jeffrey Tautrim, photo assistant
Michael Pederson, food stylist
Tracey Harlor, assistant food stylist
Betty Alfenito, prop stylist

SIMON & SCHUSTER and colophon are registered trademarks
of Simon & Schuster, Inc.

For information about special discounts for bulk purchases,
please contact Simon & Schuster Special Sales at 1-800-456-6798
or business@simonandschuster.com.

Designed by Katy Riegel

Manufactured in the United States of America

10   9   8   7   6   5   4   3   2   1

Library of Congress Cataloging-in-Publication Data

Fowler, Damon Lee.
    Damon Lee Fowler's new southern baking : classic flavors for today's cook / Damon Lee Fowler.
       p.   cm.
    Includes index.
    1. Baking.   2. Cookery, American—Southern style.   I. Title.
TX763.F58   2005
641.8'15'0975—dc22   2005051591

ISBN-13: 978-0-7432-5058-0
ISBN-10:   0-7432-5058-3

Acknowledgments

It is often said that writing is a lonely business, but that's either nonsense or else cookbook writing is an exception that proves the rule. Through the writing of half a dozen books, I have never felt alone. Indeed, my desk and my kitchen have always been crowded with what St. Paul called "a cloud of witnesses," sometimes actually, sometimes only in my imagination—which should probably worry me more than it does.

Possibly the most important material contributions to this present book have come from my friends Bonnie Carter, Melissa Emery, and Susan Todd who loaned me reliable ovens when I was ready to kick mine out of the window and into the next county. Bonnie, moreover, got me over my unnatural fear of pound cake, shared masterpieces of her own, and helped me bake through every version of that lovely staple appearing in this book.

Karen Barker, the best pastry and dessert chef I know, has, with her chef-husband, Ben, inspired me with beautiful cooking and the warmest of friendships. Her book *Sweet Stuff* has become my constant desk-side companion, and it has been a comfort to know that she has been no farther than one cheering phone call away. Likewise, author and fellow historian Greg Patent's wisdom, both firsthand and in his handsome book *Baking in America,* has helped me appreciate and reconstruct many nearly lost treasures.

What food writers and cooks did before Shirley Corriher, I have no idea. There are a lot of people purporting to be "food scientists" these days, but none who have a cook's passion mixed so intimately with a scientist's curious objectivity and the most generous of spirits. Even if she weren't a walking encyclopedia of the science of cooking and baking, I would still have lived for those calls in which Shirley would drawl "Oh no, baby—you're overbeating your egg whites—that's your problem," or some other pearl of wisdom, and then laugh like anything.

What I, personally and professionally, would have done without Nathalie Dupree is something I cannot at this point imagine. It was in large part her landmark book *New Southern Cooking* and its companion television series that inspired me to look back at the roots of Southern food, and, as we got to know one another, her gentle nudging helped turn that glance into a book and new profession. But even if she had meant nothing to me professionally, the constancy of a friendship that has spanned nearly two decades would be of immeasurable value.

Karen Hess has for nearly twenty years been my teacher, mentor, conscience, and friend. I may go for months at a time without talking to her, but her voice is always with me, especially when I am making bread. Needless to say, during this project her coaching has been steady, and her passion for, and knowledge of, good bread making is inextricably woven into these pages.

John Martin Taylor, who introduced me to Karen Hess and, with her, has been my historian's conscience, also introduced me to the joys of some of America's nearly lost historical breads, especially the rice bread of his beloved Charleston.

It could be said that my other mentor, Marcella Hazan, must have had little, directly, to do with a book on Southern baking, and yet, when I was discouraged and ready to give it all up, Marcella, with one stern look and a few spare words, let me know that quitting was not an option and renewed my commitment to see it through.

I am lucky to come from a family of good bakers—some of them far better at it than I, and I'd have been a proud fool indeed had I not taken advantage of their knowledge. The memory of my mother's and both grandmothers' breads, cakes, and pastries has helped maintain a high standard. My younger brother, Sidney, though a butcher by profession, makes the best biscuits in the family, and helped me through the kinks in the biscuit chapter of this book.

Lyn MacDonald and I met by chance, when she booked me to do a cooking demonstration for a community fund-raiser, but without her, one whole section of this book might never have happened: it was she who gave me my sourdough starter and coached me through its care and use. Now, whenever the tang of baking sourdough bread fills my kitchen, I see her brilliant smile and am warmed by her friendship. Another friend and bread baker, Rita Spitler, shared sourdough wisdom born of years of baking and wonderful sticky buns that were in part the inspiration for the sourdough sweet buns in this book.

The staff at E. Shaver, Booksellers not only sells more of my books than anybody but, once again, has been my tasting laboratory, objectively telling me when to go back to the kitchen and when to leave well enough alone.

Two of my closest friends in Savannah, Tim Hall and Alysa Smith, have also been steady and objective tasters and kept my morale up, and our friend Susan Jackson, an excellent baker in her own right, was close at hand with the loan of necessary equipment and advice.

Every writer needs a good editor, and throughout my career, I've been lucky to have had the best, from Erica Marcus on my first book, through Harriet Bell on the middle two and Mary Jane Park in my work as a journalist, to Janice Easton and Sydny Miner on *New Southern Kitchen.* I've learned from all of them, but it was Erica who first wanted me to write this book, and I eventually did write it mainly because I wanted to do it with Sydny, whose warm professional relationship and personal friendship I treasure.

Photographer Ann Stratton put together a team that produced the breathtakingly beautiful pictures in *New Southern Kitchen,* and managed to gather the same team for this book, creating pictures that are—if anything—even more beautiful.

As usual, last but by no means least, mid- and low-list writers like me often have trouble maintaining the loyalty, let alone interest, of their agents, but Elise and Arnold Goodman have been loyal champions and faithful friends.

Thank you and God bless you all!

Damon Lee Fowler

Contents

Preface

MAMA'S BREAD

They may be simple words, homey and even a little saccharin; yet nothing in all of Southern cooking is as powerfully evocative as the words "mama's bread." Whether it was a cloud-light biscuit that seemed almost to float apart as it was torn open, a delicate, butter-crusted company yeast roll, suave, elegant white bread, sliced thick for toast or wafer-thin for dainty reception sandwiches, or a lusty brown loaf of whole-meal, earthy with the spicy fragrance of molasses, the idea of bread made by our mother's hands is deeply rooted in our consciousness. It lingers in our memories, filling the imagination just as the warming aroma of toasting wheat and yeast once filled the house. The words have a power to beguile even those who have no actual memory of morning biscuits or still-hot yeast bread on cool autumn afternoons.

Perhaps there may be something in the aroma itself: when I was growing up in upstate South Carolina, the long route across the northern arc of the state to my grandmothers' houses in Anderson was punctuated by a bakery near the highway at Spartanburg. No matter how badly my brothers and I were behaving, my parents could always stave off or still a fight in the backseat by promising that we were near it, and as its aroma filled the car, they knew they could count on complete harmony for several miles to come. Even the baking aroma of that flaccid, spongy, sad excuse for loaf bread—so appropriately called "light bread" in the rural South to this day—had the power to still sibling arguments and stir bored appetites.

Yet there is something deeper and more complex than enticing aromas at work here.

When a mama's hands have worked the dough, shaped the roll or loaf, and dropped it, piping hot from the oven, into a cloth-lined basket, the deeply felt emotions behind the very word "mama" charge the aroma with that much more power—even for those who did not grow up with it. Southern novelist and essayist Lee Smith captured that power when she spoke in her soft, gentle drawl of her own mother's bread at the Southern Foodways Alliance's annual symposium in Oxford, Mississippi. Possessed of one of the South's most lucid and distinctive voices, she talked sweetly and poignantly of this bread, of how its baking filled the crisp fall air and met her at the door as she came home from school with the very essence of her mother's warmth and love. She went on to explain how, in baking the bread herself, she recaptures a little of that essence, and when she held up copies of the recipe, the old courtroom erupted like a feeding frenzy in a fish tank. Only a promise to publish the thing in the alliance's newsletter restored civilized order (and these were people who had just stuffed themselves with fresh hot biscuits). Part of that reaction may have been owed to a gifted novelist's way with words but, then again, is there any other aroma the mere idea of which is as evocative and rich with promise?

As this book matured from little more than an idea of what to do with the baking recipes left over from my first book, the one thing that stuck most in my own imagination was that moment in Oxford—and I began to notice how people reacted to the mere idea of their mama's bread.

Unhappily, mine is the last generation to grow up with such memories. Today most mothers work outside the home and spend those cool autumn afternoons shuttling budding soccer stars, junior Olympic gymnasts, and first-string cheerleaders. My own mother managed to bake often, even though her time was divided between her responsibility as principal of an elementary school and her duty to my father's ministry, but she was the exception to the rule.

A colleague once remarked that he was not worried about the future of biscuits; they were being kept alive by restaurants. It's true that in many regional dining rooms, a basket of fluffy biscuits on the table has become standard fare, and every fast-food diner in the Southeast offers them by the sackful. My own nephew, in fact, became a master at turning out such biscuits at his part-time college job. But even if they could touch the goodness of home-baked bread—and they rarely do—I would hate the idea of my nieces and nephews slipping into misty-eyed eloquence about fast-food biscuits. I'd hope they'd be recalling their grandmothers' biscuits and yeast rolls, or their father's and mother's—or even those of their odd old uncle. But more than anything, I like to think that someday their own children will be remembering bread made by their hands.

Throughout these pages are recipes for such breads, both from my own collection of surrogate mamas and grandmothers and from all the people who shared the memory of the embracing warmth of their own mama's bread with those misty eyes and watering mouths. All they require of you is a little time; what they give back may not be fully measured for a generation, but they will not be measured at all unless you take them into the kitchen, roll up your sleeves, and brave getting a little flour in your hair.

Get in there and make some memories of your own.

Lee Smith's Mama's Loaf Bread

This is the bread that Lee described so poignantly at the Oxford symposium. It turns out that her mama's bread is nothing more than a variation on the enriched "French" rolls found on page 308, but for Lee, and for the people who shared her memories that afternoon, the fact that her bread was not unique did not—and never will—matter.

This delicate, yet robustly flavored loaf is very satisfying eating with or without the nostalgia—fresh from the oven, toasted the next day, or as the base for French toast once it passes its prime. Also, like most of the enriched doughs in the yeast bread chapter, it makes very nice rolls. It will yield about three dozen, depending on the shape.

Makes two 9-inch loaves

¼ teaspoon active dry yeast or ½-ounce cake compressed fresh yeast
¼ cup lukewarm water
2½ cups whole milk
3 tablespoons sugar
1 teaspoon salt
¼ cup (4 tablespoons) lard, butter, shortening, or oil
2 large eggs, well beaten
40 ounces (about 8 cups) unbleached all-purpose flour
About 2 tablespoons unsalted butter, softened

1. Dissolve the yeast in the water and reserve; let it proof 10 minutes. Put the milk, sugar, salt, and lard or other fat in a heavy-bottomed saucepan over medium heat. Bring it almost to the boil, remove it from the heat, and pour it into a large mixing bowl. Let it cool until lukewarm (less than 110°F), and stir in the eggs and yeast. Gradually stir in the flour (about 6 cups) until the dough is too stiff to stir, then turn it out onto a floured work surface and work in the remaining flour until the dough is no longer sticky. Knead it lightly for 2 to 3 minutes—just until the dough is uniform—then clean the mixing bowl and return the dough to it, cover with a damp double-folded towel or plastic wrap, and leave it in a warm, draft-free spot to rise until it has doubled in volume, about 4 to 6 hours.

2. Turn the dough out onto a lightly floured work surface, punch it down, and knead until it is elastic and smooth, about 8 minutes. Lightly grease two 9-inch loaf pans, divide the dough in half and shape it into loaves. Place the dough in the pans and cover them with a double-folded damp cloth. Let rise until doubled and clearing the tops of the pans, about 2 to 4 hours.

3. Position a rack in the center of the oven and preheat it to 350°F. Bake the loaves for about 35 to 40 minutes, or until well browned and hollow sounding when thumped. Turn the loaves out of the pans onto a wire cooling rack, generously butter the tops while still hot, and let them cool on the rack.

DAMON LEE FOWLER'S NEW SOUTHERN BAKING

Introduction

The Southern Baker's Art in Legend and Practice

They are the stuff of legend: steaming-hot, fresh-from-the oven biscuits, crusty wheels of skillet-baked cornbread, and a lacy-edged flatbread with arguably the most enigmatic name ever devised—the "hoecake"; that equally celebrated litany of pies from chess to pecan to lemon meringue; those dense, satisfying pound cakes and delicate layer cakes with rich striations of caramel, coconut, fudge, Lemon Curd (page 201), and butter-cream; the crisp hush puppies and apple pies hot from the frying pan; the biscuit short-cakes filled with ripe strawberries or peaches and clouds of whipped cream. And that is only scratching a rather obvious surface. Many regions in America have similar specialties worth celebrating, some of them even mirroring those from the South, but nowhere else do they seem to transcend the flour, butter, and sugar that made them, becoming as es-sential to living as water and air, as inextricably woven into the cultural identity of the re-gion as sweet tea, fried chicken, and grits.

Behind all that baking is an equally powerful legend, the mythic Southern mama. Up to her elbows in flour and smelling vaguely of vanilla and lemon, her cakes were always moist and delicate, her pastries tender and flaky, her yeast rolls and biscuits airy, delicate, and meltingly tender—and there was a perpetual supply of them pouring forth from her kitchen in a steady, fragrant stream. Well. If this woman ever really existed, she has van-ished beneath her own legend, and today's bakers no longer have her hand to guide them. Yet the flavor of her legacy is still fresh on the tongues of modern Southerners, and hap-pily, much of the baking that was the foundation of that legend is not merely a memory, wispy and insubstantially glued to our consciousness by bakery-made and instant-mix imitations. Many traditional bakers may have shed that flour-dusted grandmotherly image, but they still wield their magic, and new generations are beginning to recover the pleasures of home baking.

But where did that mythic baking mama come from? To some extent, she was real. Southern baking is founded, nurtured, and grounded in the home hearth. Sustained by a largely agrarian economy, the South remained a rural culture until modern life, having long since overtaken the rest of the country, began to catch up with it in the middle of the twentieth century. Except in its port cities and few inland urban centers—where commerce still centered around farm trade—bakeries were mostly not a viable undertaking, and where they did exist, many families that had once been sustained on home-baked bread out of necessity continued to prefer it even though the need had vanished.

Baking, therefore, continued to be home-based in the South long after it was more or less relegated to professionals in other parts of the country, and the responsibility for the daily bread rested squarely on the shoulders of the housewife. The root meaning of "lady," that word so highly prized in the South as a mark of grace and good breeding, is literally "the bread giver." Even in wealthy Southern households where an African-American cook ruled the kitchen, the daily bread was the mistress's responsibility and she took that responsibility seriously, sometimes to the point of rolling up her silk sleeves and doing much of the baking herself.

This is probably the reason that, unlike the rest of Southern cooking, which changed drastically in the hands of those African cooks, baking changed the least. A glance at historical cookbooks and other written records confirms that Southern baking strayed little from its European roots. That eventually those equally legendary African-American cooks excelled at baking to the extent that they have made such celebrated classics as the fried and griddle-baked breads that had counterparts in Africa, as well as sour cream pound cake, sweet potato custard pie, and biscuits their own, clearly indicates that upper-class mistresses cannot have done all or even most of the baking. But that they tended to take more ownership of the baking and supervised it more closely cannot be denied. That said, of course, it would be naïve and irresponsible to ignore the African expertise at baking.

The overriding European influence in the South, as it was for the rest of the country, continued to be the English: Anglo culture dominated the Eastern seaboard from the eighteenth century onward and pushed its way westward with the nation's steady expansion in the nineteenth century. But the English were hardly the only influential European community, nor was the baking untouched by continental Europe: long before it found its way into American kitchens, there had been strong German and French influences on English cookery in general and on its baking in particular. There were also pockets of German and French Protestant settlers, from the Salzburger Lutherans and French Huguenots in Savannah and Charleston to the Moravians of North Carolina's Old Salem. Each in turn had something to contribute, some of which—Carolina's famed Moravian spice wafer cookies being a good example—have survived to this day. In the twentieth century, a wave of Greek settlers pushed across the Deep South, becoming restaurateurs that changed the very face of the South's meat-and-three diners and left in their wake an abiding affection for phyllo pastries and moussaka. Mexican migrant workers and settlers pushing north and east from Texas planted tortillas and tamales that have taken root in some pretty unlikely places and at the hands of some equally unlikely cooks.

Another element in the mix is Native Americans, those for whom North America had been home for centuries before the Europeans landed. Pushed out of the way and largely ignored in the written history of American culture, these peoples nonetheless had their own contribution to make, even though their hot-stone and ash-baked cornmeal cakes had European and African parallels.

All that said, the main theme of Southern baking, as it was for Southern cooking, remains a duet between white, mostly Anglo, European, and black African descendants. It is a complex melody with many themes that Southern Americans are only beginning to live with comfortably, let alone understand, particularly since "white," "black," "European," and "African" each represent not a single theme, but a collection of dozens. What we are beginning to learn is that its music can't be unraveled, for without each part the melody is incomplete. Does one call the hot-water cornbread that I learned to make from the hands of an African-American cook a Native American or African hot-stone bread or a northern European griddlecake? Would it be what it is without any of those elements? Of course not. Likewise, it is not in any way diminished by not having come from a "pure" bloodline—whatever that is. Its strength and beauty, like so much of the South's rich jazz, blues, country, and gospel music traditions, lies in its blending. It is a music that is far more beautiful for the fact that more than one voice is singing.

ABOUT THE RECIPES

Every cookbook can be described in many ways, as a collection of short stories or perhaps a novel composed of episodes that stand on their own, for each recipe tells a story within itself, and in turn, lends an element to a larger one. This particular collection was chosen deliberately with the telling of that bigger, more complex story of Southern baking at the heart of each selection. There are historical recipes that have been halfway (or completely) forgotten over time, telling of its beginnings and early blending, and there are new ideas that tell of the continuing evolution. There are stories whispering both of grace in the face of poverty and elegance born of plenty, and there are classic standards that have endured, virtually unchanged by the ravages of centuries.

Of necessity, the collection speaks broadly—sometimes generalizing, sometimes with less illuminating detail than I'd have liked, but as novelist Dori Sanders is fond of saying, every story has to have boundaries or it would never make sense, if, indeed, it got told at all. Many classics survive intact in the modern Southern bakers' repertory or differ very little from their counterparts in other regions; their story is repeated in virtually every book on Southern or American cooking. Still others are stories that I have told before. Unless I really thought I had something to add, I've left those for others to tell—even a few that are personal favorites. There is little point, for example, in giving you yet another lemon meringue pie recipe when there are hundreds of good ones in print, and I think I've told all that needs telling of my own fruitcake in other books, even though it pains me to make a baking book without it. Instead, I prefer to take the space and time that I have here to tell of other lemon pies and of Aunt Margaret's Fresh Apple Pound Cake (page 168). There was a time when a book such as this would be considered incomplete without the vast family of boiled, steamed, and baked puddings, but today they're rarely made in home kitchens and are actually more within the realm of cook than baker. Their story will have to wait.

With each telling, these stories have grown richer and more meaningful for me. I have never tired of them, and more than two decades of sharing in the enriching tales of other cultures has only made me appreciate them all the more. In sharing them with you, I hope not only to draw you in and make my own heritage a part of yours, but to inspire you likewise to embrace and celebrate your own.

Damon Lee Fowler
Savannah, Georgia
October 2004

Southern Baking Essentials

FOR THE MOST PART, a Southern baker's needs are not much different from those of any other baker. If you are well stocked for baking in general, you are mostly ready to tackle any of the recipes in this book. There are a few special regional ingredients that may not be commonplace in all parts of the country, but none that are so exotic that you should have any trouble finding them no matter where you live. This section is (at least for a mouth like mine) relatively brief. Rather than getting into a detailed discussion of every single thing required, it seemed more sensible to put that information where you will need it, with the pertinent recipes. There are, however, a few general things that are specific and pretty much universal to almost all Southern baking, so here are a few pertinent notes on those ingredients and their place in the Southern baker's pantry.

FLOUR, OR A TALE OF TWO WHEATS

Until the mid-nineteenth century, most of the wheat grown in colonial and early republican America was soft winter wheat, so-called because it was generally planted in the fall. The soft grain was easily milled by water-powered millstones and preferred both for its texture and flavor. After the invention of the steel-roller mill in the middle of the nineteenth century and the opening of the Midwestern plains, however, soft winter wheat began to be displaced by hard red summer wheat (planted in the spring). Though too hard and tough for stone milling, red wheat was ideal for roll milling and flourished in the growing conditions of the open plains. Actually, what distinguishes these related grains from one another is less when they are planted than their density and protein content: red summer wheat is higher in protein and gluten than soft winter wheat. Eventually, this made it the preferred grain for bread making, especially commercially baked bread, in part because high-gluten flour makes stronger dough that rises higher and faster, and also because it was tough enough to withstand the heavy handling of commercial baking equipment.

Soft-winter-wheat flour did not, of course, just disappear: its low-gluten content is ideal for pastry and quickbread, where glutens are the enemy of the baker. It isn't gluten free, of course, and popular wisdom aside, the glutens that it does contain are high quality, and this flour actually makes pretty good yeast bread: it is, after all, the wheat that European and early American bakers used for centuries. Its first rise may not be as fast as hard wheat flour, but when properly kneaded, it makes a fine, even loaf, and if you are interested in reproducing a historical bread, it is the only flour to use. Be aware, however, that soft wheat weighs slightly less than an equal volume of hard wheat, and hard wheat has a higher moisture absorption rate, so if you are planning to use soft-wheat flour in a recipe that calls for "bread flour," you'll need to add a bit more flour.

Here is a little more about each type of flour and what to expect from it.

BREAD FLOUR: This is flour made up from high-protein hard red wheat. It is coarser than soft-wheat flour, feeling almost grainy in your fingers, and when you squeeze a handful, it will not hold the shape but will crumble when you release it. Today, it is not usually bleached (a chemical and sometimes natural process of whitening the flour), but check the bag to make sure. Bread flour will work fine for any yeast bread, but scant measure it if you are using a recipe that calls for "all-purpose" flour. It is not suitable for quickbread, pastry, or cakes. Because soft-wheat flour is more flavorful than hard wheat, when I'm using bread flour, I throw in a handful of whole-wheat pastry flour to give the flour an added boost of flavor and a little more character from the added bit of bran. There are two advantages to hard-wheat flour: it will rise more, making a lighter loaf, and because it has a high absorption rate, it holds moisture and the loaf will not go stale as quickly as soft-wheat bread.

ALL-PURPOSE FLOUR: A blend of both soft- and hard-wheat flours, this is the most common flour in our markets. The soft- and hard-wheat proportions vary from brand to brand, and in the South, may tend to have a higher proportion of soft than hard wheat. Elsewhere, it may be the other way around. This regional difference can make it tricky to use but it will, in general, make acceptable bread. Use only unbleached flour, and when baking yeast bread with it, add a handful of whole-wheat pastry flour for flavor and character.

SOUTHERN SOFT-WHEAT FLOUR: Soft-wheat flour is as soft as its name implies, silky, fine-textured, and smooth under your fingers, and when squeezed will actually hold the impression of your fingers. In the South, except when it is labeled pastry flour, most bags of soft-wheat flour are sold as "all-purpose," which means only that the flour is not self-rising (see below). All the same, even though it may be labeled "pastry" flour, it does make pretty good yeast bread—if it has not been bleached. Unfortunately, most of the regional brands are, since many home cooks prefer bleached flour for cakes and pies. Check the bag to make sure you are not getting self-rising flour.

SELF-RISING FLOUR: This is flour premixed with baking powder and salt for use in quickbreads. Most of these flours are made from either soft-wheat flour or an all-purpose blend. I don't use self-rising flour because it is impossible to regulate the amount of leavening, it tends to leave a harsh, metallic aftertaste in baked goods, and the fact that it has leavening already mixed into it limits its usefulness. Self-rising flour can't be used in yeast breads or most pastries. I'd much rather take the extra little step of measuring in the baking powder, soda, and salt when I need it. If you choose to stock it, buy it only in small quantities, use it quickly, and be sure to store it in a carefully sealed container, since the leavening agents go stale quickly. If it gets mixed up with your other flour, a good sniff should tell you which flour is self-rising, since the sharp smell of the baking powder is quite distinct.

FINDING SOFT-WHEAT FLOUR: Southern brands of soft-wheat flour are not nationally available, except in some specialty grocers and kitchenware stores. I used to steadfastly maintain that Texas was as much a part of the South as Georgia, but began to have my doubts upon discovering that soft-wheat flour was virtually unheard of in Dallas. If you live in Dallas—or outside the South, it is good to know that the flour is the same as plain pastry flour. Don't confuse "soft-wheat" with "whole-wheat" just because the word "wheat" is in there: whole-wheat pastry flour is available in natural food groceries and some supermarkets. It will no doubt work in these recipes, but the bran and germ in it alter the whole structure of the dough and won't produce the same delicacy of flavor and texture. Whole-wheat piecrust, for example, is very brittle and susceptible to tearing.

WHERE TO GET QUALITY SOFT-WHEAT FLOUR: Here are several reliable sources.

White Lily Foods
P.O. Box 871
Knoxville, TN 37901
(800) 264-5459
www.whitelily.com

Martha White Foods
200 Butler Drive
Murfreesboro, TN 37133
(800) 663-6317
www.marthawhite.com

King Arthur Flour Company
The Baker's Catalogue

P.O. Box 876
Norwich, VT 05055
(800) 827-6836
www.kingarthurflour.com
Ask for pastry flour.

OTHER GRAINS AND DRY GOODS

RICE FLOUR: Once commonplace in the rice-growing regions of Carolina and Georgia, this flour faded from use after the rice industry collapsed in the early twentieth century, but a few of the breads it contained remain in the Lowcountry repertory, and still others are making a comeback. For those recipes, use fine white rice flour, available at most natural food, Latin, and Asian markets.

CORN FLOUR: Corn flour is finely ground cornmeal, coarser than cornstarch but finer than regular cornmeal—roughly the same texture as semolina flour. You can usually find it in Latin markets and some well-stocked supermarkets.

CORNMEAL: For the most authentic and traditional Southern flavor, use stone-ground white cornmeal. For more on cornmeal, see Chapter 2 (page 30). Good-quality cornmeal is becoming more widely available.

WHERE TO GET GOOD-QUALITY CORNMEAL: Here are a few sources if you have trouble finding it.

Anson Mills
(Meal and grits from heirloom corn and Carolina-grown rice)
(803) 256-2463
www.AnsonMills.com

Hoppin' John's
(John Martin Taylor's celebrated cookbook store on-line, for high-quality stone-ground cornmeal and grits)

(800) 828-4412
www.hoppinjohns.com

Old Mill of Guilford
Box 623, Route 1
Oak Ridge, NC 27310
(336) 643-4783
www.oldmillofguilford.com

BAKING POWDER: Not all baking powders were and are created equal. The earliest form was single-acting powder, which means it worked through only a single, liquid-activated chemical reaction between an acid and an alkali—usually cream of tartar and baking soda. Double-acting powder works through two reactions: the first, just like single-acting powder, is liquid-activated; the second is heat-activated, causing a second rising in the oven.

The recipes in this book were tested with double-acting powder and it works fine as long as it is not overused. Look for an aluminum-free brand such as Rumford for the best results and flavor. Where the amount will make a difference, I've also included an alternative amount for single-acting powder (in quickbreads and some sweets, more of it is required). If you are baking a historical recipe, single-acting baking powder is the one that will give you the most authentic results, and a few traditional cooks believe it is better-tasting because it doesn't leave behind the chemical aftertaste that they claim they can detect from double-acting powder. It is no longer manufactured commercially, but is easy enough to make at home and a recipe follows. It is not as strong as modern double-acting powder, so if you are substituting it in a modern recipe that was formulated with double-acting powder (i.e., one that has been developed within the last forty years) use roughly a third more single-acting powder than called for.

Regardless of which type you are using, always give the container a shake before you open it and measure out the powder: that which is on the very top of the can goes stale more quickly from having had more exposure to air, so shaking it up ensures that you'll get an even dose of potent powder.

Single-Acting Baking Powder

This does not keep well, so don't make it in any larger quantity than you will use in a month.

Makes 1/2 cup

3 tablespoons cream of tartar, available in many markets and drugstores
2 tablespoons bicarbonate of soda (baking soda)
3 tablespoons rice flour, cornstarch, or unbleached all-purpose flour

1. Combine all the ingredients in an airtight container and shake until thoroughly mixed.
2. Store it tightly covered and away from moisture and always shake the container before spooning out the powder.

SUGAR AND OTHER SWEETENERS

Granulated Sugar: Most Southern cooks use only pure cane sugar. Though all refined sugars are the same chemically, we still think cane sugar has the edge in flavor and texture. Aside from regular refined white sugar, several varieties of cane products are called for in this book and are indispensable in a Southern pantry.

Powdered Sugar: Powdered sugar is available to us mostly in two grades, 4X and 10X. American powdered sugars all contain small amounts of cornstarch as an anticaking agent. Unfortunately, when it is used in an uncooked frosting such as buttercream or as a dusted topping, the cornstarch can lend an unpleasantly pasty, raw aftertaste. To get around that drawback, some bakers use either superfine sugar or have developed partially cooked frostings.

Superfine Sugar: Superfine sugar is close to the texture of American 4X powdered sugar, except that it doesn't contain cornstarch. It's ideal for finishing many baked goods with a dusting of sugar because it doesn't have that pasty raw taste of cornstarch that some find objectionable. It's rarely available in regular supermarkets: look for it in specialty grocers, professional baking supply houses, or by mail order from catalogs such as King Arthur Flour Company's *The Baker's Catalogue* (see page 10).

If you can't get it, you can pulverize regular granulated sugar with a mortar and pestle or with a food processor. Process it about a cup at a time as follows: fit the work bowl with the steel blade, put in the sugar, and cover the bowl. Drape a kitchen towel over it to contain the sugar dust and process for about 3 to 4 minutes. Sift it through a fine wire mesh sieve for even texture.

TURBINADO OR "RAW" SUGAR: This type of sugar has been only partially refined, so its color is naturally blond to light brown and it has a distinctive, but delicate flavor. When I first started writing about food, it was a hard-to-get rarity for many home cooks, but thanks to the gourmet coffee craze, it's even common in most supermarkets. It looks something like commercial brown sugar, but the crystals are larger and less damp. Since they do not react in quite the same way in cooking, the two are not quite interchangeable, though sometimes they substitute for one another without a problem; if that's the case, the recipe will say so.

BROWN SUGAR: Unlike Turbinado or "raw" sugar, both light and dark commercial brown sugars are fully refined white sugar mixed with molasses. I use light brown sugar almost exclusively and it's what I used to test all these recipes. If you are in the middle of a recipe and find that you only have the dark brown variety on hand, you don't have to drop everything and go to the store: just substitute regular granulated sugar for about a third to half of its volume measure and it will be exactly the same as light brown sugar.

MOLASSES: Molasses is real sugar in the raw—the stage in its refinement between raw cane juice and crystallization. Use pure, unsulfured molasses.

SORGHUM SYRUP: Sorghum is an African grass related to sugarcane. During the War Between the States, it became a common substitute for imported cane sugar, and has been popular in the South ever since. It doesn't taste quite the same but it is pretty much interchangeable with molasses and there are many Southern cooks who prefer it.

HONEY: There are literally hundreds of regional varieties of honey available, and they're growing apace as more boutique producers take an interest in beekeeping. There are several Southern varieties that I like to use—orange blossom honey from Florida, tupelo blossom honey from the Deep South, and dense, flavorful sourwood blossom honey from the Appalachian Mountains of Georgia, the Carolinas, and Virginia. However, I tend to think that locally produced honey gives the most interesting results in baking, so experiment with a local honey until you find one that you prefer.

DAIRY PRODUCTS

BUTTERMILK: Originally, buttermilk was the liquid by-product from making butter. Lightly soured whole milk or cream was churned until the fat separated from the liquid and milk solids. That leftover liquid with its lightly curdled solids was true buttermilk. It was far less perishable than fresh milk, and could be kept for a long time in a springhouse in the days before refrigeration made prolonged storage of fresh milk possible. Consequently, buttermilk came to replace fresh milk in much of America's baking, especially in the South, where the added heat and humidity made keeping fresh milk far more difficult than in cooler climates. But buttermilk is much more than a mere substitute born of necessity: it lends tenderness to the crumb of breads and cakes, enhances the leavening action of baking soda and powder, and gives bread a distinctive flavor that most Southerners have not only grown accustomed to, but love.

Unfortunately, real buttermilk is no longer available, unless, of course, you make your own butter—and who does? Commercial buttermilk is made from whole or skimmed pasteurized milk that has been treated with cultures to make it sour. Sometimes thickeners and emulsifiers are added for texture, especially when the product has been made from skimmed milk. Whole-milk buttermilk will give better results in these recipes, because the flavor of milk that is soured with the fat still present is smoother and fuller. Skimmed milk produces an unpleasantly sharp-tasting product. Moreover, most whole-milk buttermilk does not contain thickeners, whereas skimmed or low-fat ones usually do.

Commercial whole-milk buttermilk will work fine in all these recipes, but for truly exceptional results, the better choice is a plain, all-natural whole-milk yogurt—preferably an unhomogenized product from an organic dairy. The reason to look for this kind of yogurt is not only for quality's sake: these yogurts usually don't have any thickeners added to them, and because they are made with milk that has not been homogenized, the fat mostly settles to the top of the carton and is easily skimmed away. Brown Cow, Stonyfield Farms, and Seven Stars Dairy are a few excellent nationally available brands (mostly at natural food and other specialty grocers). The flavor of these yogurts comes closer to true buttermilk because they were cultured and soured while the fat was still present.

To use yogurt as a buttermilk substitute, it will have to be thinned: some of its water content has been evaporated, and it is usually far too thick to use as is. There's no set proportion: thickness varies from brand to brand. Just stir in milk or water until the yogurt is the consistency of buttermilk.

Using Buttermilk and Yogurt in the Recipes: When using commercial buttermilk, remember that it is almost always salted. Taste it first to determine how salty it is and adjust the salt in the recipe—in some cases, you may want to just leave out salt altogether. Since yogurt is not salted, keep that in mind when you are substituting yogurt for commercial buttermilk in a recipe; you may have to add a little more salt than the recipe calls for. The recipes in this book were tested with both commercial buttermilk and yogurt, and will tell you where to adjust the salt, but you should still taste your brand of buttermilk to determine how much adjustment to make, since the amount of salt included will vary.

Fresh Milk: Though buttermilk was and still is the staple of many Southern pantries, fresh milk (often called "sweet" milk to differentiate it from sour buttermilk) is still essential to baking. Use the freshest whole milk you can find—and don't substitute skimmed milk unless the recipe says it is safe to do so.

Butter: There's not much to say about butter except to use the best-quality unsalted butter that you can get. Most baked goods, even cakes and cookies, will contain a little salt by design, but it's almost always less than the amount contained in salted butter. The unsalted variety makes the salt content much easier to control, but it also helps ensure better flavor, since salt can partly cover the taste of inferior butter. In baking, however, flavor is not the only consideration. Unlike lard, bacon drippings, suet, and similarly rendered animal fats, butter is fat extracted from a liquid, and even the finest grades will have a little liquid—anywhere from 5 to as much as 20 percent. In general, however, the better the quality the lower the moisture content. Most European butter has less moisture than American butter, except for a very few regional premium brands from small specialty dairies. Experience helps most bakers work around variable moisture in the fat, but even they can have trouble with it in pastries and quickbreads.

CREAM: Cream is a common ingredient in cakes, pies, and other pastries, but it is also an occasional and lovely addition to bread. Most cream that is available outside the restaurant supply industry is loosely graded like this: heavy cream or heavy whipping cream, usually minimum 36 percent milkfat; "whipping" cream, by law minimum 30 percent milkfat, but seldom more than 32 to 34 percent; coffee cream, also called "light" cream, falls somewhere between half-and-half and whipping cream—where seems to depend on the dairy; and cultured sour cream, which is usually no more than 24 percent and often as little as 16 percent milkfat. In the recipes, "heavy" is used for cream with a minimum 36 percent milkfat, "whipping" for 30 to 34 percent milkfat, and "light" for less than 30 percent. Use the best quality you can get, preferably not ultrapasteurized, and never even think of using so-called "low-fat" cream or sour cream, which are full of God knows what to give them a consistency like cream. They will not react in baking in at all the same way as real cream.

EGGS: Unless a recipe says otherwise, Grade-A large eggs are intended. Use the freshest eggs you can get: the fresher the eggs, the better the results in baking, especially with cakes. I use eggs laid by organically fed hens from a local farm, both because they taste better and because buying locally is one way to be sure that they're reasonably fresh. But to reassure new bakers, I tested all these recipes with supermarket eggs and got perfectly acceptable results.

Eggs perform best in baking if they are not cold, so always let them sit at room temperature for at least 30 minutes before using them. Some bakers insist that eggs separate more easily when they are cold. I can't tell enough difference to worry about it, but if you want to separate them while they're cold, do so and then cover their separate bowls and let them come up to room temperature. Don't leave them sitting out for more than half an hour once they're separated. If you've forgotten to take them out ahead of time and are in a hurry, let them sit completely covered in hot tap water for 1 minute before breaking them.

NUTS, MEAT PRODUCTS, AND OTHER PERISHABLES

PECANS AND OTHER NUTS: The most frequently used nuts in this book are pecans, a nut indigenous to the South and, therefore, less expensive in our region than elsewhere in the country. They are not, however, the only nuts used by Southern bakers. Traditionally, we've long made use of almonds, hazelnuts, walnuts, and that little subterranean legume that poses as a nut—the peanut. Today, the list is extended to include all kinds of exotica, from cashews to macadamias. All nuts have a high fat content and, therefore, turn rancid easily, but pecans and walnuts are especially susceptible: buy them from a vendor who properly stores them (in a cool, preferably dark place) and has a high turnover. If you use them up quickly, store them at home in a cool, dark place (in a hot, humid climate, that would be the refrigerator); for long-term storage, the freezer is best. Double bag them and squeeze out all the air to prevent freezer burn and keep out strong odors (the fat of nuts absorbs flavor-affecting odors more easily than other foods).

In all the recipes, it's taken for granted that the nuts are already shelled and picked clean of any of the bitter inner shell (especially found in pecans and walnuts). When it says "whole" almonds, I mean the whole, shelled nutmeat, brown skin on. Pecan or walnut meats are in two lobes that connect at the top of the nut; "whole," in their case, means one whole lobe. Pecans and walnuts that are sold shelled are, of course, already divided.

In most of the recipes of this book, the nuts are given a light toasting to intensify their flavor and to keep them from becoming flabby and flat tasting in a high-moisture bread or cake. Here's how to do it.

Toasted Pecans

Almonds, hazelnuts, and walnuts may also be toasted using this method.

Makes 1 pound

1 pound pecans

1. Position a rack in the center to upper third of the oven and preheat the oven to 375°F. Spread the nuts on a rimmed baking sheet in one layer.

2. Toast the nuts, stirring occasionally, until fragrant and just beginning to color, about 10 minutes. Watch them carefully and keep in mind that in most recipes, they'll undergo further cooking, so don't overdo them or they'll taste sharp and bitter.

DRY-SALT-CURED PORK AND PORK FAT

What's in a name? Apparently, a lot. One of the primary foundations of the Southern kitchen is one that people tend to go a little goofy over: salt-cured pork and lard—pure rendered pork fat. It's as integral to Chinese and Italian cooking as it is to Southern cooking, but people don't go quite as nutty about the pig when its nationality is Asian or Italian. In my cooking classes, I can add pancetta and prosciutto to the pot until the cows come home—and not one person will so much as blink—but if I call it ham or bacon, gasps of disapproval are inevitable. And the word "lard" will send them right over the edge every time.

The role of pork and its fat in the traditional Southern baker's pantry is not as large as it is in the stew pot, but it's still an important one. Whether it's ham, bacon, or sausage added for flavor and texture, or drippings and lard added as shortening, part of the pig's sacrifice can be found in everything from quickbreads and savory pastries to sweet pastries and cakes. It is true that lard contains both cholesterol and saturated fat but actually less than you'll find in butter, and it has none of the even more harmful trans fats caused by hydrogenation (which makes vegetable shortening and margarine solid at room temperature). More to the point, its flavors are large and distinctive: a little will go a long way, so you don't have to use much to get a maximum of flavor.

Here are a few notes on the types of pork you'll need:

DRY-SALT-CURED PORK: Lean-streaked pork side meat, known regionally as "streak-of-lean," is similar to breakfast bacon but is never cured with sugar or smoked, so it's closer to Italian pancetta. It's used in a few quickbreads and when fried until golden brown and crumbled, it can be used as a fairly good substitute for cracklings. It's not to be confused with "fatback" (sometimes called "white meat" in old recipes), which is a solid salted chunk of pure back fat with the skin (or rind) still attached.

"Old," Dry-Cured, or Country Ham: Most American ham is brine-cured (that is, cured by soaking it in a liquid salt and sugar solution), but dry-cured country ham is made in much the same way as prosciutto, except that it is usually smoked and prosciutto usually is not. Country ham is sometimes added chopped or ground to cornbread, cocktail biscuits, or quick muffins (see Savory Virginia Ham Muffins, page 50), but otherwise isn't really much used in baking. Mostly it's just sliced wafer-thin and stuffed into a biscuit, a combination that is unsurpassed.

Smoked Bacon: Identical to breakfast bacon, this is what I mean by "bacon" in the recipes that follow. It's occasionally used in quickbreads, especially cornbread, and in a few savory pastries, but it, like ham, most often turns up fried crisp and tucked into a biscuit. Use thick-sliced, preferably dry-cured bacon.

Where to Get Cured-Pork Products: Exceptional, traditionally cured hams, bacon, and sausages are available from:

S. Wallace Edwards & Sons, Inc.
P.O. Box 25
Surrey, VA 23883
(800) 222-4267
www.virginiatraditions.com

Drippings and Lard: Drippings, the fat rendered from cured pork or bacon, are most often used as fat for sautéing, but occasionally they are used as shortening in biscuits, cornbread, and occasionally yeast breads. They are also a common griddle-lubricating fat for hoecakes and griddlecakes. Because they're rendered from cured meat by frying it, drippings are full of cooking residues and trace solids, and have a distinctive flavor for which there's no real substitute. Lard, on the other hand, is slowly rendered from fresh pork fat, the finest of which comes from the grainy leaf fat found around the kidneys and saddle of the belly. It's not to be confused with what the French and Italians call lard—which is not rendered but is in solid pieces similar to fatback (see Dry-Salt-Cured Pork, page 19). Lard is still the best shortening for biscuits and can't be equaled for light, tender pastry.

Unfortunately, much of the commercially packed lard available today is treated with the same preservatives as vegetable shortening and is sometimes even partially hydrogenated to stabilize it at room temperature. Look for minimally processed lard without additives. It's often kept in the meat cooler of a supermarket. If the package has an expiration date printed on it, be sure it's still several months ahead. The package should be clean, dry, and not discolored or greasy-looking. If it's not sealed (though most of them today are), take a look inside: fresh lard is creamy white with a faint but pleasantly porky smell.

The best way to be sure of quality is to render your own, a side benefit of which is a ready supply of excellent cracklings, the flavorful brown nuggets that give so much character to bread. Though more and more butchers are getting processed pigs and not the whole animal, a few of them will still sell you fresh pork fat if you ask for it ahead of time. You will get about a pound of lard for every 1¼ to 1½ pounds of fat.

To Render Fresh Lard

Makes about 3 pounds

4 pounds pork fat, preferably leaf fat

1. Cut the fat into ½-inch cubes and wash it thoroughly in cold water. Press out the washing water and put the fat in a large, deep kettle with a heavy bottom, such as a cast-iron Dutch oven or a heavy stockpot. Turn the heat to medium and bring the fat to a good simmer. Let it cook until all the lingering traces of water have evaporated and the fat begins to melt from the solid tissues.

2. Reduce the heat to low and cook until the fat is completely rendered from the solids, checking the pot frequently: don't leave the pot unattended at this point or it could easily overheat and start to burn, at best ruining your batch of lard and at worst creating an unpleasant exercise in fire extinguishing. You will easily recognize when the lard is ready, as the solid tissue will sink to the bottom and start to brown. After that, cook the lard just long enough for the cracklings to turn golden brown (if you are using leaf fat, the cracklings will crisp, but back fat will not, so use color as your gauge). Remove the kettle from the heat and lift out the cracklings with a wire frying skimmer or slotted

spoon. Spread them to drain on brown paper or paper towels. Let the melted fat cool enough to handle safely (it should still be liquid), and carefully pour it into metal or heatproof glass containers. Cool it completely before sealing it, and store it in the refrigerator. Properly sealed, this should keep for a couple of months. Lard does not take well to freezing, since fat won't really freeze at the temperatures of most home freezers, and it easily absorbs freezer odors. Always use a clean stainless-steel utensil to scoop the lard out of its storage container to keep it from picking up things that might make it spoil sooner.

OTHER FATS

OLIVE OIL: This staple of the Mediterranean kitchen is not as commonplace in traditional Southern baking as it is in other cuisines; in fact, to be strictly honest one would have to say that it was practically nonexistent in the Southern baker's pantry of the past. But as good oil becomes increasingly available, good bakers are finding ways to use it in our traditional baking. For the few recipes in this book that call for it, use an extra-virgin olive oil that you like the taste of, since, in almost every case, the reason for using this particular fat in the recipe is flavor.

VEGETABLE OIL: The most common of these fats are extracted from coconuts, canola, corn, soybeans, palms, and peanuts. In the baker's pantry, they are mostly used for frying pastries and some quickbreads and as the fat in enriched yeast breads. Less often, but occasionally, they turn up in pastries, quickbreads, and cakes. For frying, I prefer peanut oil because of its high burning temperature, but if you or anyone who you will be feeding is allergic to peanuts any pure oil that you prefer will generally work fine. For pastries and cakes, you'll want to use an oil that is pretty much flavorless.

VEGETABLE SHORTENING: This is vegetable fat that is hydrogenated and emulsified so that its normally fluid state will be solid like animal fat at room temperature. There are recent health concerns about it and I find in most cases it is inferior to lard and butter, but because it is virtually flavorless, it is occasionally useful when the flavor of the fat would be intrusive. If you are not able to use lard, a little vegetable shortening helps tenderize pastry and gives lightness to cakes or cookies that are not butter-based.

MARGARINE: I have nothing to say about this stuff except that I neither use it nor recommend it.

OTHER ANIMAL FATS: Suet (beef fat), rendered duck and goose fat, and, occasionally, rendered chicken fat are all used in pastries. Duck and goose fat are often recommended as a substitute for lard for those who do not eat pork. Suet is available from most butchers and some supermarkets. Poultry fat is mostly rendered at home in much the same way as lard (page 21).

SPICES, EXTRACTS, AND OTHER AROMATICS

VANILLA: This may be the single most commonly used spice in the American baker's pantry. Though it was once expensive and rare, today it's almost commonplace—so commonplace that many home bakers tend to use way too much of the stuff, and in many cakes and pastries where it does not, quite frankly, belong. Rarely is vanilla meant to steal the show: most of the time it is supposed to stay in the background, blending with but not dominating the other flavors.

Master pastry chef Karen Barker makes me feel a little guilty about vanilla, because she is very particular about using the best-quality fresh beans to get maximum flavor in her baked goods and other desserts. I rarely use whole beans, except to make my own extract—the one thing that I do get very particular about. Unless some angel brings me back one of the small, perfume-sized bottles of premium vanilla extract from Mexico (Mexican vanilla is far more aromatic and flavorful than any other, but until recently, its commercial importation was forbidden by the USDA), I prefer to use my own extract, made from the best beans I can get my hands on and a good-quality, well-aged bourbon. Here is how I do it.

Homemade Bourbon Vanilla

This homemade extract is by contrast more flavorful than most commercial extracts and yet subtler; it can be used more liberally than commercial extract because it is not as harsh. Once you start making it, you'll never go back. It keeps indefinitely—as you use it, just replace the amount with an equal volume of bourbon. My batch at this writing is four years old and, had I not been working on this book, might've lasted me another two years. If you bake often and find you need a larger quantity, the recipe increases easily, allowing a whole vanilla bean for every 2 ounces (¼ cup) of alcohol. I prefer the flavor that bourbon lends to the extract, but if you prefer, you may use vodka or brandy—mind, I don't know why you'd want to, but you may.

Makes 4 ounces (½ cup)

2 whole, imported vanilla beans
4 ounces (½ cup) bourbon

1. With a sharp knife, split the beans in half lengthwise, and cut across into three equal pieces. Reserve any seeds that fall out; they're important to the flavor.

2. Put the beans and any stray seeds into a glass jar fitted with a tight lid. Pour the bourborn over them, tightly screw on the lid, and shake well. Set it aside in a cool, dark cupboard that you use frequently and shake it well every day for 2 weeks before using it. When you use the extract, replace the amount you took away with an equal amount of bourbon until you can tell from the aroma and taste that the extract is losing its potency, then use it up, discard the beans, and make a fresh batch.

OTHER SPICES: The only spices that I'm manic about grating fresh are nutmeg and gingerroot, but all of them contain volatile oils that begin to evaporate the instant they're exposed to the air, and benefit from being freshly grated or ground. Microplanes do a very good job of grating large spices such as stick cinnamon, fresh gingerroot, and nutmeg; grind small seeds like allspice, cloves, cardamom, and pepper in a mortar and pestle, an electric spice mill, or a coffee grinder that is used exclusively for that purpose.

I won't go into a long discussion of each spice here, but it will be useful for bakers with access to Middle-Eastern and Asian markets to know that the cinnamon sold in most Western markets, both the hard stick form and ground powder, is actually cassia—a bark spice that has a similar but more powerful aroma and flavor than true cinnamon. The real thing is often sold in ethnic markets: the sticks are delicate and papery, far more crumbly than cassia, and the flavor is correspondingly delicate. It isn't quite a one to one substitution. I used standard supermarket (that is, cassia) cinnamon to test all these recipes, so if you use true cinnamon, you may find that you'll need a little more than is called for.

BOURBON: Marcella Hazan once wrote that, in her entire career as a cook, she had never been without real Parmigiano-Reggiano cheese: what I'm never without is a bottle of this most Southern of whiskeys. It's such a common ingredient in much of my cooking and baking that my mostly Baptist family has had a field day with my affection for it. Needless to say, cooking with it is not the same as drinking it, but never mind. Bourbon is no mere substitute for brandy or other liquor: it lends a smooth richness to the flavor that even the best cognac can't match. By law, bourbon is any whiskey that is made from mash that is at least 51 percent corn, but within the industry, and among regional connoisseurs, "bourbon" is whiskey made only in Bourbon County, Kentucky, a distinction that Jack Daniel's honors by calling its brand "Tennessee whiskey." In cooking and baking, any good Southern whiskey will do but—as Elizabeth David and Julia Child advised about cooking with wine—don't waste a premium sipping whiskey on a cake or pie, and don't use one that you can't drink, only one you might not care to drink.

ON EQUIPMENT

There is little point in giving you a long list of tools and equipment. A Southern baker's equipment needs are no different from any other's—the usual whisks, mixers, spatulas, measuring cups and spoons, pastry cutters, rolling pins, roomy mixing bowls, and the best-quality bakeware that you can afford. For the most part, heavy and substantial pans cook more evenly and give better crust color than thin, bright pans. But while all of those things help ensure good results, they are not essential: most of the time a resourceful baker can substitute tools and bakeware and hand-mix a batter when a machine is not available. There is one piece of equipment, however, that is all-important—and that's your oven. If it isn't reliable, no amount of expertise in the mixing will save you from failure. You'll also need a good relationship with that oven if you want to be a good baker, so if it's not the best one in the world and you can't afford to replace it, learn to love it as it is. Here are a few tricks that will make that easier to manage.

Preparing the Oven

When my first cookbook on antebellum Southern cookery was published, a woman came up to me in a bookstore and happily chirped, "I think cooking has really come into its own in the last fifty years." Didn't I agree? Well, no, I did not. "Oh, but with reliable ovens and such!" she exclaimed. Reliable ovens: would that she was right. Unfortunately, most of us don't have any such thing, and the historical ovens that poor lady thought so unreliable, having been refined over thousands of years, were and are just about the most perfect baking chambers ever devised.

Before the advent of metal stoves fired by gas or electricity all baking was done either in a wood-fired domed brick oven—exactly like the currently fashionable wood-fired pizza ovens—or in a deep iron Dutch oven. The brick oven was heated by building a fire directly on its floor. When the masonry floor and walls were superheated, the coals were swept out of the oven or, if the chamber was large enough, pushed to one side. The low conductivity of the clay made it possible, once it was heated, for it to hold the heat and radiate it evenly out into the chamber. There are no hot and cold spots in an oven like that. In fact, it's so perfect that professional bakers, who know better than to reinvent the wheel, often use a similar arrangement fired with gas or electricity instead of wood.

Only wealthy households and professional bakers had such ovens. A few settlements had communal brick ovens, but most households depended on a Dutch oven for routine, everyday baking. It wasn't quite like the Dutch oven pots in our cookware sets today: made of thick cast iron, it stood on spiked legs and sported a deep-rimmed lid so that hot coals could be spread both beneath and on top of it. Iron is almost as poor a conductor as clay: it slowly absorbs heat and holds it, radiating it in the same even way as a brick oven. If you knew what to look for—and those old bakers did—these ovens were very reliable indeed. Even the cast-iron range that replaced it, with its thick iron walls, did a better job of baking than our modern ranges.

Unhappily, modern range ovens—sometimes even the wildly expensive ones—are not nearly as reliable as either one of those devices. Their thin, steel walls don't heat evenly or hold the heat for any length of time, and their roomy chambers can be drafty. The result is often uneven hot and cool spots. They cannot in any way approximate the heat-retaining properties of a brick or iron oven. To imitate the old brick ovens and even out my very temperamental range oven, I have settled on a compromise that uses a pizza baking stone or unglazed terra-cotta tiles.

You will need a ceramic baking stone, available at many cooking stores and through such catalogs as *The Baker's Catalogue, Williams-Sonoma, Sur la Table,* or *The Wooden Spoon.* Get the largest and thickest one you can find, preferably a wide rectangular one instead of a round one. If you can't find a baking stone of those dimensions, unglazed terra-cotta tiles make a good substitute. Scrub them with detergent and let them dry completely before using them. Line a rimmed cookie sheet with the tiles and use them as you would the stone. You will also need a wood baker's peel (often sold as a kit with the stone) or other flat, sturdy tool for sliding the bread into the oven. A rimless cookie sheet or sturdy piece of cardboard makes a good substitute for a peel.

Position a rack to its lowest position in the cold oven and place the baking stone or sheet of tiles on it. Turn on the oven and preheat it for at least half an hour. Never put the stone into an oven that is already hot (this could cause it to break), and always allow plenty of time for it to heat completely. Likewise, if you need to take it out of the oven, let it cool completely before doing so. To even out an especially erratic electric oven chamber, some experts recommend putting the stone directly onto the heating coil, thereby creating an even, radiant heat that rises from the floor of the oven. They then use the racks conventionally. I find it is almost as effective lifted a little above the heating element; that gives me room to spray the oven floor with water when I need supplemental steam. Besides, putting a dead weight on the coil does not seem like a good idea. I bake directly on the stone, but if you often bake on the rack or use both racks in your oven (or if it only has one rack), extra racks can be bought from an appliance dealer.

To create the supplemental steam needed for baking yeast bread that the old domed chambers trapped naturally, put a little water in a clean spray bottle and spray the oven floor, or put a rimmed metal pie plate or pan on the floor of the oven and toss about ¼ cup of water into it after you have placed the bread on the stone. Be careful not to throw large amounts of cold water directly on the stone or heating element, which could break the stone and change the element.

If you have an especially uneven oven like mine, leave the stone in it all the time, taking it out only to do high-temperature roasting. You'll find that almost everything bakes more evenly sitting directly on the heated stone. When I first started this book, I took mine out and tried to test bake these recipes conventionally, but my oven was so wildly uneven that, after being tempted to fling more than one fallen cake and soggy-bottomed pie against the wall, I put the thing back and it has been there ever since.

Regulating and Measuring Temperature

Oven thermostats are a lot like first dates: full of promise and loaded with uncertainties. They can be (and often are) off by anything from 25° to 75°F. I've learned to adjust my thermostat, compensating for its irregularities after using a hanging oven thermometer to measure the difference between the setting and actual temperature at the oven's center, but Shirley Corriher, the doyenne of kitchen chemistry, recommended a much better system to me that employs the baking stone and an instant-read probe thermometer with an outside digital register. She clamps the probe directly onto her stone, measuring the temperature of the actual baking surface rather than the uneven ambient air of the chamber. Not only does this measure the really important temperature, it also prevents heat loss from opening the door to check the thermometer. Even digital probes can be a little off, so check it in boiling water (it should read exactly 212°F) and then adjust your oven setting accordingly. When preheating the oven, rely on the temperature of the stone over the thermostatic temperature, since the ambient air will heat much faster than the stone itself, and if the stone has not been perfectly heated, it will slow down the baking.

Convection Baking

Convection ovens overcome some of the worst drawbacks of modern range ovens, evening out the temperature and compensating for the lack of even radiant heat. They usually bake a little faster than a conventional range oven. I don't own one, but did bake some of these recipes using a friend's oven—just enough to know that they are terrific. If you bake with convection, follow the manufacturer's guidelines for adjusting the baking times, since they can speed it up by as much as 10 to 15 minutes.

Quickbreads— The Southern Staple

WHETHER YOU WERE BORN and bred down South or have never been anywhere near the place, chances are, when the words "Southern cooking" meet your ears, the two images most likely to be conjured are fried chicken and biscuits. It isn't surprising: our take on the world's favorite way to cook a bird is justly famous, and biscuits, featherlight and piping hot, whether from the home bread basket or from practically every corner fast-food takeout in our region, are an icon of gracious Southern hospitality, a touchstone for many a homesick traveler, and the hallmark of everything that is good about the Southern table.

Yes, everyone knows about Southern biscuits, but what they may not know is that there is no single such thing. Celebrated Southern food writer James Villas recorded more than a hundred recipes in his book *Biscuit Bliss,* and only scratched the surface of this many-faceted family of quickbreads. The reality is that there are almost as many kinds of biscuits in the South as there are cooks. Most of them fall into three basic types: rolled and cut, drop, and hand-shaped (or "cat head" biscuits), but within those three categories are hundreds of permutations.

So commonplace has this bread become that most people presume that biscuits have always been a part of the Southern table, as old and immovable as the hills. Not so. They've only been around for about 200 years—not all that long in the larger scheme of things. Chemical leavenings of one sort or another—baking powder, bicarbonate of soda, and other bicarbonates (such as pearl ash, saleratus, sal volatile)—have been around at least since the eighteenth century and historians believe that Native American cooks used a form of chemical leavening that was a by-product of making lye from hardwood and oyster shell ashes. But such leavenings didn't become commonplace in American baking until the early nineteenth century, and even then did not dominate our bread making till much later in the century.

Well into my own living memory, biscuits were never seen on the dinner table, nor would any self-respecting hostess ever have dreamed of putting them there. This was bread for breakfast and supper or, stuffed with ham, a picnic. Rarely were they to be found on the family dinner table, and never when there was company: only yeast-leavened, or, as we used to call it, "light" bread was considered really nice enough for dinner. Today, however, biscuits are standard fare for virtually every meal in the South, appearing with great respectability on formal dinner tables from elegant homes to white-cloth restaurants, and Southern home bakers take great pride in serving up lighter-than-air biscuits to company no matter what the time of day or occasion.

Cornbread, our region's other distinctive quickbread, is, on the other hand, truly ancient and the most thoroughly American of all breads. Native Americans made a form of cornmeal ash cakes (bread baked in banked hot ashes) and probably a kind of griddlecake baked on hot stones, which hungry European settlers were quick to adapt into their diets. Over time, those of European descent began adding their own imported enrichments: soured cow's milk, chicken eggs, rendered pig fat, and sometimes even wheat flour. But even with these added refinements, cornbread, like biscuits, remained largely humble fare—good enough for the family table but not quite nice enough for high company.

Today cornbread has, like biscuits, come to know no social barriers and appears at virtually any occasion on the best tables of the land.

Of all the breads that are enjoyed in the South today, cornbread is probably the one that has been the most altered by time. Once—and not all that long ago—I could have said with reasonable authority that you would never, ever find two things in Southern cornbread: wheat flour and sugar. Most of the time, one could also take for granted that the bread would be made from white cornmeal and buttermilk. But while today there are many hard-core Southerners who still call bread made with yellow meal and/or with sugar and wheat flour "Yankee cornbread," the line has been considerably blurred. There are as many who would call themselves hard-core who find cornbread without sugar and flour too rough and bland for their tastes. For my own taste, however, I still prefer the toothsome, savory bite of traditional cornbread without those additions. The soft, spongy texture and added sweetness make it more like cake than bread—less interesting to bite into, and far less compatible with the other flavors in the meal. I am not, however, prepared to sit in judgment of those who happen to like their cornbread soft and sweet. Still, they won't get anything like that at my table.

THE ART OF THE SOUTHERN BISCUIT, OR "GETTING YOUR HAND IN"

Like most things in this life, biscuit making comes naturally only to those rare individuals who prove the rule. For the rest of us, it requires practice to get it right, and still more practice to get past merely "right" to perfection. Not that there is anything especially complicated about biscuit making; like all skills, it is easy once you get the feel of it. Southern food maven Nathalie Dupree puts it into perspective in her comparison to perfecting a golf game: a novice golfer rarely pronounces failure after his first (usually bad) game and throws his expensive clubs into a lagoon, yet when the very first try at biscuits or piecrust produces equally unimpressive results, he's all too ready to pronounce it impossible and throw in his pastry blender.

The business of practicing until you have the feel of a good dough in your fingers is colloquially known as "getting your hand in." It only sounds like voodoo magic: it's nothing more than a simple way of learning the feel of the dough, which is the only sure way to judge when a dough is a good one—whether it is for biscuits, piecrust, yeast bread, or pasta. Practice is the only way to "get your hand," but happily, bread making can be relaxing and therapeutic, requiring no special technique or finesse, and the raw material is not expensive. If you mess up, it's no big deal—just try again until you get it right. What I've tried to do here is take as much guesswork out of learning the feel of a good dough as possible. If it's your first try, I want to make it as simple and accessible for you as I can. If you are an experienced biscuit maker, I hope this will help you better understand what happens in the mixing bowl, the rolling board, and the oven.

Here are the essential elements of good biscuit making.

A LIGHT HAND: The first thing required of biscuit making, as with all pastry, is a light touch. Rough, heavy handling produces tough, heavy biscuits. Without getting too deep into the structure of flour, which is discussed in more detail elsewhere in this book (see Yeast Bread Basics, page 286), all flour contains a protein known as gluten, which activates and forms itself into interlocking chains when the dough is stretched and kneaded. This is what gives a yeast-leavened dough the tensile strength it needs to trap and hold the gas thrown off by the yeast, thereby causing the dough to rise. But what is great for trapping those gas bubbles in yeast dough actually has the opposite effect on a chemically leavened one. Because the chemical rise is instantaneous, it is actually hampered by tensile strength within the dough; those glutens hold the leavening down and lock tightly to one another in the baking, compressing the leaven and causing the dough to rise unevenly. That's why it's important to work the dickens out of yeast dough but barely handle biscuit dough. You'll want to work it just enough to make it hold together and ensure an even distribution of the ingredients, and that's all.

A LIGHT FLOUR: The next thing you need is the right kind of flour—which is the light kind. For the best biscuits and other quickbreads, Southern bakers prefer flour milled from soft winter wheat (the same kind of wheat used for national brands of pastry and cake flour). The advantage of this low-gluten flour is discussed in Chapter 1 (page 8) but to recap: the less gluten, the less likely the baker is to have tough quickbreads or pastries from overworked dough. It is possible to make perfectly good biscuits with a national brand of all-purpose flour: all it needs is a little more care in the mixing and handling, so if soft-wheat flour is not available where you live, you can certainly use all-purpose flour. Soft-wheat flour is also available by mail order (see pages 10–11).

A Light Leavening: Perhaps the most common baking mistake for novice bakers is over-leavening: they are afraid that the bread won't rise or rely on an old recipe without taking into account that today's leavening agents are not the same as even half a century ago. Active dry yeast and double-acting baking powder are not equal one-to-one substitutes for the old bakers' yeast, homemade yeast, and single-acting baking powder of the past. Both are stronger than their historical counterparts, and overusing them will have a negative impact on the quality and flavor of the baked goods. The mistake is less pronounced in yeast bread—too much active dry yeast speeds up the rising time and the texture does not develop as well, but the worst it will do to the bread is lend a heavy, slightly sour, yeasty aftertaste. Overusing baking powder, however, does nothing to speed up rising, since it will happen instantly regardless, and can, in fact, make the dough rise too much, resulting in an insubstantial, puffy texture and harsh, metallic aftertaste. For more about baking powder and other chemical leavenings that are used in biscuits, see page 12.

Balanced Moisture: In general, the more "wet" or soft the dough, the lighter the biscuits will be—up to a point; tip the balance of liquid to dry ingredients beyond that point and the bread will turn out soggy and heavy. The best and only way to be sure of the moisture content is by feel, which is why you must do the mixing by hand. The key to balancing the moisture content in the dough lies in understanding that the moisture within the flour itself will vary from bag to bag—and from batch to batch within the same bag, even when the flour is kept in a well-sealed container. There are several variables: the amount the grain contains to begin with, the amount remaining after milling and/or absorbed by the flour before it is bagged, the amount that is absorbed (or lost) through the bag in transit and storage, and finally, in storage in your kitchen at home. That is why most of the biscuit recipes give both a weight and cup measure for the flour (weight is by far the more reliable way of measuring) and a flexible amount of liquid in the ingredients. Sometimes the flour will be pretty moist already—in which case it will weigh more and will also tend to absorb less liquid in the mixing. Sometimes it will be dry and thirsty, in which case it will be lighter and will drink up all the moisture it can.

This is the other place that "getting your hand in" comes into play. Not only did the light touch aid traditional bakers, it also helped them measure out the right proportions of liquid to dry ingredients. Good traditional bakers don't bother to weigh the flour when making bread: they volume measure the liquid ingredient and adjust the proportions by feel, adding flour until the dough is no longer sticky and wet and yet still soft enough for a light, tender crumb. This kind of measuring is exactly what you should hope to get within your fingers for all your bread making—but until you can get it, weight measuring the dry ingredients is by far the more foolproof.

A QUICK OVEN: This cozy if old-fashioned way of describing the right oven temperature for baking quickbreads says far more to the baker than mere degrees on a thermostat—be it Fahrenheit or Celsius. Calibrations vary from oven to oven and their thermostats are rarely all that accurate. Even if they were, most domestic ovens are subject to uneven heat and have hot and cold spots. Because I have never quite gotten the feel of a quick and slow oven in my senses, every move to a new kitchen produces a series of baking flops—crisp biscuits with over-browned bottoms, sad-streaked pound cakes, yeast breads that don't have the right balance of crustiness and lightness of crumb, fruitcakes whose bottom gets too dark—even though I always check the thermostat's accuracy with an oven thermometer. My younger brother is an experienced biscuit maker (and, hands down, the best in our family), yet he recently began having trouble with bread that was turning out heavy and tough until he realized that his oven was running slow: the bread was baking at too low a temperature.

Give yourself time to know your oven and to get accustomed to its individual quirks and virtues. A quick way to judge its accuracy is to test it with an oven thermometer that you know to be accurate, but the only way to find the setting that is exactly right for your quickbreads is by practicing. After a few batches you will know where to set the thermostat and position the oven rack for the best results. If you can manage, in the process, to get the feel in your hand and face of a "quick," "moderate," and "slow" oven from the heat that radiates out the door, you will find that it is far more useful to you than a mechanical gauge and will serve you well in any kitchen.

Another good way to even out an inconsistent oven is to use a baking stone, even for quickbreads, pastries, and cakes. Using the baking stone is discussed on page 27. Note that it works best in the lower third of the oven—closer to the bottom heating element—so if you are using the baking stone, always put it on the bottom-most position and disregard the positioning of the rack that is called for in the individual recipes.

Southern Breakfast Biscuits

If you've never made biscuits before, or the biscuits you have tried to make have been—let's just say less than successful, please read "Getting Your Hand In" (see page 31) before you begin. Biscuits are not hard to make once you get the knack of it, but they do take practice. The recipe that follows uses a folding technique that does two important things for the bread: it ensures an even distribution of moisture in the dough and introduces even, flaky layers that give the biscuit height and make it easier to tear open. It is not the same as kneading, and requires as light a hand as possible.

Makes 12 biscuits

10 ounces (about 2 cups) Southern soft-wheat flour (see page 9), pastry flour, or unbleached all-purpose flour

3 teaspoons Single-Acting Baking Powder (page 13) or 2 teaspoons double-acting

1 teaspoon salt

4 tablespoons chilled lard

About 1 cup whole-milk buttermilk or plain whole-milk yogurt thinned with milk to buttermilk consistency

1. Position a rack in the center of the oven and preheat it to 450°F. Sift the flour, baking powder, and salt into a mixing bowl. Add the lard and cut it in with a pastry blender, fork, or two knives until it is the texture of very small peas. Do not overblend—small lumps of shortening are what make biscuits flaky.

2. Make a well in the center of the dry ingredients and pour in ¾ cup of the milk or yogurt (you may not need quite all of it—ambient humidity and the moisture of content of each bag of flour will vary virtually every time you make bread). Mix with as few strokes as possible until the dough clumps together and pulls away from the sides of the bowl, adding more milk by spoonfuls until all the dry ingredients are incorporated into a dough that is no longer crumbly.

3. Turn the dough out onto a lightly floured work surface and pat it flat (about 1 inch

thick). Fold it in half and pat flat again. Repeat this twice more, then lightly flour the surface and roll or pat it out ½ inch thick. Using a sharp, round 2-inch biscuit cutter dipped in flour before each cut, cut the dough straight down without twisting the cutter, into twelve biscuits. When you are cutting at the edges of the dough, be sure that there is a cut side all the way around the biscuits or they won't rise evenly. You will have scraps of dough left over and you don't want to waste them. They can be reworked if you use extra care. Gather the scraps together, lightly fold the dough over itself, and pat flat about three times—until the scraps just hold together. Then pat—don't roll—the dough until it is ½ inch thick and cut it into biscuits. Put the biscuits on an ungreased baking sheet and bake until they are risen and golden brown, about 8 to 10 minutes. Serve piping hot.

Old Chickahominy House Biscuits for Virginia Ham

For half a century, the Old Chickahominy House in Williamsburg, Virginia, has been celebrated for its honest, simple, and deeply traditional breakfast and luncheon fare. Their signature bread is the ultimate ham biscuit—delicately thin and generously stuffed with paper-thin shavings of the finest Virginia ham, which, for more than half a century, has been supplied by S. Wallace Edwards and Sons of nearby Surrey, Virginia (see page 20). The dough formula and initial mixing varies little from a standard biscuit; the significant difference lies in how the bread is finished. Instead of the familiar thick-rolled, round-cut shape, Chickahominy's specially trained biscuit makers roll them out almost to the thinness of a piecrust and cut them into generous squares. The rolling takes some finesse to get the hang of, and you may need to make several batches before you are satisfied, but, like any biscuit, it is less a matter of skill than practice.

Makes about 12 to 14 biscuits

10 ounces (about 2 cups) Southern soft-wheat flour (see page 9), pastry flour, or unbleached all-purpose flour

3½ teaspoons Single-Acting Baking Powder (page 13) or 2½ teaspoons double-acting

½ teaspoon baking soda

Salt

4 tablespoons chilled lard

About 1 cup whole-milk buttermilk or plain whole-milk yogurt thinned with milk to buttermilk consistency

1. Position a rack in the upper third of the oven and preheat the oven to 425°F. Sift or whisk together the flour, baking powder, baking soda, and a pinch of salt (taste the buttermilk first: if it is salty already—as many commercial brands are—you won't need much, and the biscuits should be a little bland as a foil for the salty ham). Cut in the lard until the mixture resembles coarse meal.

2. Make a well in the center and add ¾ cup of milk. Mix lightly just until a cohesive dough forms, adding milk by the spoonful as needed to form a soft but not wet dough.

3. Turn the dough out onto a floured work surface and lightly work it until the dough is smooth and even—no more than half a minute. Scrape the work surface clean, dust it with flour, and roll the dough out almost as thin as a piecrust, a little more than ⅛ inch, but not quite ¼ inch thick. Cut the dough into equal 2½-inch squares. You may lightly rework the scraps. Lay the biscuits on an ungreased baking sheet, and bake until they are golden, about 10 to 12 minutes. Serve split and stuffed with thinly sliced Virginia ham.

AHEAD-OF-TIME NOTE: Most biscuits don't really take too kindly to being reheated, but at the Chickahominy, the biscuits are made ahead and taken from the oven before they are completely browned. Just before splitting and stuffing them to order, the cooks run them briefly under the broiler to finish the coloring and reheat them.

Cat Head Biscuits

There are many folk explanations for the name of these biscuits, but the most likely candidate is the one that maintains that the smooth, round rolls resemble a fat cat's head. This is the bread that my grandmother made until she discovered canned biscuits and lost her "hand" forever. Happily, they have survived in the practiced hands of Southern cooks like Nora Williford in Wilson, North Carolina, whom I once watched deftly turn out batch after perfect batch—from start to piping-hot finish—in less than 15 minutes.

The ingredients and first mixing step of this recipe—and the baking—are virtually the same as the previous one: the primary difference lies in the amount of liquid they require and in the final mixing and shaping.

Makes about 12 biscuits

10 ounces (about 2 cups) Southern soft-wheat flour (see page 9), pastry flour, or unbleached all-purpose flour
3 teaspoons Single-Acting Baking Powder (page 13) or 2 teaspoons double-acting
1 teaspoon salt
4 tablespoons chilled lard
About 1 cup whole-milk buttermilk or plain whole-milk yogurt thinned with milk to buttermilk consistency

1. Position a rack in the upper third of the oven and preheat it to 450°F. Sift the flour, baking powder, and salt into a mixing bowl. Add the lard and cut it in with a pastry blender, fork, or two knives until it is the texture of very small peas.

2. Make a well in the center of the dry ingredients and pour in ¾ cup of the milk. Mix with as few strokes as possible until the dough clumps together and pulls away from the sides of the bowl, adding more milk by spoonfuls until all the dry ingredients are incorporated into a dough that is no longer crumbly. The dough should be a little wetter than that for cut biscuits, but not sticky.

3. Lightly flour your hands and scoop up a heaping 2-tablespoon-sized lump of

dough. Quickly and gently roll it with your hands into a smooth round. The dough should be quite soft—if it seems too firm, work a little more liquid into the remaining dough. After a couple of batches you will know exactly how the dough should feel. Place the biscuit in a 10-inch round or 9-inch square pan and lightly flatten the top with the back of your knuckles.

4. Repeat with the remaining dough, putting each biscuit into the pan so that it lightly touches the other biscuits. When they touch, they "climb" against one another as they rise and expand in the baking for a lighter, higher, and fluffier biscuit with tender, soft edges. Some cooks prefer not to let them touch at all and bake the biscuits on a baking sheet. The choice is yours, but you may want to try them touching first (that will help cover any deficiencies in your mixing). Bake for 10 to 12 minutes for touching biscuits or 8 to 10 minutes for separated ones—until golden brown.

Sour Cream Cheddar Drop Biscuits

Drop biscuits are just about the easiest ones for novices to master. They require very little handling, so there's also very little chance of overworking the dough, and they are the most forgiving of an imperfect balance of moisture. These are doubly easy since, unlike most drop biscuits, there's no shortening to cut in: it's all contained in the liquid.

Makes 12 biscuits

10 ounces (about 2 cups) Southern soft-wheat flour (see page 9), pastry flour, or unbleached all-purpose flour

3 teaspoons Single-Acting Baking Powder (page 13) or 2 teaspoons double-acting

1 teaspoon salt

1 cup (about 4 ounces) shredded sharp cheddar

1 cup sour cream

2 to 4 tablespoons whole-milk buttermilk, or plain whole-milk yogurt thinned with milk to buttermilk consistency, as needed (see step 2)

1. Position a rack in the upper third of the oven and preheat it to 450°F. Lightly grease a 9 × 3-inch baking sheet with butter, lard, or shortening and set it aside. Sift the flour, baking powder, and salt into a mixing bowl. Add the cheese and toss until it is evenly distributed and lightly coated.

2. Make a well in the center and add the sour cream and 2 teaspoons of the buttermilk. Quickly and gently work it into the flour mixture, using as few strokes as possible. The dough will be firm, but not crumbly. Work in a spoonful or so more of the buttermilk as needed until the dough holds together. Drop the dough in heaping 2-tablespoon-sized mounds onto the prepared baking sheet, spacing them about an inch apart, and bake until the biscuits are risen and golden, about 8 to 10 minutes.

Savannah Cream Biscuits

Despite the image that its name evokes, heavy cream makes light, delicate bread. These vener-able biscuits, which have a long history in Savannah, are very delicate, indeed, and as simple to make as they are delicate. Their crumb is a fine foil for ham, jam, or—for that matter—just about any sweet or savory filling. Cut very small, they are the ideal cocktail biscuit for savory and spicy fillings—and you know that Savannahians love anything involving a cocktail.

Makes 12 to 16 biscuits

8½ ounces (about 1¾ cups) Southern soft-wheat flour (see page 9), pastry flour, or
    unbleached all-purpose flour
3 teaspoons Single-Acting Baking Powder (page 13) or 2 teaspoons double-acting
1 teaspoon salt
1 cup heavy cream

1. Position a rack in the upper third of the oven and preheat it to 450°F. Sift the flour, baking powder, and salt into a mixing bowl.

2. In a separate bowl, whip the cream until it is quite thick and beginning to peak but not stiff. Fold the cream into the flour mixture until it is thoroughly combined.

3. Turn the dough out onto a lightly floured work surface and pat it out 1 inch thick. Fold it in half, pat flat, and repeat twice more. Lightly flour the dough and surface and roll or pat it out ¼ inch thick. Using a plain or decorative biscuit cutter (1½ to 2 inches round) dipped in flour before each cut, cut without twisting into 12 to 16 biscuits, depending on the size of the cutter. The scraps may be lightly reworked and cut into biscuits (see step 3 of Southern Breakfast Biscuits, page 35). Put the biscuits on an ungreased baking sheet and bake until risen and golden brown, about 8 to 10 minutes. Serve piping hot.

Sage and Olive Oil Biscuits

Perhaps the one thing that most changed American cooking during the last quarter of the twentieth century, especially in the South, was the increased availability of—and interest in cooking with—quality olive oil. As cooks began experimenting with cuisines based on oil, it inevitably began to creep into more traditional regional dishes. My mother has made her biscuits with olive oil for at least twenty years. These biscuits follow her idea, combining two of my favorite breakfast breads—her biscuits and Genoese focaccia perfumed with sage. In a way, they encapsulate my whole career as a cook, which has always been a haphazard mixture of Deep South subtlety and deeply Mediterranean sass.

Try these stuffed with shaved country ham, thick slices of applewood-smoked bacon, or sizzling-hot patties of breakfast sausage for a breakfast biscuit you won't forget any time soon.

Makes 12 biscuits

10 ounces (about 2 cups) Southern soft-wheat flour (see page 9), pastry flour, or
    unbleached all-purpose flour
3 teaspoons Single-Acting Baking Powder (page 13) or 2 teaspoons double-acting
1 teaspoon salt
1 tablespoon chopped fresh sage or 1 teaspoon crumbled dried sage
4 to 5 tablespoons extra-virgin olive oil
¾ to 1 cup whole-milk buttermilk or plain whole-milk yogurt thinned with milk to
    buttermilk consistency
About 1 teaspoon coarse sea salt

1. Position a rack in the upper third center of the oven and preheat the oven to 450°F. Sift together the flour, baking powder, and salt into a mixing bowl. Add the sage and toss until well mixed. Stir 3 tablespoons of the olive oil into ¾ cup of buttermilk or diluted yogurt.

2. Make a well in the center of the flour and pour in the olive oil–buttermilk mixture. Mix with as few strokes as possible until the dough clumps together and pulls away from

the sides of the bowl, adding more milk by the spoonful until all the dry ingredients are incorporated and the dough is no longer crumbly. You may need as much as a cup—as with traditional biscuits, a lot depends on the moisture content of the flour and the humidity of the day.

3. Turn the dough out onto a lightly floured work surface and pat it flat (about ½ inch thick). Fold it in half and pat it flat again. Repeat this five or six times, then lightly flour the surface and pat it out into a ½-inch-thick rectangle. Using a sharp knife dipped in flour before each cut, trim the edges of the dough so that all of the edges are cut, then cut the dough straight down into 2-inch-square biscuits. You will have scraps of dough left over, which can be reworked with extra care. Gather the scraps and lightly fold the dough over itself and pat flat about three times—until the scraps just hold together, then pat it out to a ½-inch-thick rectangle and cut as before. Put the biscuits on an ungreased baking sheet and gently dimple the surface with your fingers. Brush the biscuits with the remaining oil and sprinkle them lightly with the coarse sea salt. Bake until they are risen and golden brown, about 7 to 10 minutes. Serve piping hot.

Bacon and Cracked Pepper Biscuits

Bacon short biscuits were the studied pride of Miss Laurie LeGrand, the most unusual and eccentric neighbor I've ever known—and in a town like Savannah, I've known my share. Her legal name was Mrs. Laurie Campbell, but she didn't like to talk about that part of her life and steadfastly held on to her maiden name. Every election, she ran for president on her own ticket—the National Maturity Party—which had, so far as we know, only one member—Laurie. She was also possessed of an amazing patience, even fondness, for the call girls who worked the edges of our transitional neighborhood. Of all her eccentricities, I guess it isn't surprising that the one I remember best involved food: her deep and abiding affection for very dry martinis and almost anything that contained bacon fat, both of which, in her opinion, were major food groups.

Laurie went on to her reward before she shared her recipe, so this is the closest I have been able to get to it with guesswork. With plenty of the good bacon fat and less leavening than the other recipes that precede them on these pages, these crisp, flaky morsels are my tribute both to her and my other favorite fallen belles: Jill Conner Browne and her troupe of Sweet Potato Queens in Jackson, Mississippi, who equally love bacon-fat and, I think, would have made Laurie their high-priestess—if only they had known her.

Makes about 12 to 16 biscuits

10 ounces (about 2 cups) Southern soft-wheat flour (see page 9), pastry flour, or unbleached all-purpose flour
1 teaspoon Single-Acting Baking Powder (page 13) or ²⁄₃ teaspoon double-acting
1 teaspoon salt
6 tablespoons chilled bacon drippings (see Note, below)
½ to ²⁄₃ cup whole milk
Whole black pepper in a peppermill set on coarse grind

1. Position a rack in the upper third of the oven and preheat the oven to 450°F. Put the flour, baking powder, and salt into a mixing bowl. Whisk together well, then cut in the fat

with a pastry blender, fork, or two knives until the overall texture is one of damp, coarse meal, with occasional lumps the size of very small peas.

2. Make a well in the center and pour in ½ cup of milk. Mix with as few strokes as possible until the dough clumps together and pulls away from the sides of the bowl, adding more milk (if needed) by spoonfuls until the dough is no longer crumbly.

3. Turn the dough onto a lightly floured work surface and pat out ½ inch thick. Liberally grind pepper over it and fold it in half. Pat it flat again and sprinkle with more pepper. Repeat twice more, omitting the pepper unless you want the biscuits really peppery.

4. Lightly flour the surface once more and roll or pat the dough out about ¼ inch thick. Using a 1½-inch-diameter biscuit cutter dipped in flour before each cut, cut the dough straight down, without twisting the cutter, into twelve biscuits. The scraps can be reworked with care (see step 3 of Southern Breakfast Biscuits, page 35). Gather them together and lightly fold the dough over itself and pat flat about three times—until they just hold together, then pat flat and cut as above. Put the biscuits on an ungreased baking sheet and bake until golden brown, about 8 to 10 minutes. Serve piping hot.

NOTE: An average piece of thick-sliced bacon (not the extra-lean kind, which is in general not worth your notice) will yield at least a tablespoon of rendered fat. Store drippings for the short term (3 to 4 weeks), well sealed, in the refrigerator, or for up to 3 months in the freezer. Frankly, they never last that long around here.

Savannah Flatbread

Brittle, unleavened flatbreads like this one are truly ancient and variations on the theme are frequently found in Southern cookbooks. This one has, by modern legend, been connected back to Savannah's colonial days, when it was purportedly baked on the superheated floor of the old wood-fired brick ovens. In those days only a rare few wealthy Savannahians had such ovens, and the earliest recipes I've found date from the mid-nineteenth century. One recipe called it bread to serve with terrapin soup—a popular nineteenth-century delicacy. The colonial connection was popularized during the 1970s when the Desoto Hilton Hotel featured a version of it as their daily table bread under the trademarked name Brittlebread. Regardless of its provenance, this almost bland, crisp bread is a perfect foil for any soup or stew, and is fine for dipping or for slathering with a spicy or sweet spread at cocktail parties and teatime.

Makes about three dozen 3½- to 4-inch flatbreads

1 rounded tablespoon sugar

½ cup whole-milk buttermilk or plain whole-milk yogurt thinned with milk to buttermilk consistency

10 ounces (about 2 cups) Southern soft-wheat flour (see page 9), pastry flour, or unbleached all-purpose flour

Salt

Baking soda

4 ounces (8 tablespoons or 1 stick) unsalted butter, cut into bits

½ ounce (1 tablespoon) lard or shortening, cut into bits

1. Position a rack in the upper upper third of the oven and preheat the oven to 400°F. Stir the sugar into the milk and mix until dissolved.

2. Whisk together the flour, and a pinch each of salt and baking soda. Cut the butter and lard into the flour until it resembles coarse meal. Make a well in the center and pour in the milk. Quickly mix together until a soft dough is formed, turn it out onto a lightly

floured work surface, and lightly work until the dough is soft and uniform, about two or three turns.

3. Pinch off about six 1-inch-sized balls of the dough, and on a lightly floured surface, roll them into wafer-thin rounds (about 3½ to 4 inches in diameter). Place them on an ungreased baking sheet. Bake about 5 to 7 minutes, or until golden brown. The bread crisps as it cools. Meanwhile, roll out six more flatbreads and prepare them for the oven while the first batch bakes, repeating until all the dough is rolled and baked. Cool the bread completely before storing it in an airtight tin.

VARIATION

You may divide the dough into about six portions, roll them out, and cut them with a knife or zigzag pasta wheel into 3-inch squares or wedges. Bake as for the round bread.

Old-Fashioned Popovers

These are so easy to make it is almost embarrassing—so easy, in fact, that one can't help won-der why they are rarely seen nowadays. Don't take them seriously: being too careful and over-mixing them will result in bread that is too even to "pop" into the airy, hollow puffs that give the bread its name and make it so delightful to eat. Traditionally served for breakfast or tea, these make really showy and delicious dinner rolls, and are a fine thing to have with lunchtime soup or salad.

Makes 8 popovers

3½ ounces (1 scant cup) unbleached all-purpose flour, measured by spooning flour
    into the cup after sifting or whisking it
1 teaspoon salt
2 large eggs
1 cup whole milk

1. Position a rack in the center of the oven and preheat it to 450°F. Generously butter an eight-well standard muffin tin and put it in the oven to heat.

2. Whisk together the flour and salt. In a separate bowl, beat the eggs until light but not too fluffy. Stir in half the milk until smooth. Gradually mix in the flour, then the re-maining milk. Don't use a whisk or beat the batter at this point—overbeating will give the bread a texture that is actually too even and regular. Pour the batter into the hot muffin tin, filling the wells only two-thirds full. Bake in the center of the oven for about 15 min-utes without opening the oven.

3. Again, without opening the oven, reduce the heat to 350°F and bake until the popovers are crisp and golden brown, about 20 to 25 minutes longer. Make sure the sides of the popovers are firm and crisp. The popovers will collapse if they are taken from the oven before they are done. They'll still taste good, but they won't have the wonderful airy quality that is the hallmark of a well-made popover. Serve hot.

Savory Virginia Ham Muffins

Another recipe from Old Chickahominy House, these savory muffins are, of course, ideal for breakfast and lunch, or any family supper where bean soup is the main fare, but when spiced with a pinch of cayenne pepper and made in minimuffin tins, they are right at home on the cocktail circuit as a welcome hot hors d'oeuvres.

Makes 10 standard muffins or about 24 minimuffins

5 ounces (about 1 cup) unbleached all-purpose flour
3 teaspoons Single-Acting Baking Powder (page 13) or 2 teaspoons double-acting
½ teaspoon sugar
¾ cup ground cooked Virginia country ham (see page 20)
1 large egg
⅔ cup whole milk
1 tablespoon melted unsalted butter
Butter or Chutney Butter (page 52), for serving

1. Position a rack in the upper third of the oven and preheat it to 400°F. Lightly butter ten wells of a standard-sized twelve-muffin tin. Sift or whisk together the flour, baking powder, and sugar. Add the ham and toss until it is evenly mixed into the flour. In a separate bowl, beat together the egg, milk, and butter.

2. Make a well in the center of the dry ingredients and pour in the milk, egg, and butter. Quickly stir it together, using as few strokes as possible. Spoon the batter into the buttered muffin cups, filling them about three-quarters full. Bake for about 25 minutes, until the muffins are golden brown and separating from the edges of the tin. Serve hot with butter or, if you like, with Chutney Butter.

Sweet Potato Corn Muffins

Sweet potato pone—cooked or grated raw sweet potato molded into cakes with cornmeal (or, sometimes, all on their own) and baked in ashes, on a griddle, or in a hot oven—are a rough, old-fashioned bread that is rarely seen in the South today. The combination is well worth rediscovering, however; sweet potatoes lend a moist sweetness and hefty substance to the crumb of cornbread that is very satisfying to eat on a cold autumn morning, or, for that matter, any time the weather is cool and appetites are large.

Makes 12 muffins

1¾ cups stone-ground white cornmeal

¼ cup unbleached all-purpose flour

3 teaspoons Single-Acting Baking Powder (page 13) or 2 teaspoons double-acting

1 teaspoon salt

⅓ cup sugar

2 tablespoons unsalted butter, softened

1 cup hot cooked mashed sweet potato (about 1 large or 1½ medium potatoes)

1 large egg, lightly beaten

1 to 1¼ cups whole milk

Chutney Butter (recipe follows) or softened butter and orange marmalade, for serving

1. Position a rack in the upper third of the oven and preheat it to 425°F. Butter a 12-well muffin pan. Whisk together the meal, flour, baking powder, salt, and sugar.

2. In a separate bowl, stir the butter into the potato until it is melted and absorbed. Beat in the egg and 1 cup milk. Gradually mix in the meal and flour until a thick, smooth dough is formed. The batter should be thick but not stiff: if it seems too stiff, mix in up to ¼ cup milk. Spoon it into the prepared muffin pan and bake until risen, browned, and set, about 25 to 30 minutes. Serve hot with Chutney Butter passed separately. They are also great slathered with butter and orange marmalade.

Chutney Butter

This savory-sweet butter is a natural with sweet potatoes. It is also delicious with Sweet Potato Tea Bread (page 174), Sweet Potato Tea Buns (page 306), or simply spooned into a steaming-hot roasted sweet potato. You might also try it with Savory Virginia Ham Muffins (page 50), on any biscuit (pages 35–46) that is stuffed with thinly sliced country ham, or on your next ham, lamb, or turkey sandwich.

Makes about ¾ cup butter

4 ounces (8 tablespoons or 1 stick) unsalted butter, softened
¼ cup mango or peach chutney
Salt
Cayenne pepper, optional

1. With a mixer or fork, whip the butter until it is fluffy. Mix in the chutney until it is smooth. Taste the butter and add a pinch or so of salt and, if the chutney wasn't very spicy, a pinch or so of cayenne—not enough to make it hot, just to brighten the flavor. Whip until the butter is smooth and fluffy and the seasonings are incorporated.

2. Allow the butter to stand at room temperature for 15 to 20 minutes. Taste and correct the seasonings. It can be served right away or covered and refrigerated. Allow it to return to room temperature and just before serving, give it a light whip until it is fluffy.

Sour Cream Rice Muffins

For 200 years, rice was the staple money crop of the Carolina and Georgia Lowcountry—until a string of disastrous storms late in the nineteenth and early twentieth centuries devastated the rice fields, and machinery that was too heavy for the marshy fields began to replace hand labor. In those days, rice flour was a common ingredient in regional bread—either mixed with wheat or corn flour or replacing them both altogether. While rice has lingered as a staple in the diet of the region, and whole-grain rice is still occasionally used in regional breads, rice flour had all but disappeared from Lowcountry larders by the middle of the last century. These rich, simple muffins are typical of the kinds of rice-flour breads that once graced our tables. They make fine breakfast bread and are very good with luncheon or suppertime soups and stews.

Makes 12 muffins

2 cups rice flour (available at Asian markets) or unbleached all-purpose flour

3 teaspoons Single-Acting Baking Powder (page 13) or 2 teaspoons double-acting

1 teaspoon salt

1 cup cooked Carolina-Style Rice (recipe follows)

1 cup sour cream, or more (see step 2)

2 large eggs, beaten

1. Position a rack in the upper third of the oven and preheat the oven to 425°F. Lightly butter the insides of a 12-well standard muffin tin. Whisk together the rice flour, baking powder, and salt in a large mixing bowl. Add the rice and toss until it is evenly mixed.

2. In a separate bowl, beat the sour cream and eggs well. Make a well in the center of the dry ingredients and pour in the liquids. Quickly stir them together. The batter should be very thick—stiffer than cornbread batter but softer than biscuit dough. If it's too dry, add a few more spoonfuls sour cream or milk. Divide the batter among the muffin wells and bake until golden brown, about 25 minutes.

NOTE: Because of the sour cream and moisture-rich rice content of these muffins, they are very good warmed over the next day. Position a rack in the upper third of the oven and preheat the oven to 425°F. Put the muffins on a small baking sheet or metal pie plate and warm them until they are crisp on the outside and hot through, about 4 to 5 minutes.

Carolina-Style Rice

In the Carolina and Georgia Lowcountry, we prefer rice cooked until the grains are fluffy but not split, distinct and separate so that they almost "rattle" when spooned onto the plate. This is also how it is cooked for use in most of the region's rice breads.

Makes 2 cups rice

1 cup raw long-grain white rice
Scant 2 cups water
Salt

1. Wash the rice in several changes of water until the water is no longer milky, rubbing handfuls of rice between your fingers. Drain it thoroughly in a tightly woven wire sieve and rinse it one last time under cold running water. Drain thoroughly.

2. Put the water, a healthy pinch of salt, and the drained rice in a large kettle. Stir to dissolve the salt and turn on the heat to medium-high. Bring it to a boil and stir it one last time to make sure that the rice is not sticking.

3. Reduce the heat to low and set the lid askew. Let the rice simmer for 12 minutes. There should be clear, dry steam holes formed on the surface, and most, if not all, of the water should be absorbed. Gently fold the top rice under with a fork, "fluffing" not stirring it.

4. Put the lid on tight and let it sit over the heat for a minute more to build the steam, then turn off the heat. Move the pot to a warm part of the stove (if you have an electric

stove, this is its big advantage; leave the pot where it is; the residual heat in the burner should be just right). If you don't have a warm spot, put the pan in a larger pan of hot water or set it over a pot of simmering water. Let it steam for 12 to 14 minutes, until the grains are tender but still firm, distinct, and separate. Fluff by picking it with a fork before serving.

Skillet Cornbread

If I had to choose a bread that was the most characteristically "Southern" to me, it would not be biscuits, however celebrated they are. It would be cornbread baked in a preheated cast-iron skillet. With crackling-crisp crust and tender crumb, this round cake, cut into thick wedges and slathered with butter or stuffed with thinly sliced cheddar, accompanied every pot of beans, vegetable soup, or stew; in summer, the cornbread was served with the midday all-vegetable dinners that celebrated the bounty of our backyard garden. It is still the bread that satisfies and soothes my soul when I am hungry and homesick, the one that makes my mother and grandmother seem close by, that evokes a keen image of my father, in his place at the head of the table, crumbling it into his bowl of beans.

Moreover, there is no other bread that demonstrates more keenly the hybridized nature of Southern baking—combining as it does a tight weave of European, African, and Native American elements in a fabric that is impossible to unravel.

Makes one 9-inch round cake, or 14 corn sticks or muffins

2 cups stone-ground cornmeal

2 teaspoons baking powder

1 teaspoon baking soda

1 teaspoon salt

2 large eggs

1¾ cups whole-milk buttermilk or plain whole-milk yogurt thinned with milk to buttermilk consistency

4 tablespoons bacon drippings, melted butter, or olive oil

1. Position a rack in the center of the oven and preheat it to 450°F. Lightly, but thoroughly grease a 9-inch iron skillet, or iron corn stick, or muffin pan, and heat it in the center of the oven for at least 10 minutes.

2. Whisk together the meal, baking powder, soda, and salt in a large mixing bowl. In

a separate bowl, beat the eggs until smooth and stir in the buttermilk and 2 tablespoons of the melted fat.

3. When the pan is very hot, make a well in the center of the cornmeal and then pour in the milk and egg mixture. Quickly stir in the liquid only as long as it takes to blend and get rid of any dry lumps.

4. Take the pan out of the oven and add the remaining fat (if using a cornstick or muffin pan, drizzle the fat equally into each well). If I'm using a corn stick pan, I'll use a cold stick instead of melted butter, rubbing a little into each well. The butter should sizzle: if it doesn't, the pan isn't hot enough. Put it back into the oven for about 5 more minutes.

5. Quickly pour the batter into the hot pan: it must sizzle when it touches. If you are using a corn stick or muffin pan, fill each well about two-thirds full (a standard-sized muffin or corn stick pan will need about half this batter; if you have only one such pan, it can be baked in two batches). Bake until golden brown and firm but somewhat springy at the center, about 25 minutes for corn sticks or muffins and 35 minutes for a skillet cake.

6. Invert the skillet over a plate or the muffin or corn stick pans over a towel. The bread should come right out of the pan. If you are baking sticks or muffins in batches, as soon as you have dumped the first batch, add more fat to the pan and repeat as above. Roll the first batch in a linen towel (not paper towels, foil, or an insulated mat) to keep it warm while the second batch cooks. Serve hot with plenty of good butter passed separately.

VARIATIONS

CRACKLING SKILLET BREAD: Cracklings are the solids left from rendering pork fat into lard. They're an ancient favorite in the South for enriching cornbread, but the roots of the practice go back further, to some of the great regional breads of Europe. To make Crackling Skillet Bread, substitute 1 cup of broken cracklings, (broken or chopped into small ½-inch pieces), for the 2 tablespoons of fat in the batter of the preceding recipe and cut the amount of fat for the skillet to 1 tablespoon. Mix it into the meal after whisking it together with the baking powder, soda, and salt.

BACON AND ONION BREAD: Omit the bacon drippings or melted fat in the master recipe. Dice four pieces of thick-sliced bacon and sauté them in an iron skillet over medium heat until they are browned and crisp. Spoon off and reserve all but 2 tablespoons of the fat. Add 1 onion, trimmed, split lengthwise, peeled, and diced and sauté, tossing frequently, until it is translucent and softened, about 5 minutes. Turn off the heat. Mix the bread as directed in the master recipe up through step 2, omitting the melted fat and adding 1 tablespoon chopped fresh sage (or 1 rounded teaspoon crumbled, dried sage) to the dry ingredients. Add the bacon and onion and fat remaining in the pan and toss until evenly mixed. Finish mixing and baking the bread as directed in steps 3 through 6, using the remaining 2 tablespoons of the bacon drippings left in the pan for the fat in the skillet.

Fresh Corn and Herb Skillet Bread

Skillet cornbread is not just the most quintessentially Southern of breads: it also illustrates, like nothing else, the steady evolution of Southern cooking and baking during the last century. All over the South cooks have not been content with the plain and simple cake of the previous recipe, but have experimented with just about every addition imaginable, from the cracklings and onions in the variations on the previous page to jalapeño peppers, cheese, and sweet potatoes. One especially delicious addition is fresh corn, which adds sweetness, moisture, and delicacy to the bread and makes it an ideal accompaniment for luncheon salads, soups, or brunch-time egg dishes.

Makes one 9-inch round cake, serving 6

2 to 3 ears fresh white corn (preferably Silver Queen)
4 tablespoons bacon drippings or melted butter
1 cup stone-ground cornmeal
2 teaspoons baking powder
1 teaspoon baking soda
1 teaspoon salt
2 large or 4 small scallions or other green onions, chopped
1 tablespoon chopped fresh thyme or 1 teaspoon crumbled dried
1 tablespoon chopped fresh sage or 1 teaspoon crumbled dried
2 large eggs
1½ cups whole-milk buttermilk or plain whole-milk yogurt thinned with milk to
   buttermilk consistency

1. Shuck, silk, and wash the corn. Cut the kernels from the cob with a sharp knife, cutting only halfway into them, and with the back of the knife, scrape the cob to get all the kernel milk and solids out. You will need 1 cup of cut kernels. Set them aside. Put 2 tablespoons of the drippings and the scallions in a sauté pan and turn on the heat to medium-high. Sauté, tossing frequently, until wilted. Turn off the heat.

2. Position a rack in the center of the oven and preheat it to 450°F. Lightly, but thoroughly grease a 9-inch iron skillet, or iron corn stick or muffin pan, and heat it in the center of the oven for at least 10 minutes. Meanwhile, whisk together the meal, baking powder, soda, and salt in a large mixing bowl. Add the scallions and herb and toss until mixed. In a separate bowl, beat the eggs until smooth and stir in the buttermilk and reserved fresh corn kernels with their milk. When the skillet is hot, pour the liquids into the dry ingredients and quickly stir until the mixture is lightly blended and mostly free of lumps.

3. Remove the skillet from the oven and add the remaining fat. It should sizzle: if it doesn't, the pan isn't hot enough. Put it back into the oven until the fat is almost smoking hot. Quickly pour the batter into the hot pan: It should sizzle. Bake until golden brown and firm but springy at the center, about 35 minutes.

4. Carefully invert the skillet over a plate as soon as you take it from the oven and remove the bread. It should come right out of the pan. Serve hot with plenty of good butter passed separately.

Herbed Skillet Rice Bread

Quickbread baked in an iron skillet does not always contain cornmeal. This one, from the Carolina Lowcountry, where rice once reigned supreme in the economy and diet of the region, was invented as a way to recycle leftover cooked rice—something old-time Lowcountry cooks always had on hand. Though originally intended for breakfast or supper, it also makes a delicious side dish for a luncheon or dinner. The recipe is adapted from old Lowcountry recipes, enlivened with herbs, scallions, and lemon zest.

Makes one 9-inch round skillet cake

3 tablespoons unsalted butter

2 medium scallions or other green onions, thinly sliced

1 tablespoon chopped fresh thyme or 1 teaspoon crumbled dried

1 tablespoon chopped fresh sage or 1 teaspoon crumbled dried

2 cups cooked Carolina-Style Rice (page 54)

1 rounded teaspoon salt

1 lemon

2 cups unbleached all-purpose flour or white rice flour (see Note, below)

4 large eggs

¾ to 1 cup whole-milk buttermilk or plain whole-milk yogurt thinned to buttermilk consistency

1. Put 2 tablespoons of the butter and the scallions in a sauté pan and turn on the heat to medium-high. Sauté, tossing frequently, until the onions are wilted, about 2 minutes. Add the herbs and toss until fragrant. Turn off the heat.

2. Position a rack in the center of the oven and preheat it to 400°F. Put the rice, scallions, and herbs in a mixing bowl, sprinkle in the salt and grate the zest of the lemon over it. Toss it with a fork until it is well mixed. Sift the flour over the rice and work it in with a spatula or wooden spoon, taking care not to mush up the rice until it disintegrates: the grains should still have their shape. Stir in the eggs and ¾ cup of the butter-

milk and beat into a thick, slightly lumpy batter. If it seems too stiff, stir in a little more milk.

3. Heat a 9-inch, well-seasoned iron skillet in the oven until it is almost smoking hot, about 10 minutes. Add the remaining butter, swirl the pan to coat it, immediately pour in the batter, and smooth the top with the back of a wooden spoon or spatula. Bake for about 40 minutes, until it is golden brown and set at the center. Run a knife around the edge of the skillet, carefully invert it over a plate, and unmold the bread. Cut it into wedges and serve hot.

NOTE: The old recipe for this bread, from *The Carolina Housewife* (1847), was not specific about the flour. Because Miss Rutledge and her contemporaries often used rice flour in bread, they generally specified "wheat flour" in any bread that contained rice, so I am inclined to think that rice flour was the original intention. However, it makes a dense, chewy bread—satisfying, but not one most modern palates are accustomed to. The choice is yours—once you make them, you'll know what you and your family prefer.

Spoonbread

This classic soft, soufflélike bread is so closely connected with Virginia that it's often called "Virginia Spoonbread" in regional cookbooks. Many a native is ready and willing to fight for his or her claim to its invention, and since the oldest printed recipes known to us did come from Mary Randolph's The Virginia House-wife *(1824), who is to say that it wasn't? The picturesque name, probably derived from the fact that it is more like a soufflé than a bread, came late in the nineteenth century; Mrs. Randolph called it "Batter Bread" and baked it in small, individual servings rather like popovers or muffins, which would not have needed a spoon. Through time, cooks have preferred square tins, pottery pudding dishes, and china teacups or individual ramekins. Each baking receptacle gives slightly differing results, but the batter usually varies only in detail.*

Late in the nineteenth century, baking powder found its way into Spoonbread, but while many modern recipes still call for it, I prefer the flavor and consistency of the traditional bread, which relies solely on well-beaten eggs for volume and texture.

Serves 4

3 cups half-and-half
1 cup fine cornmeal
3 tablespoons butter
1 teaspoon salt
3 large eggs

1. Position a rack in the center of the oven and preheat the oven to 350°F. Put the half-and-half in a heavy-bottomed pan and scald it, stirring frequently, over medium-low heat. Gradually whisk in the meal in a thin, but steady stream, pouring it either from your fist or a spouted measuring cup. When all the meal is incorporated, cook, stirring frequently, until the mush is thick, about 3 to 5 minutes. Take the pan from the heat and beat in the butter and salt. Set it aside to cool slightly.

2. Lightly butter an 8-inch soufflé dish or round casserole (or an 8-inch square one

that is at least 2 inches deep). Separate the eggs, placing the whites into a clean stainless steel or glass bowl. Lightly beat the yolks and mix them into the mush.

3. Using a clean whisk or mixer, beat the whites until they form stiff, but not dry, peaks. Add them gradually to the mush and gently, but thoroughly fold them in. Pour the batter into the prepared dish and bake until it is risen and golden brown on the top, about 45 minutes. It should be set, but still soft, like a soufflé. Serve at once from the baking dish.

Awendaw, or Hominy Spoonbread

Lowcountry food historian and champion John Martin Taylor calls Awendaw the Lowcountry version of Spoonbread (page 63) and certainly the name of this creamy, soufflélike dish is regional, deriving from a Native American name for a real place—a tiny fishing village near Charleston, South Carolina. The first known printed recipe for Awendaw is found in Sarah Rutledge's classic The Carolina Housewife *(1847), whose recipe I offer as she presented it, save for the usual modern addition of a little salt, since Miss Rutledge's recipes were often sketches, omitting such details. Well, regardless of its pedigree, this spoonbread is delicate and delicious— homey enough for cozy family suppers, and yet elegant enough for your best company dinners.*

Serves 8

2 cups hot cooked grits, preferably whole-corn grits (see Note, below)
2 tablespoons unsalted butter
4 large eggs
2 cups whole milk
1 cup stone-ground white cornmeal
1 teaspoon salt

1. Position a rack in the center of the oven and preheat it to 375°F. Lightly butter a 9-inch round soufflé dish or deep casserole. In a large bowl, while the grits are still quite hot, mix in the butter until it is melted and absorbed. Let it cool slightly; beat in the eggs and then the milk. Gradually stir in the cornmeal and salt.

2. Pour the batter into the prepared dish and bake until it is set and lightly browned on top, about 45 to 50 minutes. Serve at once.

NOTE: To cook the grits, bring 2 cups water to a boil in a 2-quart heavy-bottomed enameled or stainless-steel pot over medium-high heat. Gradually stir in ½ cup raw whole-corn grits, adding them in a thin, steady stream. Bring the liquid back to a boil and reduce the heat to medium-low. Loosely cover and cook, stirring occasionally, until the grits are tender and creamy but moderately stiff, about an hour, adding simmering water if they become too stiff and dry before they are tender. Salt, taste, and cook another 3 to 4 minutes.

Savannah Rice Puff

This is essentially rice spoonbread, even though it is never presented as bread in local cookbooks, but more usually as a vegetable side dish. Simple and homey, yet delicately delicious, it can be dressed up as little or as much as your imagination and common sense will allow, and taken just about anywhere, as fine an addition to the most formal of dinners and luncheons as it is to the simplest family supper. The original was quite plain, containing only rice, milk, and eggs; this version has a lot in common with the custard-based macaroni-and-cheese pie that is a fixture throughout the South at church suppers, family dinners, and meat-and-three diners.

Serves 4 to 6

2 tablespoons unsalted butter

4 chopped scallions or a small, chopped yellow onion

2 large eggs

1 cup whole milk

2 cups cooked Carolina-Style Rice (page 54), cooled

1½ cups grated extra-sharp cheddar or Gruyère cheese

Salt and whole black pepper in a peppermill

1. Position a rack in the center of the oven and preheat the oven to 375°F. Lightly butter a 2-quart casserole. Put the butter and onions in a sauté pan over medium heat and sauté until translucent and beginning to color, about 4 minutes. Remove it from the heat.

2. Lightly beat the eggs in a large bowl and gradually beat in the milk. Stir in the rice, onion and butter, and 1 cup of the cheese. Season it well with a couple of pinches of salt and a few liberal grindings of pepper. Mix well and pour the batter into the prepared casserole. Top it with the remaining cheese and bake until golden on top and set, about 30 to 40 minutes.

Stove-Top Baking— Griddled and Fried Breads and Pastries

GRIDDLE BAKING may not seem much like "real" baking, but it is actually the oldest form of the process known to man. The earliest breads were baked either in the banked ashes of an open fire or on a flat, heated slab of stone. It was hundreds, maybe even thousands, of years before we learned to bake bread in domed clay chambers, and a few thousand more before the chambers became iron and steel. Yet, even after ovens were perfected, man has never lost his taste for breads and pastries baked on a griddle or in hot deep fat. Biscuits and skillet bread not withstanding, if pancakes, hoecakes, and—in the Deep South touching Mexico—tortillas, or doughnuts, beignets, and other countless deep-fried pastry fritters were all withdrawn from the American table, they would leave quite a hole.

Griddled and fried breads and pastries are still favorites in the South and not, as many detractors claim, because of an inordinate love of greasy fried food, but as a practical response to local conditions: for nine months out of the year, the climate for most of our region is hot—sometimes unbearably so. Hot griddles, skillets, and pots of boiling fat add to the heat, but not nearly as much as an oven does, nor for nearly as long.

Griddle baking and frying are in many ways easier than oven baking because you can pretty much see what is going on for the entire process. There are no worries about opening the oven and making a cake collapse, no sticking your face into a wall of heat to see if the bread has browned enough, and less guessing about whether the oven is hot or cool enough. Only frying is tricky, and that is more because of the danger in large amounts of boiling fat than because it is at all complicated. Other than getting accustomed to the signals the bread or pastry will give you from the pan—the sound it makes as it meets the hot surface or fat, the way it looks when it is browning at the right pace or too quickly, the way it smells when it is baking at just the right heat or beginning to scorch from too much of it—griddle and fry baking require virtually no extraordinary skills of the cook.

Likewise, there are very few special equipment needs. Waffles must be baked in a waffle iron, but griddle baking doesn't require a griddle (even though it does make the bread easier to handle): an iron skillet or a heavy-bottomed nonstick pan will do the job well enough. Likewise, fry baking doesn't require a deep-fat fryer: it can just as easily be done in a deep, heavy-bottomed skillet or Dutch oven. What you will need are thin, flexible spatulas, a wire frying skimmer or tongs for removing fried bread and pastry from the fat, and a big spoon with a pointed tip for measuring and pouring out even, round griddle-cakes. A frying thermometer is also a big help in keeping the temperature of the fat regulated, especially if you don't fry very often and are not used to looking for the signals that will tell you when the fat is not quite hot enough, just right, or too hot.

Many of these recipes include a step that prepares the oven to hold the cooked bread or pastry and keep it hot. In all cases, griddled and fried breads are best when they are hot from the pan, but this step will help keep them at their peak when you can't serve them that way. Position a rack in the center to upper third of the oven and set it at the lowest setting—usually 150° to 170°F (sometimes it just reads "warm"—easy enough, right?). Make sure that the thermostat isn't running hot, because you only want to keep things warm, not dry them out. If the bread or pastry is fried, line a rimmed baking sheet with a cooling rack so that no part of the bread will rest on the solid surface and get soggy or greasy; most griddle breads should just go directly onto the sheet.

Muffins

These are not the puffy, cupcakelike "muffins" of our day, but the classic griddle bread of the British Isles that we know today as "English" muffins; they were enjoyed in our country at least in the early days of the republic, and have an interesting and little-known place in the history of American baking. Thomas Jefferson appears to have been especially partial to muffins and to having them well made in Monticello's kitchen: during his tenure at the President's House, his French chef's apparent ignorance of them prompted Jefferson to beg of his daughter, Martha, ". . . Pray enable yourself to direct us here how to make muffins in Peter's method. My cook here cannot succeed at them, and they are a great luxury to me." By the third quarter of the nineteenth century, however, they were on their way out, displaced by the soft, cup-baked bread that we know as muffins today. By the century's end, old-style muffins were so little known that a professional bakery reintroducing them had to market them as "English" to save confusion and the name has stuck with them.

Most Southern recipes after Mr. Jefferson's day contained egg and many of them were made up with milk; in fact, about the only difference between the recipes for muffins, crumpets, and flannel cakes was the proportion of egg and liquid to flour. But eggs make them rather heavy and the ones that Mr. Jefferson so loved most likely did not contain them. The old recipes also baked this bread in old-fashioned muffin rings, but the dough is firm enough to bake without that support.

Makes about 16 muffins

2 cups tepid water
¼ teaspoon active dry yeast or ½-ounce cake compressed fresh yeast
20 ounces (about 4 cups) unbleached all-purpose flour, including ¼ cup whole-
   wheat pastry flour
1 rounded teaspoon salt
Rice or corn flour or fine white cornmeal, for dusting

1. Dissolve the yeast in the water and let it proof for 10 minutes. Whisk or stir together the flour and salt in a mixing bowl. Make a well in the center and pour in the

yeasted water, then gradually stir it into the flour and beat until the dough is cohesive and smooth—almost too stiff to stir but too slack to knead by hand. Cover with plastic wrap or a damp, double-folded linen towel and let rise until almost doubled, about 3 hours. The dough can also be covered with wrap and left in a cool place to rise overnight.

2. Lightly dust a baking sheet, wooden dough board, or laminate counter with rice or corn flour or cornmeal. Beat the dough down with a wooden spoon. Dust your hands and the top of the dough with all-purpose flour and scoop up even small handfuls, shaping each into a round flat cake about 2½ inches across. Place the muffins on the flour-dusted surface, spacing them at least an inch apart and let them rest for 15 to 30 minutes. If you've let the dough rise overnight, they only need a few minutes to begin recovering volume.

3. Warm a griddle or wide, shallow skillet over medium-low heat. With a wide, thin-bladed spatula, place as many muffins as will comfortably fit on the griddle with at least an inch on all sides. Bake slowly until the bottom is delicately browned, about 8 to 10 minutes; turn, lightly pressing each muffin flat with the back of the spatula, and bake until uniformly browned and set but still moist at the center, about 8 minutes longer. For instructions in the art of buttering and enjoying muffins, see page 74.

Sourdough Muffins

Sourdough makes terrific muffins. The dough handles in pretty much the same ways as the previous recipe, though actually I like to let them rise a little more than they are supposed to: the last few muffins always rise a little more than the others and as they are my favorites, I usually let them all sit for at least half an hour after shaping them.

Makes about 16 muffins

20 ounces (about 4 cups) unbleached all-purpose flour, including ¼ cup whole-wheat pastry flour
1 rounded teaspoon salt
½ cup water
½ cup whole milk
2 tablespoons unsalted butter
1 cup Sourdough Starter (page 319)

1. Whisk or stir together the flour and salt in a mixing bowl. Scald the water, milk, and butter in a heavy-bottomed saucepan over medium heat until the butter is melted. Remove it from the heat and let it cool to 110°F.

2. Stir the warm liquids into the starter, then make a well in the center of the flour and pour the liquids in. Gradually stir it into the flour and beat until the dough is cohesive and smooth—almost too stiff to stir, but too slack to knead by hand. Cover with plastic wrap or a damp, double-folded linen towel and let it rise until almost doubled, about 4 hours, or cover with wrap and set in a cool place to rise overnight.

3. Lightly dust a baking sheet, wooden dough board, or laminate counter with rice or corn flour. Beat the dough down with a spoon. Dust your hands and the top of the dough with all-purpose flour and scoop up even small handfuls, shaping each into a round flat cake about 2½ inches across. Put the rounds on the floured surface, spacing them at least an inch apart, and let them rest for 15 to 30 minutes. If you've let the dough rise overnight, it will begin to recover volume more quickly and will only need a few minutes rest.

4. Warm a griddle or wide, shallow skillet over medium-low heat. Push the sides of the muffins in with a spatula to keep them fairly straight. With a wide, thin-bladed spatula, place as many muffins as will comfortably fit on the griddle with at least an inch on all sides. Bake slowly, evening up the sides with the spatula as needed, until the bottom is delicately browned, about 8 to 10 minutes; turn, lightly pressing each muffin flat with the back of the spatula, and bake until uniformly browned and set but moist at the center, about 8 minutes longer. For instructions in the art of buttering and enjoying muffins, see below.

ON BAKING MUFFINS: While cast iron is the traditional surface for baking muffins, a wide nonstick aluminum griddle works just fine. I use a heavy-bottomed coated aluminum sauté pan, mainly because I don't have anywhere to store something so luxurious as a real griddle. As you scoop up the muffins and transfer them to the griddle, they will be very soft and the edges may be a little sticky, so dust them lightly with flour and touch them as little as possible. You'll find that you will also end up scooping some of the dusting flour. Brush it off the cooking surface between batches or it will accumulate and start to scorch.

THE ART OF EATING MUFFINS: The fine art of buttering and eating muffins hot off the griddle was a skill well understood within the Jefferson/Randolph clan. According to family lore, no less than Dolly Madison was instructed in this art by toddler Benjamin Franklin Randolph: "Why you must tear him open, and put butter inside and stick holes in his back. And then pat him and squeeze him and the juice will run out!" I cannot improve on that except to add that the tearing goes easier when the edges are loosened by piercing them with the tines of a fork. In today's cholesterol- and saturated-fat conscious society, it is not for the faint of heart, but it sure is rewarding. You need not, as little Ben directed, put holes in the muffin, but if butter doesn't run out the edges when you bite into it, you didn't use enough. Muffins don't keep well, but happily leftovers freeze and toast beautifully. They should not, as is often done in this country, be split open, but as directed above be pierced with the fork to loosen the edges, and toasted whole. It is then and only then split open and buttered.

Mrs. Hill's Crumpets

These small yeast-leavened pancakes, with their characteristic honeycomb of air holes in their tops, are almost unheard of in America today, except in isolated families and cafés or inns that serve English-style afternoon teas. But once they were almost commonplace on Southern tables and in Southern cookbooks. The batter is richer than most British crumpets, having both egg and a high proportion of milk, and sometimes either cooked rice (in the Georgia and Carolina Lowcountry) or grits (upstate and into North Carolina) are added to the mix, both of which give the crumpets a longer shelf life. This is Annabella P. Hill's formula, from Mrs. Hill's New Cook Book *(1867), and is a typical late-antebellum one.*

Makes about 2 dozen crumpets, serving 4 to 6, or 8 at tea

¼ teaspoon active dry yeast or ½-ounce cake compressed fresh yeast
¼ cup lukewarm water
10 ounces (about 2 cups) unbleached all-purpose flour
½ teaspoon salt
1⅓ cups whole milk
1 large egg
Cold butter, thinly sliced, for serving

1. Dissolve the yeast in the water and let it proof for 10 minutes. Whisk together the flour and salt in a mixing bowl. Scald the milk in a small, heavy-bottomed saucepan over medium heat and let it cool to 110°F. In a separate bowl, beat the egg lightly and beat in the milk and yeast. Gradually beat the liquids into the flour. Cover with plastic wrap and set it in a warm place until risen and full of small air bubbles, about 3 hours.

2. Position a rack in the center of the oven and preheat the oven to 150° to 170°F. Heat a griddle or wide, heavy-bottomed skillet over medium-low heat. Butter the insides of four muffin rings and lightly brush the griddle with butter. Carefully pour enough batter into each ring to fill it one-quarter inch up the sides. Bake until the tops are perforated

with air holes and are opaque and the bottoms are browned, about 6 to 8 minutes. Crumpets are not turned.

3. As the crumpets are done, put them on a baking sheet in the oven to keep them warm while the remaining crumpets are griddle-baked.

4. If you are making them to toast or reheat later, let them cool completely in a single layer, and wrap them well in plastic wrap or store in a zip-sealing plastic bag. They will keep for about 2 days. To serve them immediately, put a wafer-thin pat of butter on top of each, stack them on a warm plate, and serve warm.

Flannel Cakes

Also known as "velvet" cakes, these enriched, yeast-leavened griddlecakes were another commonplace on the American table that has all but disappeared. They fall somewhere between crumpets (page 75) and modern pancakes. Eaten hot off the griddle, with their delicate, velvety centers and crisp edges, they are terrific for breakfast, supper, or—if you have that kind of leisure—an afternoon tea. They don't hold up well if they're allowed to cool or sit for too long in a warm oven, but they do reheat beautifully on a griddle, so you will want to save leftovers (or make an extra batch) and store them, well wrapped, in the refrigerator or freezer, for a quick breakfast or suppertime treat.

Makes about 2 dozen 3-inch cakes, serving 4 to 6

¼ teaspoon active dry yeast or ½-ounce cake compressed fresh yeast
¼ cup lukewarm water
2 cups whole milk
2 tablespoons unsalted butter
2 large eggs
10 ounces (about 2 cups) unbleached all-purpose flour
½ teaspoon salt

1. Dissolve the yeast in the water and let it proof for 10 minutes. Meanwhile, scald the milk in a heavy-bottomed saucepan over medium heat. Add the butter and heat until it is just melted, remove from the heat, and let it cool to 110°F. (The milk can be heated in the microwave.)

2. Beat the eggs in a large mixing bowl. Add the milk and yeasted water. In a separate bowl, whisk together the flour and salt, then gradually beat the liquids into it; it should have the consistency of a standard pancake batter. Cover it with plastic wrap, and set it in a warm place until it is doubled, about 3 hours.

3. Heat a griddle or wide, heavy-bottomed skillet over medium heat. Generously brush the griddle with butter and pour the batter by 2-tablespoonful portions onto it. It

should pool into a cake about 3 inches in diameter. Cook until lightly browned, about 4 minutes, turn, and cook until evenly browned and set at the center.

VARIATION

YEAST-RAISED WAFFLES: This batter can also be used to make very good waffles. Heat the waffle iron to medium heat (about 350°F) and grease with butter or oil. Pour in the batter, leaving enough room on the edges for it to expand. Close the iron and bake until the steam no longer rises from the edges of the iron and the waffle smells toasty and is uniformly golden brown, about 5 to 8 minutes. For waffle cooking and storage tips, see page 92, Waffle Wisdom.

Mrs. Randolph's "Quire of Paper Pancakes"

This is a very old recipe, from Mary Randolph's landmark cookbook The Virginia House-wife *(1824). You might say that Mrs. Randolph's "quire" is an all-soprano chorus—it's made up of delicate, lacy-edged crepes flavored with wine and nutmeg. Until the twentieth century, the American understanding of the difference between a griddlecake and a pancake was distinct: griddlecakes were thick, round, sweet or savory flatbreads and pancakes were what we now call crepes. Eventually, the old-fashioned name "griddlecake" disappeared from American usage, and today's pancakes are nothing that Mrs. Randolph would have approved of, let alone recognized as such.*

Have everything at room temperature: let the eggs and milk sit out until they are no longer chilled, or warm the milk to between 90° and 110°F and let the eggs sit (in their shells) in hot tap water for 1 minute before mixing everything together.

These are best made at the moment of serving, but if you need to make them ahead, instead of stacking them on top of one another, invert them onto squares of wax paper as you take them up. Cool, stack them, and store them in a zip-sealing plastic bag. They can be re-warmed for a few seconds one at a time, top side down, in a nonstick pan over medium-high heat.

Makes about 2 dozen pancakes, serving 4

1 cup whole milk

3 large eggs

2 ounces (4 tablespoons or ½ stick) unsalted butter, melted

2 ounces (a generous ½ cup) unbleached all-purpose flour

Whole nutmeg in a grater

½ cup granulated sugar

¼ teaspoon salt

¼ cup dry white wine or sherry

Superfine sugar (see Note, below), for dusting

Your favorite fruit sauce, syrup, or sautéed seasonal fruit or wine sauce

1. Scald the milk in a heavy-bottomed saucepan over medium heat and let it cool to around 110°F. Beat the eggs until well mixed, then beat in the milk and butter until smooth. In a separate mixing bowl, sift or whisk together the flour, a generous grating of nutmeg, sugar, and salt. Gradually stir the eggs and milk into the dry ingredients, being careful not to let the flour lump. When the liquid is incorporated, stir in the wine. The batter will be quite thin. Let it rest, covered, for at least 1 hour.

2. Warm a plate and lightly dust it with superfine sugar. Heat a crepe pan or small, nonstick sauté pan over medium-high heat. Brush it lightly with butter or oil. Pour in just enough batter to thinly coat the bottom of the pan and cook until the edges are well browned, the bottom is golden brown, and the top is set and completely opaque, about 35 to 45 seconds. These crepes don't require turning. Loosen the edges, invert the pan over the plate, and let the crepe fall onto the warm plate. Lightly sprinkle with superfine sugar.

3. Repeat with the remaining batter (you will not need to grease the pan after the first pancake), stacking them one on top of the other, with a dusting of superfine sugar between each. Serve warm, cutting into wedges like a cake with the fruit sauce.

NOTE: Superfine sugar is the consistency of American 4X powdered sugar, but the cornstarch in our powdered sugar makes it a poor substitute: it gives the pancakes a pasty consistency and has a raw aftertaste. Superfine sugar is available from professional baker's suppliers and mail-order catalogs such as King Arthur Flour Company's *Baker's Catalogue* (see page 10). Failing that, pulverize granulated sugar in the food processor until it is powdery.

Batty or Corn Griddlecakes

The curious name that these cakes once went by had nothing to do with Halloween, nor was it a reflection of the cook's mental health (though sometimes my family begs to differ); it's only a corruption of "batter cakes." This is the same enriched griddle cornbread that often goes by "hoecake" in modern Southern restaurants, even though it is not at all the same bread (see page 83).

Makes about 12 griddlecakes, serving 4 to 6

1 cup stone-ground white cornmeal
½ teaspoon baking soda
2 tablespoons sugar
½ teaspoon salt
1 large egg
About 1¼ cups whole-milk buttermilk or plain whole-milk yogurt thinned
    with milk to buttermilk consistency

1. Position a rack in the center of the oven, place a large, rimmed baking sheet on it, and preheat the oven to 150° to 170°F. (the warm setting). In a large mixing bowl, whisk together the meal, soda, sugar, and salt. In a separate bowl, lightly beat the egg and beat in the milk or yogurt. Make a well in the center of the meal, pour in the egg and milk, and quickly stir them together. It should be moderately thick but should still pour easily from a spoon: if it doesn't, add a little more milk.

2. Place a griddle or wide, shallow skillet over medium-high heat, or heat an electric griddle to 325°F. The griddle should be hot enough for a drop of water to "dance" on the surface. Brush the griddle or pan with fat, just enough to give it an even sheen. Pour the batter in about a 2-tablespoon-sized portion from the end of a large spoon: just enough to pool into cakes about 3 inches in diameter. The edges will sizzle and form lacy air bubbles. Cook until the cakes are golden brown on the bottom, turn, and cook until uniformly

golden, about 2 to 3 minutes per side. Transfer the cooked griddlecakes to the baking sheet in the oven while you cook the remaining batter. Serve hot with more butter passed separately. They are often served at breakfast or supper as you would pancakes, with plenty of butter and cane syrup, maple syrup, or honey.

Hot Water Cornbread

This is the ancient bread that more properly goes by the name hoecake. *Scalding the meal with hot water softens it and gives the bread a more delicate consistency. Nita Dixon, a traditional Lowcountry cook who for years ran a café in downtown Savannah, used to serve this bread with her deeply Southern fare. Nita learned to make it from her sister, Joan Simmons, a lovely artist and free spirit who has lived all over the map and learned about hot water bread from a woman in Tennessee. One warm spring morning, Joan finally shared her secret with me: an eye for balance and a well-seasoned cast iron skillet.*

Makes about 8 griddlecakes, serving 4 to 6

About 1¾ cups water
¼ cup thinly sliced green onion (about 2 small scallions)
1 cup stone-ground white cornmeal
1 teaspoon salt
Vegetable oil or bacon drippings (or a mixture of both), for frying

1. Bring the water to a boil in a heavy-bottomed saucepan over medium heat. Stir together the onion, meal, and salt in a heat-proof mixing bowl.

2. Gradually stir the boiling hot water into the meal, beginning with 1½ cups, and adding more water by spoonfuls until a thick, almost stiff batter forms.

3. Heat a wide, well-seasoned cast iron skillet over medium-high heat until a drop of water "dances" when dropped on the surface. Film the bottom with oil about ⅛-inch deep and heat until it is almost smoking. Drop the batter onto the surface in 2 to 3 tablespoon-sized lumps. Spread it about ¼-inch thick with the back of the spoon or a spatula and cook until golden brown on the bottom, about 3 to 4 minutes, turn, and cook until golden brown and firm. The cakes should be slightly moist in the center but not mushy.

Joan's Water Cornbread

When Joan Simmons taught me to make hot-water cornbread, she also shared this elemental and basic but deeply satisfying griddlecake made without hot water. It's simplicity itself to stir together, being little more than cold water and meal stirred into a simple batter, but there's alchemy in the way that batter meets the hot fat. Lacy and crisp at its edges, yet soft and moist at the center, its golden brown flecked with bright bits of green onion, it looks as lovely as it tastes. As with hot-water cornbread, the choice of cast iron cookware is not arbitrary but essential to good results.

Makes about 8 griddlecakes, serving 4 to 6

¼ cup thinly sliced green onion (about 2 small scallions)
1 cup stone-ground white cornmeal
½ teaspoon salt
1 cup plus 2 to 3 tablespoons water
Peanut or vegetable oil, for frying

1. Toss together the onion, meal, and salt. Gradually stir in the water until a smooth batter is formed, beginning with 1 cup and adding water by the tablespoon until it forms a thick, but still pourable batter.

2. Heat a cast iron skillet over medium-high heat until a drop of water "dances" when dropped on the surface. Film the bottom with oil to completely cover it by about ⅛-inch and let it heat until it is almost smoking. Pour the batter onto the surface in about 3-tablespoon-sized rounds, spreading it with a spatula if necessary. There should be a lively sizzle as the batter meets the fat. Cook until golden brown on the bottom, about 3 to 4 minutes, turn, and cook until golden brown and firm. The edges will be thinner than the center and very crisp. Serve hot.

Sweet Potato Griddlecakes

Sweet potato added to the batter makes a subtle, delicious breakfast cake, but these are also great for supper served with bacon, ham, or spicy sausages. Serve them as you would pancakes, slathered with butter and cane or pure maple syrup—or, for old-fashioned Southern flavor, sorghum syrup.

Makes about 20 griddlecakes

1½ cups hot cooked, peeled, and mashed sweet potatoes (about 2 medium)
½ cup tightly packed light brown sugar
4 tablespoons unsalted butter
2 large eggs
About 1½ cups whole milk
1¾ cups unbleached all-purpose flour
3 teaspoons baking powder
1 teaspoon salt
1 teaspoon ground cinnamon
½ teaspoon freshly grated nutmeg

1. Position a rack in the center of the oven, place a large rimmed baking sheet on it, and preheat the oven to 150° to 170°F. (the warm setting). While the potatoes are still hot, mix in the sugar and 2 tablespoons of the butter until both are absorbed. In a separate bowl, beat the eggs well, and then beat in the milk. Melt the remaining butter and add it to the egg and milk. Stir in the sweet potato. Whisk or sift together the flour, baking powder, salt, cinnamon, and nutmeg. Gradually whisk the flour into the egg, milk, melted butter, and sweet potato. It should form a moderately thick but still pourable batter. If it seems too thick, add a little more milk.

2. Heat a griddle or wide, heavy-bottomed skillet over medium-high heat. Brush it well with melted butter, and drop the batter by generous 2-tablespoon-sized portions,

forming cakes about 3 inches in diameter. Cook until the bottom is golden brown and distinct air bubbles holes form in the center, about 3 minutes. Turn, and cook until uniformly browned, about 3 minutes longer. Transfer the cooked cakes to the baking sheet in the warm oven and repeat until all the batter is cooked.

Hominy Griddles

Leftover grits were once a daily problem for most Southern households: now one is lucky to have grits at all. In the days when there was always a surplus left in the breakfast pot, however, inventive, frugal cooks (who never wasted anything) often put that surplus to good use at suppertime, stirred into spoonbread (see Awendaw, or Hominy Spoonbread, page 65), or cut into thick squares and fried in cakes, as they are now served in trendy "nouvelle" Southern restaurants, or stirred into griddlecakes like these. They're worth making extra grits on purpose.

Makes about 24 griddlecakes, serving 4 to 6

1 cup stone-ground white cornmeal

1 teaspoon baking soda

2 teaspoons baking powder

1 teaspoon salt

2 large eggs

About 2 cups whole-milk buttermilk or plain whole-milk yogurt thinned with milk to buttermilk consistency

2 cups cooked grits (see Note for Awendaw, or Hominy Spoonbread, page 65), cooled

1. Position a rack in the center of the oven and preheat the oven to 150° to 170°F (the warm setting). Position a wire cooling rack over a rimmed baking sheet and place it in the center of the oven. Whisk together the meal, soda, baking powder, and salt in a mixing bowl. In a separate bowl, beat the eggs well and beat in the milk until smooth. Beat the grits thoroughly into the milk-egg mixture.

2. Place a griddle or wide, shallow skillet over medium-high heat, or heat an electric griddle to 325°F. When it is hot (a drop of water should "dance" on the surface), gradually beat the meal into the batter, sprinkling it in a little at a time. If the batter doesn't pour easily from the spoon, add a little more milk.

3. Brush the griddle or pan with melted butter—just enough to give it an even sheen,

and let it heat. Pour on the batter from the end of a large spoon in 2-tablespoon-sized portions. It should pool into a thin cake about 3 inches in diameter. Cook until the cakes are golden brown on the bottom, turn, and cook until uniformly golden, about 4 minutes per side. Transfer the cooked griddlecakes to the prepared baking sheet in the oven while you cook the remaining batter. Serve hot with butter and honey or cane syrup.

Rice Griddles

As the rice industry collapsed and then vanished from Carolina and Georgia, rice flour also vanished from the larder of most Lowcountry cooks, gradually replaced either by cornmeal or wheat flour—neither of which react at all the same way in cooking and baking. Cornmeal gives these cakes a different character and texture, but it can be substituted for rice flour if you have trouble finding it.

Makes about 14 griddlecakes, serving 4 to 6

½ cup rice flour (available at Asian and natural food markets) or stone-ground white cornmeal

½ teaspoon baking soda

½ teaspoon salt

1 large egg

About 1 cup whole-milk buttermilk or plain whole-milk yogurt thinned with milk to buttermilk consistency

1 cup soft-cooked long-grain white rice, cooled

1. Position a rack in the center of the oven, put a large, rimmed baking sheet on it, and preheat the oven to 150° to 170°F (the warm setting). Whisk together the flour, soda, and salt in a mixing bowl. In a separate bowl, lightly beat the egg and beat in the milk until smooth. Stir the rice into the milk and egg. Gradually beat the flour into the batter, sprinkling it in a little at a time. If the batter doesn't pour easily from the spoon, add a little more milk.

2. Place a griddle or wide, shallow skillet over medium-high heat, or heat an electric griddle to 325°F. It should be hot enough for a drop of water to "dance" on the surface but not so hot that the cakes immediately brown on the bottom.

3. Brush the griddle or pan with melted butter—just enough to give it an even sheen—and let it heat. Pour the batter in about 2-tablespoon-sized portions from the end of a large spoon—enough to pool into cakes about 3 inches in diameter. Cook until the

cakes are golden brown on the bottom and perforated with steam holes all the way into the center of the cake, about 3 minutes. Turn and cook until the second side is uniformly golden, about 3 minutes more. Transfer the cooked cakes to the baking sheet in the oven while you cook the remaining batter. Serve hot with honey or cane syrup.

Savannah Rice Waffles

Rice waffles were once a specialty of Lowcountry cooks and a signature on Savannah's best breakfast and supper tables. They were more prized then than they are today, because it was trickier to make them on waffle irons that did not have nonstick coatings and evenly regulated heating elements on both sides of the iron. We may not always appreciate how special they were in those days, nor how proud the cook must have been of having perfected their baking, but never mind: ease of preparation takes nothing away from the deep satisfaction of a crisp, well-made waffle. If you've not made waffles before, please read Waffle Wisdom (below) before beginning.

Rice waffles may be served as any other waffle would be, with fresh fruit and whipped cream, or with butter and syrup or honey, but they are also a terrific receptacle for savory toppings such as creamed chicken or turkey.

Makes about 6 large or 10 to 12 small waffles

1 cup warm cooked Carolina-Style Rice (page 54)
2 tablespoons unsalted butter
10 ounces (about 2 cups) unbleached all-purpose flour
2 teaspoons baking powder
½ teaspoon baking soda
1 teaspoon salt
2 large eggs, separated
1¼ cups whole-milk buttermilk or plain whole-milk yogurt thinned to buttermilk
    consistency with milk

1. While the rice is still warm, stir the butter into it until melted and incorporated. Set the rice aside to cool to room temperature.

2. Whisk together the flour, baking powder, soda, and salt. Beat the egg yolks and beat in the buttermilk and rice, then gradually stir in the dry ingredients. In a separate glass or metal bowl, beat the egg whites until they form soft peaks.

3. Prepare a waffle iron and heat it to medium heat. When it's hot, fold the egg whites gradually into the batter, brush the waffle iron well with fat, and spoon the batter evenly over it, leaving room at the edges for it to expand. Close the iron and bake until the steam stops rising from the iron, the fragrance changes and smells toasty, and the waffle is golden brown on both sides, about 5 to 8 minutes. Serve the waffle as soon as it comes off the iron, and repeat with the remaining batter until all of it is baked.

WAFFLE WISDOM: It is often hard to judge at first how much batter the iron will need without running over the sides, so your first batches may be less than perfect, but they will still taste good. And after the first couple of times, you'll know exactly how much batter to use. When the steam stops rising from the edges of the waffle iron, the waffles are probably done, but if it begins to smell as if it may be scorching, check it to be sure it hasn't browned too much. Don't check it while the steam is rolling out: if you open the iron before the waffle is set, it will tear up and be spoiled.

All waffles are at their best crisp and hot from the iron, but they can be made ahead and reheated on a rack in the oven or in a toaster. To store them, let them completely cool and refrigerate for up to a week or freeze in well-sealed airtight bags for up to 2 months.

Sweet Potato Waffles

While these exceptionally moist and flavorful waffles are wonderful served in the traditional way for breakfast, slathered with butter and syrup or perhaps a spoonful of fresh seasonal fruit, they are wonderful with those classic latke accompaniments, applesauce and sour cream, and really shine with sliced ripe bananas and/or strawberries and whipped cream. They are also delicious with just about any hot berry sauce, and make a terrific and elegant dessert when topped with a scoop of ice cream and a drizzle of fresh fruit sauce or strawberries and freshly whipped cream.

Please see Waffle Wisdom (page 92) before beginning.

Makes about 6 large waffles

1 medium hot cooked sweet potato, peeled and mashed (about 1 cup)

3 tablespoons unsalted butter, softened

¼ cup firmly packed light brown sugar

1 cup milk

2 large eggs, well beaten

8 ounces (about 1¾ cups) unbleached all-purpose flour

2 teaspoons Single-Acting Baking Powder (page 13)
    or 1⅓ teaspoon double-acting

1 teaspoon ground cinnamon

½ teaspoon freshly grated nutmeg

½ teaspoon salt

1 teaspoon Homemade Bourbon Vanilla (page 23) or vanilla extract

1. While the sweet potato is hot, add the butter and brown sugar and mix until both are melted and incorporated; stir in the milk and eggs until smooth.

2. In a separate bowl, whisk or sift together the flour, baking powder, cinnamon, nutmeg, and salt. Gradually beat it into the sweet potato batter until it is smooth and free of lumps. Beat in the vanilla. Heat the waffle iron to medium heat (about 375°F). Brush

both sides lightly with melted butter, spoon in enough batter to just cover it, then close the iron and bake until the steam no longer rises from the iron, and the waffle begins to smell toasty and is a deep golden brown. Remove it from the waffle iron and repeat with the remaining butter and batter. Serve hot, in any of the ways suggested above. To store leftover waffles for reheating later, see Waffle Wisdom, page 92.

Hush Puppies

Hush puppies are the traditional bread served with any fish fry in the South, and hot and crisp from the fat that the fish were cooked in, they can be one of the most satisfying fried breads in the world. Unfortunately, they can also be leaden and depressing, especially when they are not piping hot and fresh from the pan. The memory of my own mother's feathery light hush puppies from my childhood—which she unhappily no longer makes—has inevitably led me to vague disappointment in nearly every fried cornbread I've had ever since, my own included. But when I was styling a recipe for fresh corn fritters from Edna Lewis and Scott Peacock's The Gift of Southern Cooking *for a newspaper story photograph, the first bite brought back a rush of memories that told me what had been missing: separately beaten egg whites made the fritters light and airy—and very much like my mother's elusive hush puppies.*

Makes about 2 to 2¹/₂ dozen hush puppies, serving 6 to 8

³/₄ cup stone-ground white cornmeal

¹/₄ cup white corn flour (available at Latin markets and the ethnic food section of some supermarkets)

¹/₂ teaspoon baking soda

1 teaspoon baking powder

¹/₂ teaspoon salt

1 medium scallion or other green onions, trimmed and minced

1 large egg

About 1 cup whole-milk buttermilk or plain whole-milk yogurt thinned with milk to buttermilk consistency

Lard, peanut oil, or any pure vegetable oil, for frying

1. Whisk together the meal, flour, soda, baking powder, and salt in large mixing bowl. Add the scallion and toss until well mixed. Separate the egg, setting the white aside in a glass or metal bowl, and beat the yolk with ³/₄ cup of buttermilk. Stir this into the dry in-

gredients, mixing well. It should be about the consistency of thin mush: if it seems too stiff, add more milk by the tablespoonful.

2. In a heavy-bottomed deep pot or deep-frying skillet, put at least 1 to 2 inches of fat, but no more than halfway up the sides. Place it over medium-high heat and heat it to 375°F. Position a rack in the upper third of the oven and preheat the oven to 150° to 175°F. (the warm setting). Set a wire cooling rack over a rimmed baking sheet and put it in the oven.

3. When the fat is almost ready, beat the egg white with a whisk or handheld mixer until it forms soft peaks. Fold them gently but quickly into the batter. Drop the batter into the fat in rounded tablespoonfuls until the pan is full but not crowded. Fry until golden brown, turning once, if necessary. Remove the hush puppies with tongs or a wire frying skimmer (not a spatula or slotted spoon), blot briefly on absorbent paper, and transfer them to the wire rack. Hold it in the oven while you fry the remaining batter. Serve piping hot.

Chicken (or Skillet) Biscuits

On the farmsteads of hardworking rural Southern families, appetites have always been large and chickens rather small. Moreover, killing enough birds to give every single person at the table the kind of portions that we expect today would have wiped out the barnyard's population in a real hurry. A popular way, therefore, of making the precious chicken stretch farther— was to flavor morsels of bread dough by frying them in the fat leftover from cooking the bird itself. It's rather on the same order as hush puppies, only the bread is a traditional Southern biscuit dough that "bakes" in hot deep fat instead of an oven—rich, golden brown, and irresistibly delicious. Kentucky cooking diva Ronni Lundy, from whom I learned to make these, cuts her chicken biscuits with a star-shaped cookie cutter. The fanciful shapes do make them a lot more fun at the table, but you can just cut them in squares with a knife or into regular round biscuits if you prefer.

Makes about 18 small biscuits

10 ounces (about 2 cups) unbleached all-purpose flour or pastry flour
2 teaspoons baking powder
1/2 teaspoon salt
1/2 teaspoon each finely crushed dried sage and thyme
Whole pepper in a peppermill, optional
2 tablespoons (1 ounce) lard or unsalted butter
Leftover fat from frying chicken, or fresh lard, peanut oil, or other vegetable oil,
    for frying
1 cup whole-milk buttermilk or plain whole-milk yogurt thinned with milk to
    buttermilk consistency

1. Whisk together the flour, baking powder, salt, herbs, and, if you like, a few liberal grindings of pepper in a mixing bowl. Add the lard and cut it into the flour with a pastry blender or two knives until the mixture resembles coarse meal.

2. Put enough fat in a skillet or heavy-bottomed Dutch oven to come 1 to 2 inches up

the sides of the pan (but no more than halfway). Turn on the heat to medium-high and heat it until hot but not smoking—about 325°F (see Note, below). Make a well in the center of the flour and pour in the buttermilk. Quickly stir together, working it as little as possible. It should be the consistency of Southern Breakfast Biscuits (page 35). If it seems too dry, add milk by spoonfuls until you get the right consistency. Lightly flour the dough and gather it into a ball.

3. Lightly flour a work surface and put the dough on it. Gently pat it out into a flat cake about ½ inch thick. Fold it over, give it a quarter turn, and gently pat it out again. Lightly flour it again if it begins to stick. Repeat this four times and then pat it out ½ inch thick.

4. Quickly cut the dough either with a knife into squares or with a cookie or biscuit cutter into rounds or fanciful shapes. When the fat is ready, add the biscuits one at a time until the pan is full but not crowded. Fry, turning once, until risen and golden brown, about 3 to 5 minutes. Take them up with a wire frying skimmer and transfer them to the wire rack in the oven while you fry the remaining batter. Serve piping hot.

NOTE: If you are using leftover fat from frying the chicken, it will already be somewhat tempered and won't heat to as high a temperature as fresh fat, especially if you are frying in the same pan that you cooked the chicken in: there will be solids that will considerably lower the burning point of the fat. You can raise its burning temperature by adding a little fresh fat to the pan, but the best you will likely get is 325°F. before it starts to smoke. That is plenty hot enough for the biscuits: in fact, I prefer to fry biscuit dough at a slightly lower temperature than most other deep-fat frying.

Rice Pups, or Savory Rice Fritters

Rice fritters can be found in the Americas wherever there are descendants of rice-growing West African slaves, especially in the rice-growing regions of the Carolina and Georgia Lowcountry. Dr. Jessica Harris, who has spent a lifetime studying the culinary cross-current of the trade winds between Africa and the Americas, uses the connection as a kind of kitchen road map that she calls "the fritter factor." Where fritters are perfected anywhere on the Atlantic rim, an African hand has almost always been in the pot, and when the fritters also contain rice, you can pretty much bet on it.

Makes about 2 to 2½ dozen fritters

½ cup raw long-grain white rice or 1 cup leftover cooked long-grain rice

2 cups water (only if using raw rice)

Salt

½ cup white rice flour

1 teaspoon baking powder

½ teaspoon baking soda

Ground cayenne pepper

Whole black pepper in a peppermill

1 large or 2 small scallions or other green onions, trimmed and minced

1 large egg

1 cup plain whole-milk yogurt

Lard or vegetable oil, for frying

1. If you are using cooked rice, skip to step 2. Otherwise, bring 2 cups water to a boil over medium-high heat. Stir in the rice and a large pinch of salt. Let it return to a boil and reduce the heat to low. Simmer gently until the rice is quite soft, about 20 minutes. Drain off any excess moisture and set it aside, uncovered.

2. Whisk together the flour, a small pinch of salt, the baking powder, soda, a pinch of cayenne pepper to taste, and several generous grindings of black pepper in a large mixing

bowl. Add the rice and scallion and toss until well mixed. The rice should still hold its shape, so don't overwork it.

3. Separate the egg, setting the white aside in a glass or metal bowl. Beat the yolk into the yogurt. Make a well in the center of the rice and flour mixture and stir the yogurt into it lightly, but thoroughly until there are no dry, crumbly bits left.

4. Position a rack in the upper third of the oven and preheat the oven to 150° to 170°F. (the warm setting). Fit a wire cooling rack over a rimmed cookie sheet and place it in the upper third of the oven. Choose a deep, heavy-bottomed pot or skillet and put in enough lard or vegetable oil to come 1½ to 2 inches up the sides of the pan, but no more than halfway. Turn on the heat to medium-high and heat the fat to 375°F.

5. When the fat is hot, beat the egg white with a wire whisk or handheld mixer to soft peaks. Fold it gently but quickly into the fritter mixture. Drop the batter by rounded tablespoonfuls into the fat until the pan is full but not crowded, and fry them, turning once, until they are a uniform, rich golden brown. Remove them with a wire frying skimmer and transfer them to the wire rack in the oven while you fry the remaining fritters. Serve hot.

Classic Creole Calas

These are the true, original calas of New Orleans, the ones that now vanished legendary street vendors once hawked in the old French Quarter with cries of "Belle calas! Tout Choud!"— *"Beautiful calas! Very hot!" Unhappily, they, like those old vendors, have almost disappeared, having been mostly replaced by fritters leavened with baking powder instead of yeast. Though these take longer to rise, they are much more delicate than the modern baking powder fritters, and well worth waiting for. Classic calas are flavored only with nutmeg, but I like the added flavor of a touch of grated lemon zest.*

Makes about 1 dozen calas

½ cup raw long-grain white rice
2 cups water
Salt
½ teaspoon active dry yeast
½ cup lukewarm water
3 large eggs, lightly beaten
½ cup granulated sugar
8 ounces (about 1¾ cups) unbleached all-purpose flour
Whole nutmeg in a grater
Grated zest of 1 lemon
Lard, peanut oil, or other vegetable oil, for frying
Superfine sugar or confectioners' sugar, for dusting

1. The night (or at least 8 hours) before you plan to serve the calas, put the rice in a heavy-bottomed saucepan with 2 cups of water and a large pinch of salt. Turn on the heat to medium-high and bring the water to a boil. Reduce the heat to medium-low, stir, and cook until the rice is quite soft, about 20 minutes. Meanwhile, dissolve the yeast in the ½ cup of lukewarm water and let it proof for at least 10 minutes. Drain the rice and let it

cool until it is just warm, then beat the yeast and water into it, cover it well with plastic wrap, and let it rise overnight or for at least 8 hours.

2. The next morning, beat in the eggs and granulated sugar, then gradually beat in the flour, and finally a generous grating of nutmeg and the lemon zest. It should be the consistency of cooked oatmeal. Cover and let it stand for at least half an hour.

3. Position a rack in the upper third of the oven and preheat the oven to 150° to 170°F (the warm setting). Fit a wire cooling rack over a rimmed baking sheet and place it on the rack in the oven. Put in enough fat to come at least 2 inches up the sides of a heavy-bottomed Dutch oven and heat it over medium-high heat to 375°F.

4. Drop the batter into the fat by rounded tablespoonfuls, using another spoon or rubber spatula to push the batter off the spoon, until the pot is full but not crowded. Fry, turning once, until golden brown, about 4 to 6 minutes altogether. Remove the calas from the fat with a wire frying skimmer. Put them on the wire rack in the oven while you fry the remaining batter. Dust well with superfine sugar and serve hot.

Quick Calas

Though not as delicate as the previous recipe, modern baking-powder-leavened calas can still be quite good, and have the advantage of quick mixing on the morning you plan to serve them, which is probably why they eventually replaced the yeast-leavened fritters of the old days. If you have leftover rice, the mixing is even quicker: use a generous cup of cooked rice for the quantities given here and omit step 1. The big drawback of these fritters is that, aside from lacking the delicacy of yeast-leavened calas, they do not keep well. They can be reheated the same day in a hot (400°F) oven or by refrying them briefly, but they are leaden and hopeless by the second day. If you want to make fewer servings, the recipe easily divides by half to make an even dozen, serving up to four.

Makes about 2 dozen calas, serving 6 to 8

½ cup raw long-grain white rice

2 cups water

Salt

Lard, peanut oil, or other vegetable oil, for frying

1 cup unbleached all-purpose flour

2 teaspoons baking powder

⅓ cup granulated sugar

½ teaspoon salt

½ teaspoon ground cinnamon

½ teaspoon freshly grated nutmeg

1 lemon

2 large eggs, well beaten

Superfine sugar or confectioners' sugar, for dusting

1. Put the rice in a heavy-bottomed saucepan with 2 cups water and a large pinch of salt. Turn on the heat to medium-high and bring to a boil. Reduce the heat to medium-

low, stir, and cook until the rice is quite soft, about 18 to 20 minutes. Drain it well and let it cool until it is just warm.

2. Position a rack in the upper third of the oven and preheat the oven to 150° to 170°F (the warm setting). Fit a wire cooling rack over a rimmed baking sheet and place it on the rack in the oven. Put in enough fat to come at least 2 inches (but no more than halfway) up the sides of a heavy-bottomed Dutch oven and place it over medium-high heat. Heat it until it is hot but not quite smoking, 375°F.

3. Meanwhile, whisk together the flour, baking powder, sugar, ½ teaspoon salt, cinnamon, and nutmeg. Grate the zest from the lemon into the flour. Mix in the rice and eggs. Cut the lemon in half and squeeze in the juice from one half through a strainer. If needed, add a few spoonfuls of water to make a stiff batter the consistency of cooked oatmeal. When the fat is hot, drop in the batter by heaping tablespoonfuls until the pot is full but not crowded. Fry, turning once, until golden brown, about 5 to 6 minutes. Remove the calas with a wire frying skimmer and transfer them to the prepared pan in the oven while you fry the remaining batter. Dust liberally with superfine sugar and serve hot.

Carolina Rice Jam Fritters

Creole New Orleans is not the only place where West African sweet rice fritters turn up. A version of these old-fashioned jam fritters from the Carolina Lowcountry were included in my last book, Damon Lee Fowler's New Southern Kitchen, *but they are so good that they are well worth repeating here. Vary them by substituting orange zest and about a tablespoon of freshly squeezed orange juice for the lemon zest and juice, and use a good-quality orange marmalade for the filling.*

Serves 4

2 cups whole milk or half-and-half
½ cup granulated sugar
1 cup raw long-grain white rice
1 tablespoon unsalted butter
Whole nutmeg in a grater
1 lemon
¼ cup unbleached all-purpose flour
2 large eggs
½ cup raspberry, blackberry, strawberry, or damson plum jam or preserves
1 cup fine cracker crumbs or dry bread crumbs
Lard or peanut oil, for frying
Superfine sugar or confectioners' sugar, for dusting

1. Put the milk in a 2-quart saucepan and stir in the sugar until it is dissolved. Turn on the heat to medium-high and bring the milk to a simmer, stirring frequently. Stir in the rice and bring it back to a simmer. Reduce the heat to a bare simmer, loosely cover the pan, and cook, fluffing the rice occasionally with a fork to be sure it isn't scorching, until the rice is very soft, about 20 minutes. Turn off the heat.

2. Stir in the butter and a generous grating of nutmeg. Grate the zest from the lemon into the rice, cut the lemon in half, and squeeze the juice from one half through a strainer

into the rice. Sprinkle the flour over all and mix well. Spread the rice on a plate or platter to cool. When it is almost room temperature, stir in the eggs, spread the mixture again, and cover it with plastic wrap. Refrigerate until it is cold and set, about 2 hours.

3. Moisten your hands and scoop a tablespoon of the rice into one hand. Make an indentation in it with your thumb and spoon about half a teaspoon of jam into it. Scoop up another tablespoon of the rice and place it over the jam. Seal the two pats of rice together and shape the whole into a ball. Lightly roll each ball in fine cracker crumbs and put them on a clean, dry plate. Refrigerate until you are ready to cook them.

4. To a deep skillet or cast-iron Dutch oven, add enough lard to come halfway up the sides. Turn on the heat to medium-high and heat the fat until it is hot but not quite smoking (375°F). Fry the fritters in batches, turning them once if necessary, until they are uniformly golden and cooked through, about 3 minutes. Remove them from the fat with tongs or a wire frying skimmer to a wire rack. Drain thoroughly and transfer them to a clean serving platter. Dust generously with superfine sugar and serve at once.

Creole *Pets-de-Nonne* (Souffléed Fritters)

This is the Creole version of an ancient French souffléed fritter pets-de-nonne, *which is usually prettily translated into English as "Nun's Sighs" (though what it literally means is "Nun's Farts"). They're a variation of the famous beignets of classic French and Creole cooking; they differ in that they are lightened with separately beaten egg whites. They puff spectacularly—no doubt the inspiration for their rather colorful name—and the delicately crisp, amber-gold crust envelopes a light-as-air and yet creamy center.*

Makes 2 to 2½ dozen fritters

½ cup whole milk
½ cup water
2 tablespoons butter
2 tablespoons granulated sugar
Salt
¾ cup unbleached all-purpose flour
Grated zest of 1 lemon
½ teaspoon freshly grated nutmeg
3 large eggs, separated
Lard, peanut oil, or pure vegetable oil, for frying
Superfine sugar, or confectioners' sugar, for dusting

1. Put the milk and water in a heavy-bottomed saucepan. Stir in the butter, sugar, and a tiny pinch of salt. Bring it to the boiling point over medium heat, stirring occasionally, and let it simmer about 2 minutes. Off the heat, gradually beat in the flour: it will quickly become thick and pasty. Return it to the heat and beat until it is satiny smooth, pulling away from the sides, and leaving a film on the bottom of the pan. This will take less than a minute and the paste will begin to clump in a big ball around the spoon. Remove it from the heat and beat until it is cooled slightly.

2. Beat the lemon zest and nutmeg into the paste and then the egg yolks, one at a time, and beat until the paste is satiny and very smooth. It will still be very stiff.

3. Put enough lard or oil into a heavy-bottomed Dutch oven or deep frying pan to come about 2 inches, but no more than halfway, up the sides. Turn on the heat to medium-high and heat it to 375°F. Fit a wire cooling rack over a rimmed baking sheet. Meanwhile, beat the egg whites in a metal or glass bowl until they form soft peaks and fold a third of them into the paste to loosen it some. Fold in the remaining whites (there will be lumps of paste) and then beat until the batter is smooth and glossy once again.

4. When the fat is hot, drop the paste into it by rounded teaspoonfuls. Fry, turning once, until they are puffed and a rich golden amber brown, about 3 minutes. Remove with a wire frying skimmer to the wire rack while you fry the remaining fritters. Dust generously with superfine sugar and serve hot.

VARIATION

BEIGNETS: This fritter paste is a classic pâte à choux—the same paste that makes cream puffs and beignets (which along the Eastern seaboard are known as Bell Fritters because they are hollow and bell-like). The difference is that the eggs are not separated before being beaten into the paste. Beat them in one at a time and beat the paste for a full minute after the last egg is added. They still puff magnificently and delicately.

Rosemary- and Ginger-Scented Fried Apple Pies

Fried fruit pies, properly made only with dried fruit, are a perennial favorite all across the South, but the pies can and do vary from place to place. My grandmother's fried pies, made with a kind of modified biscuit dough for the crust and cooked in a pan lubricated with barely enough butter to keep them from sticking, were very different from the deep-fried versions that I've had in other people's homes since childhood. These pies can be of either persuasion, and while the traditional filling is given a lift with a touch of rosemary, fresh ginger, and lemon, it's still the same satisfying homespun pastry that many homesick Southerners crave.

Makes 12 pies

8 ounces dried apples

⅓ cup granulated sugar

2 large sprigs fresh rosemary (at least 3 inches long; do not use dried)

2 quarter-sized slices fresh ginger

1 lemon

2 ounces (½ stick or 4 tablespoons) unsalted butter, cut into teaspoon-sized bits

1 recipe Basic Pastry (page 210)

Butter (for sautéeing); peanut oil or vegetable oil, for deep-frying

Superfine sugar or confectioners' sugar, for dusting, optional

1. Put the apples in a heavy stainless or enameled saucepan with the sugar, rosemary, ginger, and enough water to completely cover. Turn on the heat to medium-high and bring to a boil; reduce the heat to medium-low and simmer, stirring occasionally, until the apples are tender and the liquid has mostly evaporated, about 45 minutes. Remove and discard the rosemary and ginger. Grate the zest of the lemon into the apples, cut the lemon in half, and squeeze in the juice from one half, to taste. (Save the remaining lemon half for another use.) Roughly crush the fruit with a potato masher. Mix in the butter until dissolved.

2. Divide the pastry into twelve equal balls. Roll each out on a lightly floured surface

into a circle about 5 inches across and ⅛ inch thick. Put a rounded tablespoon of apples in the center of each, brush the edges with a little water, and fold the pastry over the filling to form a half-circle, gently pressing the edges together with the tines of a fork. If the edges are a little ragged, even them up by trimming them with a knife or zigzag pastry wheel.

3. The pies may be either sautéed or deep-fried. To sauté them, heat a heavy-bottomed skillet over medium heat, brush it with butter until it is well coated, and sauté the pies until they are golden brown, about 4 to 5 minutes per side. The pastry will be soft but flaky.

4. To deep-fry them, put enough lard or oil in a deep, heavy-bottomed skillet or Dutch oven about an inch deep but no more than halfway up the sides. Turn on the heat to medium-high. Meanwhile, fit a wire cooling rack over a rimmed baking sheet. When the fat is hot, but not quite smoking (375°F.), put in enough pies to fill the pan without crowding. Fry until the bottoms are nicely browned, about 3 minutes, turn, and fry until uniformly browned, about 3 minutes more. Drain them well on the wire cooling rack. If you like, dust them lightly with superfine sugar. Serve hot or at room temperature.

VARIATION

FRIED PEACH PIES WITH ORANGE: Substitute dried peaches for the apples, omit the rosemary and ginger, and season the peaches with a generous grating of nutmeg and a tablespoon of bourbon. Use orange zest and juice instead of lemon. Assemble and cook the pies as directed in steps 2, 3, and 4.

Chicken Mushroom Puffs

Deep-fried meat-filled pastries are standard fare at tailgate parties during the season for that modern Deep South religion, collegiate football, but the tradition long predates the tailgate party. Annabella Hill included delicate meat-filled puffs of deep-fried pastry in her 1867 classic, Mrs. Hill's New Cook Book *and, of course, there are the famed meat pastries from Natchitoches, Louisiana. Most modern versions of these pies make use of ground beef or bulk sausage meat, which is convenient if a little dull. Here, diced chicken, mushrooms, and other savory flavors are combined for a more interesting balance of flavors and textures. They are as good if not better at room temperature, and would be welcome in any tailgate basket on a cool autumn afternoon—whether you are heading for a game or just a bright spot of fall foliage.*

Makes 3 to 3½ dozen small pies

1 ounce dried cèpes or porcini mushrooms

1 cup boiling water

6 ounces fresh brown (crimini or baby bella) mushrooms

2 tablespoons unsalted butter

1 small or ½ medium yellow onion, trimmed, split lengthwise, peeled,
    and minced

1 large or 2 medium cloves garlic, lightly crushed, peeled,
    and minced

1 tablespoon chopped fresh sage or 1 teaspoon crumbled dried

1 tablespoon chopped fresh thyme or 1 teaspoon crumbled dried

8 ounces (about 1 generous cup) small diced cooked chicken

Salt, whole black pepper in a peppermill, and ground cayenne pepper

Whole nutmeg in a grater

1 cup heavy cream

1 recipe Basic Pastry (page 210)

Lard or vegetable oil, for frying

1. Put the dried mushrooms in a heatproof bowl and pour the boiling water over them. Let them soak at least 15 minutes, until softened. Meanwhile, wipe the fresh mushrooms clean with a dry cloth or paper towel and chop them.

2. Lift the reconstituted dried mushrooms out of the soaking liquid, dipping them several times to remove any sand or dirt that may be clinging to them, and roughly chop them. Put them in a small saucepan. Strain the soaking liquid through a coffee filter or undyed paper towel and add it to the pan. Turn on the heat to medium-high and cook, stirring occasionally, until the liquid is absorbed into the mushrooms and almost completely evaporated. It should not dry up completely and scorch, so watch it carefully.

3. Put the butter in a large sauté pan or skillet and turn on the heat to medium-high. When it is just melted, add the onion and sauté, tossing frequently, until it is colored deep gold. Add the garlic and herbs and sauté until fragrant, about a minute longer. Add both mushrooms and sauté until they are beginning to color, about 4 minutes.

4. Add the chicken and toss until it is heated through. Season to taste with salt, black and cayenne pepper, and freshly grated nutmeg. Pour in the cream and bring it to a boil. Cook, stirring occasionally, until the cream is lightly thickened enough to coat the back of the spoon. Turn off the heat. Transfer the filling to a wide, shallow bowl and let it cool. Cover and refrigerate until thoroughly chilled. The filling can be made a day ahead up to this point.

5. Roll out the pastry and cut it with a biscuit cutter into 3-inch circles. Put a slightly rounded teaspoon of filling at the center of each. Moisten the edges with a little water and fold the pastry in half. Gently press the edges together with a fork.

6. Position a rack in the upper third of the oven and preheat to 150° to 170°F (the warm setting). Fit a wire rack over a rimmed baking sheet and place it in the oven. Put enough lard or oil to come halfway up the sides of a deep skillet or a heavy-bottomed Dutch oven and place it over medium-high heat. Heat the fat to 375°F (hot, but quite not smoking). Slip enough pastries into the fat to fill the pan without crowding and fry, turning once, until they are golden brown, about 5 to 6 minutes.

Cookies—Short and Sweet

THE ONLY POSSIBLE EXPLANATION for why the serpent used a tree full of fruit to tempt Eve is that cookies had not yet been invented. It is certain that had she presented Adam with a cookie instead of some suspicious-looking fruit, he'd have bitten right in and asked questions later. Ever since these little morsels came along, they've been used by temptresses the world over—by brides to please a new husband and win over reticent mothers-in-law or nosy neighbors, by mothers and grandmothers to tame unruly children, by little girls (of all ages) to lure little boys into a modicum of civilized behavior (or trouble, depending on how old they are).

Often called "little cakes" in old cookbooks ("cookie,"

adapted from a Dutch word, did not come into common American usage until late in the nineteenth century), these sweet little bites of temptation have been a part of American baking from the beginning, but not in the commonplace, taken-for-granted role they occupy today. Once reserved for special occasions, today they fill entire aisles of most supermarkets, and have become our easy answer to virtually every daily whim, from a reward for a good mood to a salve for depression. Ready-baked confections may satisfy as a quick fix, but they can't replace the irresistible aroma of cookies baking in your own oven, which is probably why as much as half the dairy case is taken up with cylinders of prepared cookie dough, ready to slice off and bake—or, as is often the case nowadays—to pinch right off the cylinder and eat raw.

The puzzling thing about the proliferation of this ready-to-bake dough is that making your own is not much more work than slicing off a hunk of the stuff, and it is a lot more rewarding. Whether they are artless, almost thrown-together confections such as shortbread and bar cookies, delicately subtle lacy wafers, or savory, spicy-crisp cheese straws, cookies require no special skills and are accessible to the most inexperienced baker. It's no wonder that they're often the first thing children learn to bake on their own. All they require is first-rate ingredients, carefully measured, a little care in the mixing, and very little of the cook's attention once they go into the oven. About the hardest thing about cookie baking is remembering not to wander off and forget them until that unmistakable and depressing odor of over-browned flour and sugar brings you running back—too late—to the kitchen.

Beyond simply paying attention while the things bake, here are a few cookie basics:

* Eggs and butter (and, if you live in a hot, humid climate and store your flour in the fridge, that too) should all be at room temperature unless noted otherwise.
* All-purpose flour is fine for most cookies: the mix of soft and hard-wheat flours usually does just fine in these simple doughs. Only a few of them benefit from the low glutens of soft-wheat flour, and I've so noted where it applies.
* A kitchen timer is useful in helping you not to forget to check a baking batch, but only after you have gotten used to your oven and know how hot or cool it tends to run. Set the timer for a minute or two before the time indicated.
* After a while, your nose will be the best indicator of doneness: you'll know by smell

when they are still underdone, just right, or beginning to overcook. Pay attention to those smells: once you get accustomed to them, they will never fail you.

* Most cookie doughs (except bar cookies and wafers) can be made ahead and refrigerated or frozen. You can make a batch to have on hand or bake part of a batch and store the leftover dough to use later and have fresh-baked cookies all along. Often, chilling the dough makes it easier to handle, and I've indicated as much in the pertinent recipes.

Julie's Lemon Squares

Lemon squares have long been an American standard, so much so that it always rather surprises me when a bakery declines to share its recipe for this simple confection—when, in fact, their version seldom varies from the hundreds that can be found throughout the country, and few of them ever surpass those made by my friend Julie Hooper. Julie is a good, if cautious, cook but a fearless, natural-born baker. The secret to her intensely lemony squares is simple: she uses more fresh-squeezed lemon juice and zest than most recipes call for and believes that life is too short not to use first-rate butter.

Makes about 3 dozen bar cookies

FOR THE SHORTBREAD CRUST:

½ cup confectioners' sugar
2 cups unbleached all-purpose flour
Salt
8 ounces (1 cup or 2 sticks) unsalted butter, softened

FOR THE CUSTARD FILLING:
4 eggs, well beaten
2 cups granulated sugar
Grated zest of 1 lemon
⅓ cup plus 1 tablespoon freshly squeezed lemon juice
    (about 2 large or 3 medium lemons)
¼ cup unbleached all-purpose flour
½ teaspoon baking powder
Superfine sugar or confectioners' sugar, for dusting

1. Position a rack in the center of the oven and preheat the oven to 350°F. Make the shortbread crust: sift together the sugar, flour, and a pinch of salt. Work the flour into the

butter with your fingers, or begin by cutting it in with a pastry blender and then finish it with your hands until the butter is evenly incorporated and the dough is crumbly but uniform and holds together when you press a lump in your hand. (The initial cutting-in can be done in the food processor. Process until the mixture resembles coarse meal and then finish it by hand.) Clean your hands and press the dough evenly over the bottom of a 9 × 13-inch sheet cake pan. Thoroughly prick the dough with a fork to prevent it from puffing. Bake in the center of the oven until the edges are golden brown and the top is beginning to color, about 20 minutes. Remove from the oven and cool slightly.

2. While the crust bakes, make the custard filling: stir together the eggs, granulated sugar, lemon zest, and juice. Sift the flour and baking powder over the top and stir them in until the custard is smooth. Pour the custard evenly over the baked shortbread crust, return the pan to the oven, and bake until the custard is set, about 25 minutes.

3. Cool completely and then sift the superfine sugar evenly over the top. The squares usually pull away from the sides of the pan as they cook, but if they don't, run a thin, sharp knife around the edge of the pan and cut evenly into 1½- to 2-inch squares.

Bourbon Pecan Squares

This rich kissing cousin to lemon squares combines two famed Southern baking traditions in one sumptuous mouthful: Southern-style shortbread, laced with a little cornmeal for texture, and a brown sugar, bourbon, and pecan topping reminiscent of those delectable little Southern confections, pecan tassies. Best of all, they are even easier than tassies to make—and dangerously irresistible.

Makes 2 dozen bar cookies

2 cups whole pecan halves

10 ounces (about 2 cups) Southern soft-wheat flour (see page 9) or unbleached all-purpose flour, plus 1 tablespoon

2 tablespoons extra-fine white cornmeal

1 cup granulated sugar

Salt

10 ounces (1¼ cups or 2½ sticks) unsalted butter, softened

3 large eggs

½ cup firmly packed light brown sugar

2 tablespoons bourbon

1. Position a rack in the center of the oven and preheat the oven to 375°F. Spread the pecans on a baking sheet and place them in the oven. Toast until beginning to color, about 8 to 10 minutes. Remove the pecans from the oven, cool, and roughly chop them. Reduce the oven temperature to 350°F.

2. Sift or whisk together 2 cups of the flour, the cornmeal, ½ cup of granulated sugar, and a small pinch of salt. Add 8 ounces (1 cup or 2 sticks) of the butter and work it into the flour until it forms a smooth dough. You may do the first part of this step in a food processor fitted with a steel blade. Put in the flour, meal, sugar, and salt and pulse several times to sift. Add the butter and process until the mixture resembles coarse meal. Turn it

out into a mixing bowl and finish blending the dough by hand. Wrap and chill for 30 minutes, or until manageable.

3. Press the dough into a 9 × 13-inch sheet cake pan in a uniform layer over the entire surface and press slightly up the sides. Lightly prick it with a fork and place it in the oven. Bake for 20 minutes, until it is beginning to color, then remove it from the oven and let it cool slightly.

4. Melt the remaining butter and let it cool slightly. Beat together the butter, eggs, remaining granulated sugar, brown sugar, and a small pinch of salt. Stir in the bourbon and pecans. Sift the remaining tablespoon of flour into the mixture and stir it in until smooth. Spread the topping over the shortbread crust and smooth it with a spatula.

5. Bake until the topping is golden and set, about 25 minutes. Cool in the pan on a wire rack and cut into twenty-four squares.

Aunt Margaret's Congo Squares

Southern families are endlessly convoluted, and sorting them out is not helped by the fact that most of us grew up with "aunts," "uncles," "Big Mamas," "Ma-Mas," "Paw-Paws," and "Grannies" that were not really blood relatives—at least not in any way that was ever acknowledged. Margaret Snelgrove was not my mother's sister, but her best friend, and yet I never knew her as anything but "Aunt." If you are Southern, you already understand, and if you aren't—well, explaining why is way too complicated. What's to the point is that Aunt Margaret was a terrific, old-fashioned Southern cook and baker, and any visit to her house always included plenty of good things to eat. For us children, that usually meant a big stash of these luscious, chocolate-studded blond brownies—or so I used to think. It was only while I was working on this book that my mother confessed that Aunt Margaret always had them on hand when we visited because they were Mama's secret favorite.

There are several folk explanations for this cookie's name, some more complicated than explaining about Aunt Margaret, but the most plausible is that they are named for Congo Square in New Orleans.

Makes 2 dozen bar cookies

6 ounces (¾ cup or 1½ sticks) unsalted butter, melted

2¼ cups firmly packed light brown sugar

3 large eggs, well beaten

2¾ cups unbleached all-purpose flour, measured by spooning it into the cup

2½ teaspoons baking powder

½ teaspoon salt

6 ounces (1 cup) semisweet chocolate chips

1 cup Toasted Pecans (page 18), broken up or roughly chopped

1. Position a rack in the center of the oven and preheat the oven to 325°F. Lightly butter and flour (see page 155) two 7½ × 11-inch pans (that's what Aunt Margaret used) or one 9 × 13-inch sheet cake pan. In a large mixing bowl, stir together the butter and

sugar until smooth. Stir in the eggs one at a time, mixing well until they are smoothly incorporated.

2. Sift together the flour, baking powder, and a pinch of salt onto a large sheet of wax paper or into a separate bowl. Gradually stir it into the batter, a little at a time. By the end, the batter will be fairly stiff, like cookie dough. Fold in the chocolate and pecans. Scrape the batter into the prepared pans, even it out with a spatula, and bake for 25 to 30 minutes, or until lightly browned and set in the center. The smaller pans will cook more quickly and produce slightly thinner cookies than the sheet cake pan. Cool the cookies in the pan on a wire rack, and then cut into twenty-four uniform squares.

Chocolate Mint Cream Cheese Brownies

Like Chocolate Irish Lace (page 142), these minty brownies, marbled with pale green cream cheese, are a by-product of Savannah's raucous St. Patrick's Day celebration, when everybody and everything turns Irish (and/or green) for about three long days. But you need not feel obliged to serve them only during March; they are fine picnic fare all summer long, and make a welcome, warming treat with hot tea or coffee on cool autumn afternoons.

Makes 2 dozen brownies

1¼ cups unbleached all-purpose flour, plus 2 tablespoons

1 teaspoon baking powder

1 teaspoon salt

4 ounces unsweetened chocolate

¼ pound (½ cup or 1 stick) unsalted butter

2¼ cups sugar

6 large eggs

1 tablespoon Homemade Bourbon Vanilla (page 23)
    or 1 teaspoon vanilla extract

1 pound (two 8-ounce packages) cream cheese, softened

¼ cup green crème de menthe liqueur

1. Position a rack in the center of the oven and preheat the oven to 350°F. Lightly butter and flour a 9 × 13-inch sheet cake pan (see page 155). Sift together 1¼ cups of the flour, baking powder, and salt onto a sheet of wax paper.

2. Put the chocolate and butter in a saucepan and melt it over medium-low heat, stirring occasionally. Stir in 2 cups of sugar and beat in 4 eggs, one at a time. Stir in the vanilla, then gather up the wax paper and pour in the flour mixture. Mix it in until the batter is smooth.

3. With a mixer, beat the cream cheese until fluffy, then beat in the remaining 2 eggs, ¼ cup sugar, and 2 tablespoons flour. Add the liqueur and mix until smooth. Pour half the

chocolate batter into the baking pan and level it with a spatula. Spoon the cream cheese batter evenly over it, and spoon in the remaining chocolate batter over the top. Make marblelike swirls through the batter with the tip of a knife blade. Bake for about 30 minutes, or until set but still soft. Let the brownies cool in the pan for 15 minutes, then cut them into uniform squares.

Jerome's Cookies

Variations of these graham-cracker layer cookies are frequent in community cookbooks all over the Southeast, and often come with a claim that the recipe originated with the author. In consequence, the true origin has become a tangle that is almost impossible to unravel. The version my family has used for three generations came from my cousin Dot Merritt in Hartwell, Georgia. She got the recipe from a coworker named Jerome, who often made them for the office, hence our name for them. Hey, it's as good a version as any.

Until my grandmother MaMa died, these cookies were at the heart of a running battle she had with my mother. Jerome toasted the coconut topping by running the cookies under the broiler before chilling and cutting them. Mama never toasted the topping, but my grandmother faithfully followed old Jerome, so when people asked Mama for her recipe, MaMa would inevitably have a fit, because she never mentioned that last step. That the person wanted them the way my mother had made them fell on deaf ears. MaMa would cross her arms and hotly insist, "You're s'posed to toast it!" Well, God rest her: I'm on my mother's side here. I never toast them, but you can make my grandmother happy in heaven if you want to.

Makes about 4½ dozen cookies

FOR THE COOKIES:

16 ounces (one 1-pound box) whole graham crackers

8 ounces shredded coconut

1 cup pecans, chopped

6 ounces (1½ sticks) unsalted butter

1 cup granulated sugar

1 large egg

½ cup milk

FOR THE BUTTERCREAM ICING (SEE NOTE, BELOW):

1 cup confectioners' sugar

4 tablespoons (½ stick) unsalted butter, softened

3 to 4 tablespoons whole milk

½ teaspoon vanilla extract

1. Line the bottom of a 9 × 13-inch sheet cake pan with whole graham crackers, cutting them if necessary to fit the pan. Set aside sufficient crackers to cover the top and crush enough of those remaining to make 1 cup. Mix the crushed crackers, 7 ounces of the coconut, and all the nuts together in a medium-sized mixing bowl.

2. Melt the butter in a small saucepan over medium heat and stir in the sugar. Break the egg into a separate bowl, beat it lightly, and then beat in the milk. Stir this into the butter-and-sugar mixture and bring it to the boiling point, stirring constantly.

3. Pour the custard over the cracker crumbs, coconut, and nut mixture and stir until evenly mixed. Pour it into pan lined with crackers. Spread the filling with a spatula until it evenly covers the entire layer. Place the reserved whole crackers on top of filling, pressing lightly, until the filling is completely covered.

4. Make the icing by beating the sugar into the softened butter. Add the milk by tablespoonfuls until the icing is spreadable and stir in the vanilla extract. Immediately spread the icing over the cookies and sprinkle the top evenly with the remaining coconut. Cover and refrigerate until firm, about 4 hours. Cut into 1 × 2¼-inch bars. Keep refrigerated.

NOTE: Some cooks double the amount of icing for a thicker coating, but I think these are sweet enough as it is. If more frosting appeals to you, just double all the ingredients.

Old-Fashioned Tea Cakes

Everything about these cookies seems old-fashioned: the very name whispers of Victorian parlor sets, floral china teapots, and grandmother—as if anyone's grandmother nowadays is sitting around in the parlor serving forth tea and cakes. That may be why this simple cookie is so frequently neglected by serious bakers. It may not be flashy or showy, but it's well worth adding back to any baker's repertory, for there's no basic dough more versatile or satisfying. Dozens of different cookies can be made from this simple base, merely by changing its flavorings, varying the toppings, or, as is done in the two recipes that follow, by mixing in nutmeats.

Makes about 8 dozen cookies

1 pound (2 cups or 4 sticks) unsalted butter, softened

1 pound (2 cups) sugar

3 large eggs, lightly beaten

Grated zest of 2 lemons or 1 orange, optional

1 tablespoon rose or orange-flower water, Homemade Bourbon Vanilla (page 23) or
    1 teaspoon vanilla extract

28 ounces (about 5½ cups) unbleached all-purpose flour

2 teaspoons Single-Acting Baking Powder (page 13) or 1½ teaspoons double-acting

½ teaspoon salt

1. In a mixing bowl that will hold all the dough, cream together the butter and sugar. Beat in the eggs, one at a time. Stir in the citrus zest, if using, and the flavoring extract (if you're using the citrus zest, use rose or orange water with the lemon zest, orange flower with the orange, or any of them if you are not using zest).

2. In a separate bowl, whisk together the flour, baking powder, and salt. Gradually work it into the butter-sugar-egg mixture, mixing until the dough is smooth, stiff, and no longer sticky. Cover and chill at least half an hour. This will make it much easier to roll and cut.

3. Position a rack in the center of the oven and preheat the oven to 375°F. Lightly

grease a baking sheet. Dust a work surface with flour and roll out the dough fairly thin—no more than ³⁄₁₆ inch—thinner, if you can manage it. Cut the dough, using a round or fancy-shaped cutter, and transfer the cookies to the baking sheet with a spatula spacing them an inch apart. Bake, in batches if necessary, until they are lightly browned, about 15 minutes. Cool on wire racks.

NOTE: For sugar cookies, dust the tops with granulated or turbinado sugar just before baking them. The tops can also be iced once they are baked: see pages 195–200 for appropriate icing recipes.

Pecan Spice Tea Cakes

Pecan shortbread cookies (also known as "sandies") are a standard for home bakers in the Deep South, where pecans are a major crop and therefore less of an extravagance than they are elsewhere. These delicately spiced tea cakes are an unusually tasty variation.

Makes about 8 dozen cookies

1 pound (2 cups or 4 sticks) unsalted butter, softened
1 pound (2 cups) sugar
3 large eggs, lightly beaten
28 ounces (about 5½ cups) unbleached all-purpose flour
2 teaspoons Single-Acting Baking Powder (page 13) or 1½ teaspoons double-acting
½ teaspoon salt
1 teaspoon ground cinnamon
1 teaspoon freshly grated nutmeg
1 cup finely chopped Toasted Pecans (page 18)

1. In a mixing bowl that will hold all the dough, cream together the butter and sugar. Beat in the eggs, one at a time. In a separate bowl, whisk together the flour, baking powder, salt, cinnamon, and nutmeg. Add the pecans and toss until evenly mixed into the flour.

2. Gradually work the dry ingredients into the butter, sugar, and egg, mixing until the dough is smooth, stiff, and no longer sticky. Cover and chill for at least half an hour.

3. Position a rack in the center of the oven and preheat the oven to 375°F. Lightly grease a baking sheet. Dust a work surface with flour and turn the dough out onto it. Roll it out fairly thin—about ³⁄₁₆ inch. Cut the dough using a round or fancy-shaped cutter, and transfer the cookies to the baking sheet with a spatula about an inch apart. Bake, in batches if necessary, until they are lightly browned, about 14 to 16 minutes. Cool on wire racks.

ALMOND TEA CAKES: Substitute chopped toasted almonds (made as for Toasted Pecans, page 18) for the pecans and beat ½ teaspoon almond extract into the creamed butter and sugar in step 1.

Coconut Tea Cakes

Coconut tea cakes first began to turn up in Southern cookbooks in the second quarter of the nineteenth century and remain popular to this day. Most of the old recipes called for freshly grated coconut, and that is what I faithfully used for years, but nowadays I've come to actually prefer the unsweetened dried grated variety: though it loses some of the subtlety of freshly grated coconut, its flavor is more concentrated. I'd like to say the discovery was keen baker's intuition, but it was a complete accident.

After my first cookbook was published I did some baking for Brighter Day, a natural food grocery in downtown Savannah. Owners Janie and Peter Brodhead and I did a lot of experimenting with all-natural, minimally processed ingredients that the store sold and championed. Two especially delectable successes were a whole-wheat shortbread and a macaroon-like variation of these cookies, made with dried grated coconut that the store sold in bulk (see Variation, below). Because its moisture content was extremely low, the coconut absorbed the egg and butter almost the same way that flour would do and made a chewy, crunchy and altogether wonderful macaroon. To top it off, the flavor was more distinctive and intense than freshly grated coconut.

Makes about 8 dozen cookies

1 pound (2 cups or 4 sticks) unsalted butter, softened

1 pound (2 cups) sugar

3 large eggs

4 cups unsweetened finely grated coconut, preferably dried (see Note, below)

2 teaspoons baking powder

½ teaspoon salt

10 ounces (about 2 cups) unbleached all-purpose flour (see step 2)

6 ounces (1 cup) bittersweet chocolate, roughly chopped

1. In a mixing bowl that will hold all the dough, cream together the butter and sugar. Beat in the eggs, one at a time. Mix in the coconut, baking powder, and salt.

2. Gradually work in enough flour to make a smooth, stiff, and no longer sticky dough—you will probably not need all of it. Cover and chill for at least a half hour.

3. Position a rack in the center of the oven and preheat the oven to 375°F. Lightly grease a baking sheet. Dust a work surface with flour and roll out the dough about ¼ inch thick. Cut the dough using a round or fancy-shaped cutter and transfer the cookies to the baking sheet with a spatula about an inch apart. Bake in batches until lightly browned, about 14 to 16 minutes. Cool on wire racks.

4. While the cookies cool, bring 1 inch of water to a simmer in the bottom half of a double boiler over medium heat. Put the chocolate in the top half and melt it over the simmering water, stirring occasionally until smooth. Put the chocolate in a squeeze bottle or keep it warm over the hot water. Line the counter with wax paper and put the cookies on a wire cooling rack over it. Squeeze thin crisscrossed lines of chocolate over the cookies or scoop up small amounts of the chocolate on a spatula and flip it over them in irregular ribbons.

NOTE: Unsweetened, dried coconut is available in bulk at natural food grocers, most Asian markets, and even a few supermarkets. Grated fresh or frozen, unsweetened coconut can be substituted, but the moisture content in both will require more flour.

VARIATION

COCONUT MACAROON COOKIES: To make the flourless macaroon cookies described in the Headnote above, you will need at least 4 generous cups dried coconut, maybe more if the dough is too loose and sticky to handle. Omit the flour and baking powder. Generously dust the work surface with rice flour, butter your hands, and pat out the dough ¼ inch thick. Using a cutter or knife dipped in rice flour, cut the dough into shapes or squares, transfer them with a spatula to a lightly buttered cookie sheet, and bake as above until golden brown. You may top them with chocolate as in the recipe or leave them plain.

Southern Shortbread

From France to Scotland, England to America, everyone loves these buttery-rich and yet delicate cookies—and everyone seems to have a favorite variation. Perhaps its popularity is due in part to the fact that it is an easy, artless confection, made up of little more than softened butter, flour, and sugar rubbed together with no particular care or technique—as easy to make as they are to gobble down by the handful. In the South, many cooks give the crumb a toothsome crunch by adding a handful of stone-ground cornmeal. For a more delicate cookie, you can substitute an equal volume of corn flour or cornstarch for the cornmeal.

Makes about 2 to 3 dozen cookies, depending on the chosen size and shape

½ cup sugar
Salt
12 ounces (about 2¼ cups) Southern soft-wheat flour (page 9)
    or soft-wheat pastry flour
¼ cup fine stone-ground white cornmeal
8 ounces (1 cup or 2 sticks) unsalted butter, softened

1. Whisk together the sugar, a small pinch of salt, the flour, and the cornmeal. With your fingers or a pastry blender, work the butter into the flour until the mixture has the texture of coarse meal. Keep blending with your hands until it is smooth. Gather it into a ball, wrap it in plastic wrap, and chill it for at least 30 minutes—until it is firm but not hard.

2. Position a rack in the center of the oven and preheat the oven to 325°F. To shape the cookies, you may simply pat the dough flat on a cookie sheet in large rounds or rectangles a little less than ¼ inch thick and prick the dough at regular intervals with a fork; or pinch off small (1-inch diameter) lumps, roll them between your hands into a tight ball, then press each one flat on a cookie sheet with a cookie stamp or the palm of you hand; or lightly flour a flat work surface, dust the dough with flour, roll it out just under ¼ inch

thick, and cut it with a cookie cutter. Transfer the cut cookies to a cookie sheet with a spatula, spacing them about an inch apart.

3. Bake for 20 to 22 minutes, until the edges are lightly browned. Let the shortbread cool on the cookie sheet. If you have baked it in one large piece, while it is still warm and soft cut it into pieces about 1 inch wide by 2 to 2½ inches long, or, if in rounds, into wedges, Scottish style. Let the cut cookies cool before removing them from the baking sheet.

Telfair Currant Tea (or Derby) Shortbread

An indomitable Southern spinster of the old school, and leader of old Savannah society, Mary Telfair was a brilliant woman of letters who was responsible for the founding of the first art museum in the Southeast, the Telfair Academy of Arts and Sciences. Like most society women in Savannah, she was not expected to cook, but every Christmas, she and her sister not only gave all their servants the day off, they refused all invitations, rolled up their sleeves, tied on aprons, and cooked Christmas dinner for the entire household. Several manuscript cookery books, attributed variously to Miss Telfair, her sister, and her mother, survive and are an interesting look at the tastes of upper-class Savannah during its heyday in the early to mid-nineteenth century. This delicate, very old-fashioned cookie is adapted from one of those books.

Makes about 5 dozen cookies

1 cup sugar, plus more, for dusting the tops of the cookies
16 ounces (about 3½ cups) unbleached all-purpose flour
½ teaspoon salt
1 teaspoon ground cinnamon
1 teaspoon freshly grated nutmeg
8 ounces (2 sticks) unsalted butter, softened
1 cup currants
1 large egg, separated
½ cup whole milk
1 tablespoon water

1. Whisk together 1 cup sugar, the flour, salt, and spices in a large mixing bowl. Rub the butter into it with your fingers until the mixture resembles coarse meal. Add the currants and toss until evenly mixed. In a separate bowl, lightly beat the egg yolk and add the milk, beating until it is evenly mixed.

2. Make a well in the center of the dry ingredients and pour in the egg and milk. Mix

together into a smooth, moderately stiff dough. Cover it with plastic wrap and let it rest in the refrigerator for half an hour.

3. Position a rack in the center of the oven and preheat the oven to 325°F. Flour a work surface and the dough and roll it out about ¼ inch thick. Cut into cookies with a 2-inch round or small decorative cutter and transfer them to ungreased baking sheets about an inch apart.

4. Lightly beat the egg white with the water until smooth. Brush the egg wash over the cookies, dust them with sugar, and bake until lightly colored, about 16 to 20 minutes. Cool them on the baking sheets and then store them in an airtight jar or tin.

Chocolate Chip Pecan Wedding Shortbread

As a boy, my favorite store-bought cookies in the world were those fancy little Danish wedding cookies (also sometimes called Mexican wedding cookies—go figure), dainty bits of shortbread enriched with nuts and nuggets of chocolate and rolled in confectioners' sugar. They actually were popular at wedding receptions—which, being a minister's child—I probably saw more of than most children. They're kissing cousins to kourabiedes, the highly addictive sugar-dusted butter cookies from Greece, and to the South's own pecan shortbread. These airy morsels, studded with pecans and bits of bittersweet chocolate, are my own version of that childhood favorite. You do not, needless to say, have to wait for someone to get married to enjoy them.

Makes about 5 to 5½ dozen cookies

12 ounces (about 2¼ cups) Southern soft-wheat flour (page 9) or pastry flour
¼ cup cornstarch
½ teaspoon salt
1 teaspoon ground cinnamon
½ teaspoon freshly grated nutmeg
½ cup granulated sugar
8 ounces (2 sticks) unsalted butter, softened
½ cup finely chopped Toasted Pecans (page 18)
½ cup bittersweet chocolate minimorsels
About 1½ cups confectioners' sugar, for coating the cookies

1. Whisk together the flour, cornstarch, salt, cinnamon, nutmeg, and granulated sugar. Add the butter and work it into the flour with your fingers or a pastry blender until it resembles coarse meal. Continue working the dough until it is smooth. Sprinkle the toasted pecans and chocolate minimorsels over the dough and work them in until they are evenly distributed. Gather the dough into a ball and flatten it into a disk about an inch thick. Wrap it well with plastic wrap, and refrigerate for at least 30 minutes.

2. Position a rack in the center of the oven and preheat the oven to 325°F. Store the

dough in the refrigerator until you are ready to work with it. Pinch off small (¾-inch diameter) lumps, roll them between your hands into a tight ball or oval, and put it on the baking sheet, spacing them about an inch apart.

3. Bake for 18 to 20 minutes, until the edges and bottoms are lightly browned. Let them cool until they are no longer soft and crumbly, and while they are still warm, roll them in confectioners' sugar until well coated. Cool completely and store in airtight tins.

Crunchy Peanut Butter Chocolate Chip Cookies

Those perennial American favorites, old-fashioned peanut butter cookies, with their charac-teristic ridges or tic-tac-toe pattern pressed into their tops with the tines of a fork, are really nothing more than shortbread enriched with peanut butter. These take a trip over the top with the added crunch of chopped peanuts and chocolate chips. They were made for eating with an ice-cold glass of milk—and I am not talking about the skimmed kind, either. Virtue is its own reward.

Makes about 3½ to 4 dozen cookies

5 ounces (about 1 cup) unbleached all-purpose flour
½ teaspoon salt
1 teaspoon baking powder
4 ounces (½ cup or 1 stick) unsalted butter, softened
1 cup firmly packed light brown sugar
1 large egg
1 cup all-natural peanut butter, preferably fresh-ground (see Note, below)
½ cup roasted unsalted peanuts, roughly chopped
¾ cup milk chocolate chips

1. Position a rack in the center of the oven and preheat the oven to 375°F. Whisk together the flour, salt, and baking powder. In a separate bowl, cream the butter and sugar with a mixer or wooden spoon until fluffy and smooth. Beat in the egg and then the peanut butter.

2. Add the flour in three parts, mixing well after each addition. Work in the peanuts and chocolate chips until they are evenly distributed in the dough. Take 1-inch lumps of dough and roll them into a ball between your palms. Place them on an ungreased cookie sheet, spacing them about 1¼ inches apart. Press the balls flat with the backside of a regular dinner fork, then press it crosswise to make a tic-tac-toe checkered pattern in the top. Bake until golden brown, about 10 to 12 minutes. They will still be quite crumbly when

they first come out of the oven; cool them on the cookie sheet before transferring them to an airtight storage container.

> NOTE: All-natural peanut butter is preferred for these cookies because it contains nothing but peanuts. Freshly ground peanut butter, available from specialty grocers (especially natural food markets) will not only taste fresher, it gives the cookies a richer, more intensely peanuty flavor.

Lemon-Ginger-Scented Benne Wafers

A lingering reminder of the slave trade with West Africa, benne (or sesame) seeds have become practically indigenous in the Carolina and Georgia Lowcountry, and almost every cook has her own version of these delicate cookies. Some are more like brittle candy than a cookie; some are so airy and delicate that they practically evaporate on your tongue. These tend toward the latter variety—delicately scented and yet intensely flavorful.

You can usually find sesame seeds in the spice aisle of supermarkets, but they are fresher and much more economical at Asian and natural food markets, where they are often sold in bulk. The kind of seed you want for this cookie is white, or hulled, sesame.

Makes about 4 dozen cookies

¾ cup white (hulled) sesame seeds
¾ cup unbleached all-purpose flour, measured by spooning it into the cup
¼ teaspoon salt
¼ teaspoon baking powder
6 ounces (¾ cup or 1½ sticks) unsalted butter, softened
1½ cups firmly packed light brown sugar
1 large egg, lightly beaten
Grated zest of 1 lemon
1 tablespoon grated fresh ginger
1 tablespoon freshly squeezed lemon juice

1. Position a rack in the center of the oven and preheat the oven to 350°F. Spread the sesame on a 9-inch metal pie plate or cake pan and put the pan in the center of the oven. Toast, stirring frequently, until they are a rich golden brown. Remove from the oven and let cool. Reduce the oven temperature to 300°F. Line two large cookie sheets with parchment or silicone baking pads (parchment can be reused once). Whisk together the flour, salt, and baking powder.

2. In a separate mixing bowl, cream the butter and sugar until light and fluffy. Beat in

the egg and then mix in the flour, sesame, lemon zest, ginger, and lemon juice. Drop by scant half-teaspoonfuls onto the parchment or silicone pads, leaving at least an inch between them (the cookies will spread more on the pads).

3. Bake in batches until nicely browned, about 10 to 12 minutes. Place the pans on wire cooling racks and let the cookies cool completely before peeling them off the parchment or pads. Store in airtight tins.

Chocolate Irish Lace

Thanks to an old, established Irish community, Savannah hosts one of the largest St. Patrick's Day celebrations in the country, and for several days, the old city is awash with green: from the river, to the fountains, to the beer, to—I am not making this up—the grits and hot dog buns. Less hair-raising are the many treats that sport Irish names and sometimes even contain Irish ingredients. These delicate and delicious lace cookies, for example, are about as Irish as Queen Elizabeth, but they are crunchy with Irish oats and mellowed with a judicious dose of good Irish whiskey.

Makes about 4½ to 5 dozen cookies

4 ounces (½ cup or 1 stick) unsalted butter, softened
½ cup confectioners' sugar
½ cup firmly packed light brown sugar
1 large egg
1 teaspoon Homemade Bourbon Vanilla (page 23) or vanilla extract
2 teaspoons Irish whiskey (your choice, but I am a Jameson's man, myself)
¼ teaspoon salt
2 tablespoons unbleached all-purpose flour
1 cup quick-cooking oats
4 ounces bittersweet chocolate

1. Position a rack in the center of the oven and preheat the oven to 350°F. Line four large baking sheets with parchment or silicone baking pads (parchment can be reused once).

2. With a mixer, cream the butter and both sugars until light and fluffy. Beat in the egg, vanilla, whiskey, and salt. Add the flour and oats and mix well. Drop by level half-teaspoonfuls onto the prepared pans, leaving at least 1½ inches between (these spread a lot, especially on silicone pads).

3. Bake in batches to a rich golden brown, about 7 minutes per batch. Cool the cook-

ies in the pans set over wire cooling racks. Meanwhile, prepare the bottom of a double boiler with about 1 inch of water and bring it to a simmer over medium heat. Put the chocolate in the top half, place it over the simmering water and melt it, stirring occasionally, until it is smooth. Remove it from the heat. (Alternatively, you may melt the chocolate in the microwave: put it in a microwave-safe bowl and cook at medium power for 2 to 3 minutes, stirring halfway through.)

4. When the cookies have cooled, spread a dab of melted chocolate on the bottom of a cookie, leaving space on the edges for the chocolate to spread. Gently press another cookie into the chocolate, bottom-side-in, until the chocolate spreads to the edges. Cool until the chocolate is hardened (you may do this in the refrigerator), and store the cookies at room temperature in an airtight tin.

Spicy Cheese Straws

This venerable Southern classic is a standard for any hostess worth her iced tea, and, happily, the food processor makes short work of it. The best cheese for straws is a very old, super-sharp cheddar—the kind that is so sharp that it'll practically take the roof off your mouth. If you cannot get such wonders, mixing in a bit of grated real Parmesan gives it just the right kick. Orange cheddar lends the most traditional color to these spicy little tidbits, and is the only kind that a traditional Southern cook would use, but white cheddar will, of course, work just as well, if you have this snob thing against the coloring.

Makes about 10 dozen straws

¾ pound (12 ounces) well-aged extra-sharp cheddar
¼ pound (4 ounces) Parmesan, preferably Parmigiano-Reggiano
4 ounces (½ cup or 1 stick) unsalted butter, softened
1 generous teaspoon ground cayenne pepper, or more, to taste
½ teaspoon salt
10 ounces (about 2 cups) Southern soft-wheat flour (see page 9) or unbleached all-purpose flour

1. Grate the cheese with a rotary cheese grater, through the fine holes of a box grater, or with the fine shredding disk in the food processor. In a food processor fitted with a steel blade or with a mixer, cream the cheddar, Parmesan, and butter until fluffy and smooth.

2. Add the cayenne, salt, and flour and process or work it into the dough until smooth. Gather it into a ball, wrap well in plastic wrap or wax paper, and chill it for at least half an hour or up to 1 hour, but don't let it chill hard. If you make the dough ahead to bake later, let it soften somewhat at room temperature so that it is still cool but pliable.

3. Position a rack in the center of the oven and preheat the oven to 325°F. Put the dough in a cookie press fitted with the star die (or a pastry bag fitted with a star tip) and press it out onto an ungreased baking sheet into narrow 2½-inch straws, leaving about ½ inch clear between. You may also roll the dough out: lightly flour a work surface and roll

the dough out ¼ inch thick. Cut it with a sharp knife or a zigzag pastry wheel into strips ½ inch by 2½ inches, laying them on a buttered baking sheet as you go. Or for a more decorative straw without the cookie press, roll them out a little thicker than ⅛ inch, cut them as directed above, and gently twist each straw into a spiral. Bake for about 18 to 20 minutes, being careful not to let them brown on top. The bottoms should be golden but the tops and sides should not color. Cool on the pan before transferring them to an airtight storage container.

Blue Cheese Straws

Clemson University, where I studied architecture some of the time and subjected dozens of my classmates and professors to my early attempts at cooking and baking for the rest of it, is the birthplace of one of the Southeast's oldest regional cheeses—a creamy, richly blue-veined cow's milk cheese known simply as Clemson Blue. Once aged in old tunnels dug by the Confederate army for reasons that are now lost to time and legend, today it is cured in modern cellars—an environment that is, perhaps, a little less romantic, but far more dependable, since artificial lakes and booming land development have forever changed the climate of that formerly pastoral, and once much cooler, region.

This variation on the classic cheese straw pays tribute to my alma mater's prize dairy product, but it can be made with any high-quality blue—Maytag, Danish blue, or even Roquefort or Gorgonzola.

Makes about 10 dozen straws

½ pound (8 ounces) extra-sharp white cheddar
½ pound (8 ounces) well-aged blue cheese
4 ounces (½ cup or 1 stick) unsalted butter, softened
½ teaspoon ground cayenne pepper, or more, to taste
1 teaspoon freshly ground black pepper
½ teaspoon salt
10 ounces (about 2 cups) Southern soft-wheat flour (see page 9) or unbleached all-purpose flour

1. Finely grate the cheddar with a rotary cheese grater, a box grater, or the shredding disk of a food processor. Crumble the blue cheese into the bowl of a food processor fitted with the steel blade or into the bowl of a mixer. Add the cheddar and butter and cream them together until fluffy and smooth.

2. Add the cayenne, black pepper, salt, and flour and work it into a uniform dough. Gather it into a ball, wrap well in plastic wrap or wax paper, and chill for at least half an

hour to 1 hour. Don't let it get hard, and, if you are making it ahead to bake later, allow enough time for it to soften at room temperature until it is pliable but still cool.

3. Position a rack in the center of the oven and preheat the oven to 325°F. Put the dough in a cookie press fitted with the star die (or a pastry bag fitted with a star tip) and press it out onto an ungreased cookie sheet into 2½-inch straws, leaving about ½ inch clear between. You may also roll the dough out and cut it into strips or spiral twists: see step 3 of Spicy Cheese Straws (page 144). Bake for about 18 to 20 minutes, until lightly browned on the bottom and pale gold on top. Cool on the pan before transferring them to an airtight storage container.

Lemon Pepper Benne Cocktail Bits

Toasted sesame seeds are a well-known crown for rolls and loaf bread, where they really add more texture than flavor, but in the Lowcountry they are used plentifully, and for their flavor as much as their texture. Frequently stirred into candies and cookies (see Lemon-Ginger-Scented Benne Wafers, page 140), another popular way that we use them is in this well-loved cocktail biscuit, rolled thin and cut into wafers, or thick-cut in nuggets and called "bits" or "bites." This recipe is a variation on one from my favorite partying experts, the Parent Teacher Organization at Savannah's St. Andrews Academy, published in their award-winning cookbook First Come, First Served . . . in Savannah. *Now, these ladies are some serious party hounds, and their book is almost as much fun as one of their impromptu gatherings.*

Makes about 4 dozen biscuits

½ cup white (hulled) sesame seeds
1 cup unbleached all-purpose flour, measured by spooning it into the cup
½ teaspoon salt, plus more, for sprinkling
¼ teaspoon freshly ground black pepper
¼ teaspoon ground cayenne pepper, more or less, to taste
8 tablespoons unsalted butter, 4 tablespoons cut into ¼-inch bits
Grated zest of 1 lemon
1 generously rounded tablespoon chopped fresh rosemary (do not use dried)
2 to 3 tablespoons ice water
1 tablespoon freshly squeezed lemon juice
2 cloves garlic, crushed and peeled but left whole

1. Position a rack in the center of the oven and preheat the oven to 350°F. Spread the sesame on a 9-inch metal pie plate or cake pan and put the pan in the center of the oven. Toast, stirring frequently, until colored pale gold. Remove the pan from the oven and let them cool.

2. Whisk together the flour, salt, pepper, and cayenne in a mixing bowl until the pep-

per is evenly distributed. Add the 4 tablespoons of cut-up butter and work it into the flour with your fingers until the mixture resembles coarse meal. Add the sesame, lemon zest, and rosemary and toss until it is evenly mixed. Sprinkle in 2 tablespoons ice water and the lemon juice and work it into a smooth dough, until it just clumps together and holds its shape, adding water by teaspoonfuls as needed. Gather the dough into a smooth ball, wrap well in plastic wrap, and let it rest in the refrigerator for 30 minutes.

3. Sprinkle a work surface with flour and roll the dough out slightly thicker than a piecrust—just over ⅛ inch thick. Cut the dough into rounds with a 1-inch or decorative cookie cutter of roughly the same diameter. Transfer them to an ungreased baking sheet, and bake until they are beginning to color, about 10 minutes. Meanwhile, melt the remaining butter in a small saucepan over medium heat, add the garlic, and simmer, stirring and mashing the garlic, until it is beginning to color. Turn off the heat and let stand. When the wafers are beginning to color, remove and brush them with the garlic butter, lightly sprinkle them with salt, and return them to the oven. Bake until golden brown, about 3 to 6 minutes minutes longer. Cool on the baking sheet and store them in an airtight tin.

Cakes—Ancient and Modern

CAKES HAVE AN ALMOST magical allure, a power to which few people are immune. For Southern cooks, they are part and parcel of our very identity. We pride ourselves on the lightness and delicacy of our layer cakes, the smooth, sad-streak-free substance of our pound cakes, the airy, almost ethereal crumb of a sponge or angel food. Indeed, a cake is often the first thing that a Southerner will learn to make—even before biscuits. Probably my earliest cooking memory is of making cakes with my grandmother; to this day, the smell of creaming butter and sugar evokes her memory more cleanly and clearly than just about anything else. In the end, it's the quality of my cake baking, not my pastry or bread making, nor even chicken-frying, that gives me my culinary identity and is my own gauge for my real prowess in the kitchen. The time in my life when I've felt the most like a failure was the period when I couldn't make a pound cake that didn't fall.

But outside the kitchen, that powerful allure continues. A cake is an event in itself: dessert at the end of the meal is just dessert, but a cake turns that meal into a special occasion, a celebration, a culinary milestone. Nothing gets more attention at one of those famed communal gatherings, the covered-dish supper, than a well-made cake. Not only do they disappear in a hurry, nothing else will be more talked of than whether or not the baker will part with her recipe—and if so, whether or not her recipe is missing her real secret. Until recently, "What's your secret?" was the most frequently asked question, but today whole generations have grown up without baking grandmothers, so the questions have become more elemental, and, depressingly, often conclude with, "Can you make it from a mix?"

There's a lot of speculation about why mixes have become so commonplace, and the most usual argument involves time, some variation of "people have busy lives; most women work; nobody has time to bake from scratch anymore." But a mix doesn't really take that much less time than a batter made from scratch: what it does take less of is skill. The biggest advantage of a mix is that the dry ingredients are premeasured and assembled in one box; there's no danger of getting too much flour or overdoing the baking powder, and no taking three or four containers out of the cupboard. The chemical leavening covers up inadequate creaming (and in some cases replaces it altogether) and their mixing is seemingly artless. I submit that the reason most people use a mix is less speed than fear: they think they don't know enough about it to make a cake from scratch, and a mix gives them the confidence to go where they would otherwise fear to tread.

If you are one of the fearful, take heart: though cake making does take a certain amount of skill, and that skill is honed with practice, it is not as complicated as it appears to be. Remember: for thousands of years it has been accomplished by thousands of ordinary people. Julia Child once said of her popularity as a cooking teacher that it had less to do with her own knowledge and skill than her very ordinariness: "They look at me and think, 'If she can do it, surely I can do it.' "

Do you know what? She was right.

CAKE-MAKING BASICS

* Have all the ingredients, especially the eggs and butter, at room temperature. If you've ever tried to cream cold, hard butter, you know partly why this is important, but egg whites also whip better when they're not refrigerator cold, and both hold volume better at room temperature. It is possible for butter to be too warm, but that is usually not the problem. To speed up the warming process, eggs (in the shell) can be submerged in hot tap water for a minute, and butter can be cut into small bits. Never try to warm eggs or soften butter in a microwave: not only does it not work, it is inviting disaster.

* Always use the freshest eggs you can get. Eggs actually lose moisture as they age; a freshly laid egg is heavier than an egg that is a week old. Their ability to hold volume after beating is affected as well.

* If you don't bake often, get a reliable scale and weigh the flour: there are too many variables in volume measures, including ambient humidity, moisture content within the flour, and compacting in the storage bin. Experienced bakers can tell when a cake batter is too thin or too thick at a glance, but most of us don't bake often enough to have that kind of eye. For example, the first time I baked the Brown Velvet Cake on page 186, because I am hopelessly nearsighted I not only used half the baking powder it called for, I was in a hurry and didn't weigh the flour, but scooped it out of a newly opened bag. My instincts told me that last quarter cup was too much, but I put it in anyway. Well, the cake rose to only half its proper volume and the excess flour made it dry so that it went stale within a day. My hurry and careless measuring ended up being wasteful in the long run.

* If you must rely on a dry measuring cup, measure the flour for a cake by spooning it into the cup, then sweep off the excess with a knife or pastry scraper. This will measure a little lighter than scooping directly out of the canister or bag.

* The initial creaming is the single most important step in ensuring volume and lightness in a cake. Although beaten egg whites are sometimes used to leaven cakes, most of the trapped air in a batter that is essential for giving the finished cake texture and height is that which is caught in the fat, not the eggs.

* If you are a worrier, this will be hard for you, but develop a habit of leaving the oven

door alone. Too much peeking can lead to collapse, and, with something like a true pound cake, *any* peeking will not just lead to it, but ensure it.

* Bake often. The best way to perfect cake baking is to make them over and over until you know exactly how the batter should look, feel, and smell. The prize cake bakers of my childhood were not champions because they were always tinkering with some new recipe, but because they had a favorite cake that they were known for, and they made that cake over and over again. After a while, you'll also know by smell when a cake is done. Some traditional cooks, like Edna Lewis, develop an ear for baking too: she puts an ear close to the cake and listens: when it stops "singing" to her, she knows it's done.

THE TECHNIQUE

One of my baking mentors is pastry chef Karen Barker, who with her chef-husband Ben operates Magnolia Grill in Durham, North Carolina, a small college town that has become something of a culinary Mecca for new Southern cooking. Rightly observing that while cake baking is more of an exacting science than the baking of most breads and pastries, relying less on technique than on precision in measuring, in her wonderful dessert book *Sweet Stuff* Karen discusses three techniques that are critical to successful cake making. They are creaming, whipping, and folding. When a cake has failed because of the mixing, nine times out of ten it is because the baker has fallen short with one of these three techniques. Without going into a dissertation, here is what home bakers need to know about them. If the science of this kind of thing thrills you, seek out *Sweet Stuff,* Rose Levy Berenbaum's *Cake Bible,* and Shirley Corriher's cookbook/how-things-work manual *Cookwise.*

CREAMING: The single most important step in ensuring the correct volume and texture in a cake is this frequently used technique. It is the process of beating the fat—usually with the sugar—until it is fully and thoroughly aerated. Sometimes the creaming is done in two steps: the fat is beaten until it is soft and fluffy, then the sugar is gradually beaten into it. Creaming accomplishes two things: obviously, it traps air in the batter, but it also helps to form a smooth emulsion, keeping the fat evenly suspended in the dough. Before chemical leavening came on the scene, this step was very important indeed, but it is no less important for even texture and volume in a baking-powder leavened cake than in a pound cake. The fat, especially when the fat is butter, must be at room temperature (around 70°F), softened but still holding it shape, and not in the least oily-looking. If it is too warm, it won't suspend the sugar and air, and will oil rather than fluff. Creaming can be done with a mixer fitted with rotary beaters or a paddle, a rotary eggbeater, or a wooden spoon. Obviously hand-creaming with a spoon or eggbeater will take longer than using a mixer, but time is not the most useful way to judge when the fat has been well creamed. It is far better to learn what to look for: properly creamed fat will change color, getting lighter, (this is more true of butter than other fats, but even shortening and lard will look a little whiter) and will be very fluffy and light, and yet hold its shape well.

Whipping: This technique involves beating eggs (usually the whites but sometimes the yolks), cream, or sometimes the entire batter to incorporate air into them, thereby introducing further volume. Whipping can be done with a fork, a wire whisk, a rotary eggbeater, or a mixer fitted with whisk or rotary beater attachments—the idea is strands of metal that slice into the ingredient leaving bits of trapped air in their wake. The conditions for optimum whipping of egg whites and cream are an exercise in extremes: while cream must be quite cold to whip properly, egg whites must be at room temperature or even a little warm. Underwhipping cream or egg whites is possible, but in some ways more damage can be done by overwhipping them: overbeaten cream can break down into butter and separate, and overbeaten egg whites become stiff and brittle. Neither of them will fold evenly into a batter and will not hold their volume as well.

Folding: The second most common failure in baking is the misunderstanding of this simple technique wherein whipped egg whites, cream, dry ingredients, and sometimes, floured fruits, nuts, or other solids are incorporated into a batter. It's called "folding" because that is exactly what one does: the lighter ingredient is literally folded—as you would fold a letter around a picture or a keepsake—within the heavier batter. The object of folding is to suspend the folded ingredient in the batter, bringing all the ingredients together without stirring or beating out the air you have gone to so much trouble to incorporate. The technique differs from stirring or mixing in that it requires a light, gentle, and yet quick hand. Here's how to do it: the ingredient to be folded into the batter (usually the lighter or drier of the two parts) is laid on top of it. Dip down into the center of the batter with a large mixing spoon, or better, a flexible rubber spatula, going all the way to the bottom of the bowl and scooping up batter onto the spoon's bowl or spatula blade as you go. Bring it up the side closest or farthest from you (whichever is the most comfortable), twisting so that it is parallel with the batter as you bring it out. Bring it up and gently flip the utensil over, letting the batter on top of it fall over the ingredient that is to be folded in. Slightly rotate the bowl and repeat this until the ingredient is evenly incorporated. As Karen observes, a few stray streaks of egg white or cream are fine and are preferable to overfolding the batter, but the mixture should be light and mostly evenly colored.

When the folded ingredient is full of trapped air, as in whipped cream or egg whites, it is helpful to fold a little of it into the batter first so that the batter is lighter and looser and better able to fold itself around the aerated ingredient. Scoop about a third of the egg whites or cream onto the batter and fold it in as described above. You'll find that the remaining whites or cream are much easier to incorporate evenly after that. When the ingredient is dry, especially flour, it must be sprinkled over the top a little at a time and folded in gradually or the batter will have uneven dry pockets.

EVENING THINGS OUT: Once the cake batter is in the pan, it will need to be leveled and, though it may seem a contradiction after all that creaming and whipping, large pockets of air will need to be removed so that the texture of the finished cake will be even. There are several techniques for doing this. Spooning the batter (especially a hefty one like a pound cake) rather than pouring it into the pan is a big help. You may then level it off by smoothing the top with a spatula or, as *Baking in America* author Greg Patent suggests, by grasping the pan firmly with both hands and half-rotating it first in one direction and then in the other. Some bakers tap the pan firmly on the counter, which both levels the batter and knocks loose any large air pockets. This is my method, but I do caution not to get too slaphappy and knock it too hard or you'll lose the even distribution of minuscule air bubbles that give the cake its texture and volume. Another way to remove those big air pockets in a pound cake or cake baked in a loaf or Bundt pan is to run a table knife or palette knife through the batter in an S-shaped motion.

PREPARING THE PAN: The last technique to cover before going on to the recipes is preparing the pan for the batter. Most cake pans are greased and floured so that the cake won't stick. For further insurance in a layer cake pan, many bakers line the bottom of the pan with a piece of buttered wax paper or cooking parchment. To grease and flour pans, save the butter wrappers: there's usually just enough butter film left on them to coat a couple of 9-inch round pans. Lightly rub the pan with butter or shortening until it is completely coated, then put in a tablespoon of flour. Gently turn and tap the pan until the entire surface is coated and turn out the excess. Bundt pans release best if coated with dry bread or cake crumbs instead of flour. Do it the same way as greasing and flouring, allowing about ¼ cup of dry crumbs for a full-size Bundt pan, about 1 tablespoon for a mini-Bundt pan.

Pound Cakes Old and New

This ancient European classic, which came into America by way of the English bakers' tradition, has been a part of the Southern table for so long that many Southerners believe we invented it. The old, traditional formula for the cake was, of course, based on weight—a pound each of flour, butter, sugar, and (ideally) eggs—hence the name, but it has evolved over time, and the pound cake that most Americans make today, while similar in structure and texture, follows a different, lighter, volume-based formula: equal volumes of flour and sugar to half the volume in fat and (more or less) eggs.

The old formula, dense, rich, and substantial, survives among traditional cooks, and remains the classic and best base for just about any fruitcake. Yet the fact that it is treated almost as an anachronism in community cookbooks, appearing under such names as "Grandma's," "Old-Fashioned," or "Old Time," is telling. It deserves a place of respect in any home baker's repertory other than as a charming anachronism. That's not to suggest that there's anything wrong with the newer cakes with their sweeter, lighter, and a bit less dense crumb, but their place is beside the old one, not instead of it.

Pound cakes were originally leavened only with the air that was beaten into the batter, mainly into the fat: that's why the old recipes directed to beat the heck out of the butter and sugar. Some also included separately beaten egg whites, like a genoise, which made for a cake that was lighter but more prone to sad streaks (a damp, heavy uneven texture caused by a partial collapse in the structure of the cake). The whites can contract a little as they cool, causing the cake to fall a little, the same way a soufflé sinks as it cools. At any rate, with or without beaten egg whites the old cake didn't need baking powder, but many of the modern ones, with their low ratio of fat and a high ratio of liquid, do.

Classic Old-Style Pound Cake

This is the original formula—made up with a pound of everything. Some of the old recipes were so specific about equal weights that they went so far as to recommend weighing a dozen eggs and using this weight to proportion the butter, sugar, and flour. It isn't as sweet as most modern cakes, but its richness and body are more satisfying.

Makes 1 round tube cake, or 2 loaf cakes, serving 12 to 16

1 pound unsalted butter, softened
1 pound (2 cups) sugar
Salt
8 large eggs (see Headnote, above)
1 pound (about 3½ cups) Southern soft-wheat flour (see page 9)
    or unbleached all-purpose flour
½ cup heavy cream
1 tablespoon Homemade Bourbon Vanilla (page 23), or rose water or orange flower
    water, or 1 teaspoon vanilla extract and 2 teaspoons bourbon

1. Position a rack in the center of the oven and preheat it to 325°F. Butter and flour the pan as directed on page 155. With a wooden spoon or a mixer fitted with a paddle or with rotary beaters, cream the butter, beating until it is light and fluffy, then beat in the sugar and a small pinch of salt and cream until very light and fluffy.

2. Beat in the eggs one at a time alternating with the flour, a little at a time, until both are incorporated. Don't overbeat it at this point. Finally stir in the heavy cream and liquid flavoring and spoon the batter into the prepared pan. Slip a table knife blade into the batter and run it through it in a back and forth S motion to take out any large air bubbles. Give the pan a couple of firm taps on the counter—just enough to bring any large air pockets to the surface.

3. Bake for 1½ to 2 hours, depending on the shape of your pan, until a straw inserted

into the center comes out clean. Don't open the oven door for the first 1¼ hours. Make sure the cake is completely done before taking it from the oven, but don't overcook it or it will be dry and heavy. Cool the cake for 15 minutes in the pan, then turn it out onto a cake plate and let it cool completely before cutting it.

Indian Pound Cake

The name of this very old-fashioned cake has nothing directly to do with Native Americans: it comes from the fact that it is made with cornmeal, which was often called "Indian" meal until late in the nineteenth century. The formula is basically the old European pound cake adapted for our native grain. Recipes for it were common until late in the nineteenth century, but virtually disappeared over the course of the last century, except in such rare historically slanted collections as Bill Neal's classic Biscuits, Spoonbread, and Sweet Potato Pie *and Greg Patent's handsome* Baking in America. *Perhaps one reason it has vanished is that it doesn't keep well, but its toothsome crumb and delicate flavor make it very satisfying eating—it's a terrific foil for fresh fruit and cream—and leftovers are delicious slathered with butter and toasted. It deserves to be returned to an honored place in the modern American repertory.*

Makes one 10-inch tube cake or two 9-inch loaf cakes, serving 12 to 16

2 cups extra-fine cornmeal or corn flour (see Note, below)
5 ounces (1 cup) Southern soft-wheat flour (see page 9) or cake flour
1 teaspoon ground cinnamon
1 teaspoon freshly grated nutmeg
Salt
8 ounces (1 cup or 2 sticks) unsalted butter
2 cups granulated sugar
7 large eggs
¼ cup bourbon
1 tablespoon Homemade Bourbon Vanilla (page 23) or 1 teaspoon vanilla extract
     and 2 teaspoons bourbon
Superfine sugar or confectioners' sugar, for dusting

1. Position a rack in the center of the oven and preheat it to 325°F. Butter and flour the pan as directed on page 155. Whisk or sift together the cornmeal, flour, spices, and small pinch of salt. With a wooden spoon, or a mixer fitted with a paddle or rotary beat-

ers, cream the butter, beating until it is light and fluffy, then gradually beat in the sugar and cream until very light and fluffy.

2. Beat in the eggs one at a time, then *stir* in the flour mixture in three or four additions. Don't beat it at this point. Finally, stir in the bourbon and vanilla and spoon the batter into the prepared pan. Slip a table knife blade into the batter and run it through in a back-and-forth S motion to take out any large air pockets. Give the pan a couple of firm taps on the counter—just enough to bring those air bubbles to the surface.

3. Bake for about 1¼ hours, until a straw inserted into the center comes out clean. Don't open the oven door for the first hour. Remove the pan to a wire rack and let it cool for 10 to 15 minutes, then loosen from the pan and invert it onto a cake plate. Cool completely and dust generously with superfine sugar. Use a serrated knife to cut the cake.

NOTE: You may use either white or yellow cornmeal in this cake—the choice is yours. Yellow meal gives the cake a rich golden color and its flavor is a little sweeter and more pronounced than white meal, but they provide exactly the same structure. It is delicious with either one.

Bonnie's Sour Cream Pound Cake

Sour cream pound cake has become a standard in the Southern baker's repertory and is often one of the first cakes a young woman will venture to make on her own. Once you taste it, you will know why: it is moist, rich, and heavenly. This version comes from my pound cake mentor, Bonnie Carter, an accomplished home baker who has helped me bake through all the pound cakes in this book. Bonnie's advice on pound cakes is not to fuss with them too much and relax: pound cakes, she says, know when you are afraid.

Makes one 10-inch tube cake, serving 12 to 16

15 ounces (about 3 cups) unbleached all-purpose flour
Salt
Baking soda
8 ounces (2 sticks) unsalted butter
3 cups sugar
6 large eggs
1 cup sour cream
1 teaspoon almond extract, Homemade Bourbon Vanilla (page 23),
    or vanilla extract

1. Position a rack in the center of the oven and preheat the oven to 325°F. Butter and flour a tube cake pan (see page 155). Whisk or sift together the flour, and a dash each of salt and baking soda. With a mixer, at medium speed, cream the butter and sugar until very light and fluffy—about 2 minutes.

2. Mix in the eggs one at a time and then the sour cream. Mix in the flour in several additions until smooth. Stir in the flavoring. Spoon the batter into the prepared pan, run the blade of a table knife through it in an S motion to get out any large air pockets, and give it a few solid taps on the counter to bring big air bubbles to the surface.

3. Bake about 1¼ hours, or until a straw, toothpick or cake tester inserted in the cen-

ter comes out clean. Don't open the oven door for the first hour. Remove the cake to a wire cooling rack and cool it in the pan for 10 to 15 minutes, then invert it onto a plate and let cool completely before cutting. Bonnie always inverts her cake onto a plain plate, then lays a cake plate onto the bottom and inverts it again so that the crusty top is face up.

Bourbon Brown Sugar Pound Cake

One of the best pastry chefs in America today is Karen Barker, who with chef-husband Ben owns Magnolia Grill in Durham, North Carolina. Karen was born and raised in Brooklyn, but has lived in North Carolina for so long that she cooks, thinks, and—yes, talks—like a Southerner. Her inspired desserts reflect a love for the traditions of her childhood, respect for those of her adopted home state, and an endless curiosity. One of her signatures is a sumptuous brown sugar pound cake studded with fresh pears, which is the inspiration for this one.

Makes one 10-inch tube cake or two 9-inch loaf cakes, serving 12 to 16

15 ounces (about 3 cups) unbleached all-purpose flour

1 teaspoon ground cinnamon

1 teaspoon freshly grated nutmeg

½ teaspoon salt

1 teaspoon baking powder

12 ounces (1½ cups or 3 sticks) unsalted butter

1 cup granulated sugar

2 cups firmly packed light brown sugar

6 large eggs

½ cup bourbon

1 tablespoon Homemade Bourbon Vanilla (page 23) or 1 teaspoon vanilla extract
    mixed with 2 teaspoons bourbon

1. Position a rack in the center of the oven and preheat it to 325°F. Butter and flour the pan as directed on page 155. Whisk or sift together the flour, cinnamon, nutmeg, salt, and baking powder. With a wooden spoon, or a mixer fitted with a paddle or rotary beaters, cream the butter, beating until it is light and fluffy, then gradually beat in both sugars and cream until very light and fluffy.

2. Beat in the eggs one at a time alternating with the flour-and-spice blend, a little at a time, until both are incorporated. Don't overbeat it at this point. Finally stir in the bour-

bon and vanilla and spoon the batter into the prepared pan. Slip a table knife blade into the batter and run it through in a back and forth S motion to take out any large air pockets. Give the pan a couple of firm taps on the counter—just enough to bring any air pockets to the surface.

3. Bake for about 1½ hours, depending on the shape of your pan, until risen, golden brown, and a straw inserted into the center comes out clean. Don't open the oven door for the first 1¼ hours. Make sure the cake is completely done before taking it from the oven, but don't overcook it or it will be dry and heavy. Turn off the oven, and let it cool for 10 minutes, then crack the door and let the cake cool completely before taking it out of the pan.

Applesauce Raisin Pound Cake

Fruitcakes are a truly ancient part of the Western baker's art, and once got much more respect than they do today. Not limited by the constraints of any holiday, based on a buttery rich pound cake base, and unencumbered by today's syrupy, artificially colored candied fruit, they were the delectable heart of every celebration—the original wedding cake (the fruit was supposed to both symbolize fertility and increase the couple's chances in that department), and the best cake for commemorating a birthday, anniversary, or just about any other milestone. Eventually, it eclipsed plum pudding as the centerpiece of the Christmastide dessert board and, in turn, began to lose ground in other celebrations.

The early fruitcakes were much simpler than the candylike stuff we endure today, often containing little more than raisins, currants, and some variety of nuts, but there were dozens of variations, some of which, like this moist, delectable cake, contain fruit that modern fruitcakes rarely see. Here the fruit does several jobs beyond merely studding the cake with juicy, sweet morsels: the applesauce contributes moisture, adds richness, and provides leavening as its natural acidity reacts with the soda.

Makes one 10-inch tube cake, serving 12 to 16

2 cups seedless raisins (about 12 ounces)

1 cup water

14 ounces (about 3 light cups) unbleached all-purpose flour

1 teaspoon baking soda

½ teaspoon salt

1 teaspoon ground cinnamon

½ teaspoon freshly grated nutmeg

8 ounces (1 cup or 2 sticks) unsalted butter, softened

2 cups sugar

3 large eggs

Grated zest of 1 lemon

2 cups applesauce

1 tablespoon Homemade Bourbon Vanilla (page 23) or 1 teaspoon vanilla extract
   and 2 teaspoons bourbon, mixed
1 cup roughly chopped pecans

1. Position a rack in the center of the oven and preheat the oven to 300°F. Butter and crumb a Bundt pan (see page 155). Put the raisins in a heatproof bowl, bring the water to a boil, and pour it over them. Let them plump for 10 minutes and drain them thoroughly. After measuring the flour take up ¼ cup and set it aside. Whisk or sift the remaining flour with the soda, salt, cinnamon, and nutmeg.

2. Beat the butter until fluffy and gradually beat in the sugar, beating until fluffy and light. Mix in the eggs one at a time and then the lemon zest. Alternately add the flour mixture and the applesauce, beating well between additions. Finally mix in the vanilla.

3. Combine the raisins and pecans in a mixing bowl and toss them with the reserved flour. Fold them into the batter and then pour the batter into the prepared pan and run the blade of a table knife through it in an S motion to take out any large air pockets and lightly tap the pan on the counter several times. Bake the cake until a straw, toothpick, or cake tester inserted into the center comes out clean, about 2 hours. Cool it in the pan for 10 minutes, then carefully invert it over a cake plate and lift the pan away. Cool completely before cutting.

Aunt Margaret's Fresh Apple Pound Cake

This cake follows the modern volume pound cake formula but with an unorthodox twist: the batter contains oil instead of solid shortening, which makes an exceptionally moist cake. Otherwise, it is a straightforward, old-fashioned fruitcake—that is, a pound cake batter studded with fruit and nuts—along with a steaming mug of coffee or tea, the perfect thing to warm up with by the fire on a cool autumn afternoon or evening.

Makes one 10-inch tube cake, serving 12 to 16

FOR THE CAKE:

2 cups granulated sugar

1½ cups vegetable oil

4 large eggs

3 cups unbleached all-purpose flour, measured by spooning it into the cup

1 teaspoon baking soda

1 teaspoon salt

3 cups tart pie apples (such as Winesap, Arkansas Black, or Granny Smith), peeled, cored, and diced

1 cup grated coconut

1 cup chopped pecans

2 teaspoons Homemade Bourbon Vanilla (page 23) or 1 teaspoon vanilla extract

FOR THE TOPPING (OPTIONAL):

4 ounces (8 tablespoons or 1 stick) unsalted butter

1½ cups firmly packed light brown sugar

½ cup chopped pecans

1 tablespoon whole milk

1. Position a rack in the center of the oven and preheat it to 325°F. Butter and flour a tube cake pan (see page 155) and set it aside. Combine the sugar and oil in a mixing bowl and beat until well mixed. Beat in the eggs, one at a time.

2. Set aside ½ cup flour and sift together (or combine in a mixing bowl and whisk together) the remaining flour, soda, and salt. Beat it a little at a time into the sugar-oil-egg mixture and beat in the vanilla. Put the apples in a mixing bowl and lightly sprinkle them with the reserved flour. Toss to coat and then add the coconut and pecans and toss to mix. Fold the apples and nuts into the batter and pour the batter into the prepared pan. Run a knife through the mixture to get out the air bubbles and lightly tap the pan on the counter several times.

3. Bake for 1 hour and 20 minutes, or until a straw or cake tester inserted into the center comes out clean. Do not open the oven door during the first hour of baking. Cool the cake in the pan for about 15 minutes and then remove it from the pan to a serving plate. Cool the cake completely before topping it.

4. To make the topping, melt the butter in a heavy-bottomed saucepan over medium heat. Add the sugar, nuts, and milk, stirring until the sugar is melted. Raise the heat to medium-high and bring the mixture to a boil. Cook, stirring frequently, until it reaches the soft-ball stage (234° to 240°F on a candy thermometer). Let it cool until it is warm and pour it over the cake. The cake is also good without the topping, and you may omit it if you want a simpler, less rich dessert.

Candy's Blueberry Pound Cake

This lovely cake has become a modern American classic. Its rich, dense, velvety and yet delicate crumb, studded with contrasting deep purple-blue, tart-sweet berries is a perfect study in balanced contrast. This version comes from friend Candy Hall in Virginia, a fine cook and baker whose two amazing and beautiful daughters are among the great joys of my life. This cake was once strictly a summer sweet, made during the blueberry season that can be as early as June in the Deep South and as late as September to the north, but both Candy and Baking in America *author Greg Patent say that individually quick frozen berries work fine here. Don't thaw them first, but dust them with flour and fold them into the batter while they're still frozen solid.*

Makes one 10-inch tube cake or two 9-inch loaf cakes, serving 12 to 16

1 pint blueberries, washed and well drained
14 ounces (about 3 light cups) unbleached all-purpose flour
1 teaspoon baking powder
½ teaspoon salt
8 ounces (1 cup or 2 sticks) unsalted butter, softened
2 cups sugar
4 large eggs
2 teaspoons Homemade Bourbon Vanilla (page 23) or 1½ teaspoons vanilla extract
Freshly squeezed lemon juice, to taste

1. Position a rack in the lower third of the oven and preheat the oven to 325°F. Butter and flour a 10-inch tube pan or two 9-inch loaf pans (see page 155). Dust the berries with ¼ cup of the flour. In a separate bowl, whisk or sift together the remaining flour, baking powder, and salt.

2. With a mixer fitted with a paddle or rotary beaters, cream the butter until fluffy. Gradually add the sugar on medium speed until fluffy and very light. Beat in the eggs one at a time, beating well after each addition, then beat in the vanilla and lemon juice.

3. Fold the flour into the batter a little at a time until well blended and gently stir in

the berries. Pour it into the prepared pan, run a table knife through the batter in an S motion and tap the pan firmly on the counter a couple of times to break up any large air bubbles and bring them to the surface.

4. Bake for about 1 hour and 10 minutes or until a cake tester or straw inserted into the center comes out clean. Don't open the oven door during the first hour. Cool the cake on a wire rack for 10 minutes before taking it out of the pan. Cool completely before cutting.

Candy's Lemon Tea Bread

Loaf cakes for the tea table have a long-standing tradition in the South. Though often called "bread" and baked in a way that resembles it, many of them—like this one—are nothing more than a pound cake baked in a loaf pan. I like to spread the glaze on this cake while it is still warm. It will run down the sides, but once the glaze cools and sets, it loses that raw pasty taste that confectioners' sugar–based icings can sometimes have.

Makes one 9-inch loaf cake

7 ounces (about 1½ cups) unbleached all-purpose flour
1½ teaspoons baking powder
¼ teaspoon salt
½ cup (4 ounces or 8 tablespoons) unsalted butter or vegetable shortening
1 cup granulated sugar
2 large eggs
½ cup whole milk
Grated zest of 1 lemon

FOR THE GLAZE:
1 cup sifted powdered sugar
2 tablespoons freshly squeezed lemon juice (about 1 lemon)

1. Position a rack in the center of the oven and preheat the oven to 350°F. Butter and flour a 9-inch loaf pan (see page 155). Whisk or sift together the flour, baking powder, and salt.

2. With a handheld mixer, cream the butter or shortening until fluffy and light; gradually add the sugar, beating well at medium speed. Add the eggs, one at a time, beating well after each addition. Add the flour mixture and milk alternately, beginning and ending with flour. Finally, stir in the grated lemon zest.

3. Pour the batter into the prepared pan, tap it on the counter to break up any air bub-

bles and bring them to the surface. Bake for 50 to 55 minutes or until a cake tester, straw, or toothpick inserted into the center comes out clean. Cool the bread in the pan on a wire rack for 10 to 15 minutes, then remove from the pan and let it cool completely on a rack.

4. While the bread cools, make the glaze by stirring together the powdered sugar and lemon juice until it is smooth. Pour the glaze over the cooled bread.

Sweet Potato Tea Bread

Here is another pound cake masquerading under the name "bread." This one really sits at the crossroad between true pound cakes and nut-studded sweet breads that have become practically universal in American home baking. Sweet, moist, and surprisingly delicate, it doesn't have to be confined to the tea table, of course, but is equally good with coffee or an ice-cold glass of milk.

Makes one 9-inch loaf cake

10 ounces (about 2 cups) unbleached all-purpose flour

3 teaspoons baking powder

¼ teaspoon salt

1 teaspoon ground cinnamon

½ teaspoon freshly grated nutmeg

2 ounces (¼ cup or ½ stick) butter, softened

¾ cup firmly packed light brown sugar

2 large eggs

1 cup cooked mashed sweet potato (about 1 large potato)

¼ cup whole milk

Grated zest of 1 lemon

1 tablespoon Homemade Bourbon Vanilla (page 23) or 1 teaspoon vanilla extract
    and 2 teaspoons bourbon

½ cup pecans, roughly broken

1. Position a rack in the center of the oven and preheat the oven to 350°F. Butter and flour a 9-inch loaf pan (see page 155). Whisk or sift together the flour, baking powder, salt, and spices.

2. In a separate mixing bowl with a handheld mixer, cream the butter until fluffy and gradually beat in the sugar, creaming until it is very light and fluffy. Beat in the eggs, one at a time, then mix in the sweet potato, milk, lemon zest, and vanilla. Stir in the flour and

the pecans until smooth. Spoon the batter into the prepared pan and tap it on the counter several times to get out any large air pockets.

3. Bake in the center of the oven until risen and golden brown, about 55 minutes. A straw or toothpick inserted into the center should come out clean. Set the pan on a wire rack and let the bread cool in the pan for about 10 minutes, then turn out onto a wire rack and cool completely before cutting.

Plain or 1, 2, 3, 4 Cake

This is the traditional all-purpose yellow layer cake formula—its easily recalled name a short-hand for the main ingredients: 1 cup of shortening, 2 cups of sugar, 3 cups of flour, and four whole eggs. It's the cake my grandmothers and so many others have used as their basic yellow-layer cake, the name and character of the finished cake depending entirely on what was slathered over it: rich fudge frosting made it chocolate cake, snowy layers of coconut-crusted seven-minute or sour cream frosting made it coconut cake—well, you get the idea. While researching my first cookbook, I found that this recipe was so commonplace that it often appeared as nothing more than a title and list of ingredients but with no directions whatsoever, as if any baker worth her mixing bowl would know what to do.

Makes three 9-inch round layers or two 9-inch square layers

8 ounces (1 cup or 2 sticks) unsalted butter

2 cups sugar

4 large eggs (see Note, below)

14 ounces (about 3 light cups) unbleached all-purpose flour

2 teaspoons baking powder

1 teaspoon salt

1 cup whole milk

1½ teaspoons Homemade Bourbon Vanilla (page 23)
    or 1 teaspoon vanilla extract

1. Position a rack in the center of the oven and preheat the oven to 350°F. Butter and flour three 9-inch round or two 9-inch square cake pans (see page 155). In a large mixing bowl, cream the butter and gradually beat in the sugar until the mixture is light and lemon-colored. Beat in the eggs, one at a time.

2. In a separate bowl, sift or whisk together the flour, baking powder, and salt. Beat the flour and milk, alternating, in four additions, into the batter, beating well between each one.

3. Divide the batter equally among the pans, then tap them sharply on the counter several times to make any large air bubbles rise to the top of the batter. If the oven won't hold all the pans on one rack without touching, stagger them on two racks in the middle of the oven. Bake for about 25 minutes, or until the tops are lightly colored and a toothpick inserted in the center comes out clean.

NOTE: To make this cake lighter and more delicate, separate the eggs. Add the yolks to the batter where indicated in step 1. Beat the whites in a separate bowl until they form firm but not dry peaks. Fold a little of the batter into them, and then fold the whites into the batter at the end of step 2. Bake as indicated. Their rise will be a little higher, but they'll also settle a little as they cool, like a soufflé.

4. Remove the pans to wire racks and let the cake cool completely before taking them out of the pan and icing them.

White Layer Cake

Sometimes this delicate cake, pale because it contained only the whites of the eggs, could be found in old cookbooks and manuscript recipe collections under picturesque names like "lady" or "silver" cake. Its pale color of course is not truly white unless the baker has used lard or shortening instead of butter, but let's not split hairs. The ideal base for many of the elegant layer cakes filled with fruit, including the legendary Lady Baltimore cake of the Carolina Lowcountry or Emma Rylander Lane's prize cake, which now carries her name, and those curd-and-custard "jelly"-filled confections of the late-nineteenth century that carried patriotic names like "Robert E. Lee Cake."

Makes one 9-inch cake with 2 thick or 3 thin layers

7 large eggs

8 ounces (1 cup or 2 sticks) unsalted butter

2 cups sugar

12 ounces (about 2⅔ cups) unbleached all-purpose flour

3 teaspoons Single-Acting Baking Powder (see page 13) or 2½ teaspoons double-acting baking powder

½ teaspoon salt

1 cup whole milk

1 lemon or 1 tablespoon Homemade Bourbon Vanilla (page 23) or 1 teaspoon vanilla extract

1. Preheat the oven to 375°F. Butter and flour two or three 9-inch round cake pans (see page 155). Separate the eggs, placing the whites into a metal or glass bowl, and set aside the yolks, covered and refrigerated, for another use such as Lemon Curd (page 201).

2. With a mixer set on medium speed, cream the butter and sugar until light, fluffy, and lemon-colored.

3. Sift the flour, baking powder, and salt together. Gradually add it, alternately, with the milk to the butter and sugar, beating the batter well after each addition. Beat in the

flavoring. (If you are using lemon, grate the rind into the batter and then squeeze the juice into the batter through a strainer.)

4. With a whisk or the mixer refitted with cleaned beaters or a whisk attachment, beat the egg whites to soft peaks. Carefully, but thoroughly, fold them into the batter by hand with a spatula or wooden spoon. Divide the batter equally among the pans and bake in the center of the oven (make sure that the pans don't touch) for 25 to 30 minutes, until a toothpick inserted into the center comes out clean.

MaMa's Coconut Cake

This is my maternal grandmother's prize cake and one of the most extraordinarily moist cakes you will ever encounter. The secret for its moist richness is also the reason MaMa's cake always tasted more intensely of coconut than any other: she saved the fresh coconut juice, lightly sweetened it, and basted it over each layer of the cake. Except for the brief heating to melt sugar into that juice, no part of the coconut was cooked, so the taste stayed lively and fresh. This practice appears to be concentrated mainly in upstate Georgia and Carolina, where coconut cake is a tradition at Christmas, and actually both my grandmothers did it—a fact that my father's side of the family did not fail to point out when I made my first attempt at MaMa's recipe in Classical Southern Cooking. *Well, with all due respect to Granny Fowler, who was hands down the best chicken fryer I ever knew, MaMa had a delicate touch with baking that even Granny could never quite match.*

Makes one 9-inch 3-layer cake

1 recipe Plain or 1, 2, 3, 4 Cake (page 176), baked in three layers
1 medium fresh coconut, with plenty of juice (it should slosh when shaken)
2 to 3 tablespoons sugar
1 recipe Seven-Minute Frosting (page 195), not made ahead,
   but when indicated in step 2 below

1. While the cake is baking, prepare the coconut: pierce all the holes at one end with an ice pick or other pointed object such as a screwdriver, tapping it with a hammer. I do this sitting down with the coconut held firmly between my knees. Drain the juice through a strainer into a bowl, shaking the nut gently to get it all. Lay the coconut on its side on a concrete floor or brick-paved patio or door stoop and tap it firmly with a hammer at the middle. Roll it, tapping steadily until it cracks and splits in half. Turn each half dome side up and tap at the top until it cracks and breaks apart. Slip a wide sturdy knife such as an oyster knife between the shell and the meat and pry it loose. Peel off the brown skin with a vegetable peeler, rinse the white meat and grate it into a large

bowl with a rotary cheese grater, a box grater, or the fine shredding blade of the food processor.

2. Measure the reserved coconut juice. If it is less than a cup, add enough water to make a full cup of liquid. Put it in a saucepan with 2 to 3 tablespoons of sugar, to taste, and warm it over medium-low heat, stirring occasionally, until the sugar has dissolved. Turn off the heat. Make the frosting according to the recipe.

3. Invert the first layer of cake over the plate and carefully remove the pan. Spoon about ¼ cup of the sweetened coconut juice over it, gently spread it with a thin layer of frosting, and sprinkle one quarter of the coconut evenly over the top.

4. Invert the second layer over the frosted layer and carefully remove its pan. Spoon another quarter of a cup plus a tablespoon of coconut juice over it, frost it, and sprinkle it with coconut as before, and then invert the final layer over it.

5. Spoon another quarter cup of the coconut juice over the top and frost both the top and sides of the cake, turning it as you work to ensure an even cover. Pat the rest of the coconut evenly over the top and sides of the cake and spoon the remaining juice slowly over the cake, letting each spoonful soak in before adding more. Cover with a cake dome or dome of aluminum foil that does not touch the cake at any point and let it rest for 24 hours before cutting it. Once it is cut, keep it well covered, and, after the second day, refrigerated.

Old-Fashioned Lemon Jelly Cake

Jelly cakes like this—made in layers rather than a rolled spiral—are rarely seen anymore, and may be thought a bit old-fashioned, but not so long ago they were the pride of Southern house-wives from Virginia to Mississippi. Variations of it can still be found in historical collections carrying such regionally patriotic (and now politically incorrect) names as "Robert E. Lee Cake." But they live in more than history, even among those who grew up in the last half of the twentieth century. When I brought it to a recent church reception, my friend Lynne Carreker's eyes lit up as she exclaimed excitedly, "Oh, my goodness—that was my father's favorite cake! I haven't had it since I was a little girl!"

Don't wait as long as she did.

Seven-Minute Frosting really makes this cake shine. Its drawback is that, despite the Lemon Curd, there will be a lot of leftover egg yolks. If you prefer, you can frost the cake with Mock Lemon Buttercream.

Makes one 9-inch 3-layer cake

1 recipe White Layer Cake (page 178), baked in 3 layers
About 1½ cups Lemon Curd (page 201)
1 recipe Seven-Minute Frosting (page 195), flavored with lemon, or Mock Lemon
    Buttercream (page 200), not made ahead but at the point indicated in step 3
½ cup Candied Citrus Threads, made with lemons (page 203)

1. Allow the cake layers to cool and take them carefully out of the pans. If the cakes have "domed" a little in the center, you can carefully slice off the excess to level the layers with a serrated bread knife. Place one layer top side up on a cake plate. Cover the top thickly with some of the lemon curd, leaving about ½ inch uncovered at the edges (the filling spreads when the next layer is added. Invert the second layer over it and carefully set it in place.

2. Thickly cover the top of the second layer with curd, again leaving about ½ inch around the edges uncovered. Invert the third layer over it and set it in place.

3. Make the Seven-Minute Frosting and, as soon as it is made, spread it evenly over the top and sides of the cake, swirling it decoratively with the spatula. Let the cake stand for at least an hour to allow the frosting to set. Sprinkle it with Candied Citrus Threads just before serving.

VARIATION

ORANGE OR KEY LIME JELLY CAKE: Substitute Orange Curd (page 202) and Candied Citrus Threads made with orange zest, or Key Lime Curd (page 202) and use either lemon zest or green Persian lime zest for the Candied Citrus Threads—or omit them. The Seven-Minute and Mock Buttercream frostings can also be flavored with orange.

Bubber's Key Lime Cake

Since so many Southern men are named after a daddy who had in turn been named for his own daddy, many a Southern family has half a dozen members with exactly the same name. In order to distinguish each from the other, almost every Southern male has a boyhood nickname that he somehow never loses no matter how ridiculous it sounds to call a six-foot-tall man something like "Little Joe." Bubba, probably a corruption of "Brother," is the most common and notorious of those nicknames, with dozens of variations of which Bubber is just one. The Bubber in question here is Adam Howard, an accomplished cook and wicked storyteller from McClellanville, South Carolina.

Makes one 9-inch 2-layer cake, serving 8–10

3 cups sifted cake flour (sift or whisk before measuring)
3¼ teaspoons baking powder
¾ teaspoon salt
½ teaspoon baking soda
⅔ cup unsalted butter or vegetable shortening
1⅔ cups sugar
1 tablespoon grated lemon zest (not lime zest)
¼ cup freshly squeezed Key lime juice or 2 tablespoons each Persian lime juice and
    lemon juice
2 large eggs
1¼ cups whole milk
1 recipe Key Lime Cream Cheese Buttercream (recipe follows)

1. Position a rack in the center of the oven and preheat the oven to 375°F. Butter and flour two 9-inch layer cake pans (see page 155). Sift or whisk together the flour, baking powder, salt, and soda.

2. In a large mixing bowl, cream the butter or shortening until fluffy. Gradually add the sugar and cream until light and fluffy, then beat in the zest, juice, and eggs, one at a

time, and continue beating until light. Fold in the flour and milk, alternating, beginning and ending with the flour.

3. Divide the batter between the prepared pans and bake until golden and a straw or toothpick inserted in the center comes out clean, about 25 minutes. Cool in the pans on wire racks.

4. Invert one layer on a cake plate and carefully remove the pan. Cover it generously with one-third of the frosting, invert the second layer over it, remove the pan, and cover the top and sides with the remaining frosting. Chill the cake before serving and store any leftovers, well covered, in the refrigerator.

Key Lime Cream Cheese Buttercream

Makes about 3 cups buttercream, enough for one 9-inch 2-layer cake

One 8-ounce package cream cheese, softened
4 ounces (½ cup or 1 stick) unsalted butter, softened
½ teaspoon grated lemon zest (do not use lime zest)
2 tablespoons freshly squeezed Key lime juice or 1 tablespoon each Persian lime juice and lemon juice
4½ to 4¾ cups confectioners' sugar, sifted

1. Cream the cheese and butter together until fluffy. Add the zest and juice and beat until fluffy.

2. Gradually beat in the sugar until the frosting is light, fluffy, and spreadable. Spread at once.

Brown Velvet Cake with Dark Fudge Frosting

One of the most popular and legendary cakes in the modern American repertory is red velvet cake—a light cocoa-flavored cake whose naturally ruddy color is enhanced by a big dose of red food coloring. Its popularity is pointed up by a charming but completely bogus urban legend about its origins that suspiciously echoes that equally bogus Neiman Marcus 250-dollar cookie story regularly circulating on the Internet. We Americans love those stories almost as much as we love to play with names and put a spin on old ideas, so it was just a matter of time till red velvet cake began to have spin-offs without food coloring, like the all-egg-yolk spin-off of the legendary Lady Baltimore cake that logically goes by the name "Lord" Baltimore. This one, with its satisfyingly chocolaty, truly velvet-like layers, is no mere spin-off, however; it's an improvement.

Most versions of velvet cake—whether red or brown, are usually iced with a plain white sugar frosting—as pretty to look at as it is boring to eat. A cake with velvet in its name deserves a finish that is equally luscious and indulgent, and rich, silky old-fashioned fudge frosting fits the bill handsomely.

Makes one 9-inch 2-layer cake

2 cups Southern soft-wheat flour (see page 9) or pastry flour, measured by spooning the flour into the cup

2 teaspoons baking soda

½ teaspoon salt

3 ounces (3 squares) unsweetened chocolate

8 ounces (1 cup or 2 sticks) unsalted butter, softened

1½ cups firmly packed light brown sugar

2 large eggs

1 cup whole-milk buttermilk or plain whole-milk yogurt thinned with milk to buttermilk consistency

2 teaspoons Homemade Bourbon Vanilla (page 23) or 1 teaspoon vanilla extract

1 recipe Old-Fashioned Dark Fudge Frosting (page 197), not made ahead, but when indicated in step 3 below

1. Position a rack in the center of the oven and preheat the oven to 350°F. Butter and flour two 9-inch layer cake pans (see page 155). Whisk or sift together the flour, baking soda, and salt. Melt the chocolate in a double boiler over simmering water (or in the microwave at half power); remove it from the heat but keep it warm.

2. Cream the butter, then add the sugar and cream until fluffy and light. Beat in the eggs, one at a time, and then stir in the melted chocolate. Mix in the flour and buttermilk a little at a time, alternating, beginning with and finishing with the flour. Stir in the vanilla. Divide the batter between the prepared pans, tap them lightly on the counter to remove any large air bubbles, and bake for about 20 minutes, or until a straw or toothpick inserted into the center comes out clean.

3. Cool the cakes in the pans on wire racks before frosting them. While they cool, make the frosting as directed. Invert one cake layer over a cake plate and carefully remove the pan. Cover it thickly with about one-third of the frosting. Invert the second layer over it, remove the pan, and then frost the top and sides with the remaining frosting. Let the frosting set before cutting, at least an hour.

Appalachian Stack Cake

This delicate and beautiful cake was once the standard by which cooks all along the Blue Ridge of the Appalachian Mountains were measured. It had all but disappeared from Southern tables, but in recent years, it has made a comeback among both home cooks and professional pastry chefs whose exploration of old traditions has sparked a renewed interest in regional dishes like this one. Though generally served plain, just before serving it can be frosted with 2 cups of lightly sweetened whipped cream, or dusted with superfine or confectioners' sugar.

Makes one 9-inch round cake

FOR THE FILLING:

1 pound dried apples or peaches (see Note, below)

1 teaspoon ground cinnamon

1 teaspoon freshly grated nutmeg

Salt

1 cup firmly packed light brown sugar

1 lemon

FOR THE CAKE LAYERS:

12 ounces (about 2⅔ cups) unbleached all-purpose flour

1 teaspoon baking powder

1 teaspoon baking soda

½ teaspoon salt

1 teaspoon powdered ginger

⅓ cup unsulfured molasses

1 cup firmly packed light brown sugar

4 ounces (½ cup or 1 stick) unsalted butter, softened

2 large eggs

1. At least 8 hours (or the night) before, wash the dried fruit and put it in a glass bowl. Add in enough water to cover them by an inch, cover with a towel, and set it aside in a cool place.

2. Put the reconstituted fruit, its soaking water, the cinnamon, nutmeg, salt, and the brown sugar into a saucepan. If the mixture appears too dry, add half a cup or so of water. Turn on the heat to medium-low and simmer, stirring occasionally, until the apples are tender and the liquid has evaporated, about 20 minutes. Remove it from the heat, grate in the zest of the lemon, cut the lemon in half, and add lemon juice to taste. Let cool.

3. Whisk or sift together the flour, baking powder, soda, salt, and ginger. In a separate bowl, beat together the molasses, sugar, butter, and eggs until smooth. Gradually mix in the dry ingredients, mixing until it is completely smooth. It will be very stiff, like a firm sugar cookie dough. Cover the bowl and chill the dough for at least half an hour.

4. Position a rack in the center of the oven and preheat it to 350°F. Butter and flour six 9-inch round cake pans (see page 155) or reuse three pans in batches, wiping clean, buttering, and flouring them after the first batch. Divide the dough into six equal lumps. Lightly flour a work surface and roll them out into 9-inch rounds. Put them into the pans and gently press to fit to the edges. Bake the layers three at a time until golden, about 15 minutes. Cool them completely before removing them from the pans.

5. Roughly mash the filling with a potato masher, leaving the fruit rather chunky. Put one layer on the bottom of a cake plate. Cover it thickly with one-fifth of the filling. Add another layer, cover it with another one-fifth of the filling, and continue until all the layers are stacked. Leave the top dry.

6. Cover with a cake dome or foil and let it sit for several hours before cutting. The layers will absorb much of the moisture in the filling and become soft.

NOTE: Sliced, dried fruits are widely available year-round in Southern markets, and should be available in most supermarkets and natural food grocers. Look for unsulfured fruit.

Pecan Upside-Down Cake

Many historians believe that American fruit-topped cakes that bake upside down (with fruit and a buttery syrup at the bottom of the pan) are derived from the French apple confection tart tatin, *and as if to back up that theory, some of the oldest recipes for upside-down cake are in fact made with apples and not the practically ubiquitous rings of canned pineapple that are today almost synonymous with the name. This unusual coffee cake is really a cross between those fruit upside-down cakes and a pecan and syrup-coated biscuit confection known region-ally—for reasons lost in legend—as monkey bread.*

Makes one 9-inch cake

1½ ounces (3 tablespoons) unsalted butter
¾ cup firmly packed light brown sugar
1½ teaspoons ground cinnamon
¼ cup honey
1 tablespoon boiling water
1 generous cup whole Toasted Pecans (page 18)
5 ounces (about 1 cup) Southern soft-wheat flour (see page 9)
    or unbleached all-purpose flour
½ teaspoon freshly grated nutmeg
1 teaspoon baking powder
¼ teaspoon salt
2 large eggs
¾ cup granulated sugar
½ cup whole milk
1 lemon, zest grated and reserved, halved,
    and juiced through a strainer
1 tablespoon Homemade Bourbon Vanilla (page 23) or 1 teaspoon vanilla extract
    mixed with 2 teaspoons bourbon
Bourbon Whipped Cream (recipe follows)

1. Position a rack in the center of the oven and preheat the oven to 325°F. Butter a 9-inch round cake pan. Put the butter in a heavy-bottomed saucepan and melt it over medium heat. Stir in the brown sugar and 1 teaspoon of the cinnamon, honey, and boiling water, bring it to a simmer, and cook 2 minutes. Turn off the heat. Pour the syrup into the prepared cake pan and carefully (the sugar mixture will still be quite hot) place the pecan halves flat side up in concentric circles in the pan, completely covering the bottom.

2. Whisk together the flour, the remaining ½ teaspoon of cinnamon, the nutmeg, baking powder, and salt. Separate the eggs, putting the yolks in a mixing bowl and the whites in a separate glass or metal bowl. Beat the yolks until light and gradually beat in the sugar until fluffy and light. Alternately add the spiced flour and milk, mixing well between additions. Fold in the lemon zest, 2 tablespoons of lemon juice, and vanilla.

3. With a clean whisk or handheld mixer beat the egg whites until they hold soft peaks. Fold a spoonful into the batter and then fold in the remainder. Pour the batter evenly over the sugar syrup and pecans in the cake pan and bake until a straw, toothpick, or cake tester inserted into the center comes out clean, about 30 to 35 minutes. Let the cake cool in the pan for 10 minutes, then run a knife around the edges to loosen it; lay a flat cake plate over it, then invert the pan and plate carefully and unmold the cake. Serve warm or at room temperature with Bourbon Whipped Cream.

Bourbon Whipped Cream

This cream enhances just about any pie or pound cake, and is delicious spooned over a simple compote of fresh summer fruit. The bourbon flavor should be subtle and elusive, enriching but not intoxicating, so don't be tempted to add more.

Makes about 1½ cups whipped cream

1 cup very cold heavy cream
3 tablespoons sugar
1 tablespoon bourbon

1. Put the cream in a glass or stainless-steel bowl and whip it with a whisk or handheld mixer at medium-high speed until frothy.

2. Sprinkle in a spoonful of sugar and beat until the cream is thick, then beat in the remaining sugar and whip until the cream holds stiff peaks. Fold in the bourbon. Let stand for at least 10 minutes before using.

VARIATIONS

WHIPPED CREAM: Omit the bourbon or substitute ½ teaspoon vanilla extract, folding it into the whipped cream at the end of step 2.

MINT WHIPPED CREAM: Substitute green crème de menthe for the bourbon, and add a drop or two of oil of mint, to taste, folding both into the whipped cream at the end of step 2.

Peach Upside-Down Ginger Cake

Peaches and ginger are just made for one another, and this luscious, drop-dead-easy cake brings the two together in an especially handsome union. The cake is nothing more than soft ginger-bread, and those who have made pineapple upside-down cake will recognize the fruit topping that bakes in a brown sugar and butter syrup on the bottom of the pan. It is best cooked in a cast-iron skillet, because the heat-retaining iron helps make the sugar and butter topping especially luscious, but you can bake it in a round or even square cake pan.

Makes one 9-inch cake, serving 6 to 8

4 ounces (½ cup or 1 stick) unsalted butter
1 cup firmly packed light brown sugar
1 teaspoon ground cinnamon
3 medium slightly underripe peaches
1¼ cups Southern soft-wheat flour (see page 9) or unbleached all-purpose flour
1 teaspoon baking powder
½ teaspoon salt
½ cup unsulfured molasses
1 large egg
¼ cup whole milk
¼ cup bourbon
2 tablespoons freshly grated gingerroot
Grated zest of 1 lemon

1. Position a rack in the center of the oven and preheat the oven to 350°F. Put 2 ounces (4 tablespoons) of the butter in a 9-inch iron skillet and melt it over medium heat. Turn off the heat and sprinkle in ¾ cup of brown sugar. Stir until blended and sprinkle half a teaspoon of cinnamon evenly over it. Keep it warm but not hot. Scrub the peaches well under cold running water, dry them thoroughly, and peel them with a vegetable peeler or paring knife.

2. Whisk or sift together the flour, baking powder, salt, and remaining ½ teaspoon cinnamon. In a separate bowl, cream the remaining 4 tablespoons butter until fluffy, add the remaining sugar, cream until fluffy and light, then beat in the molasses and egg. Alternately add the flour and the milk and bourbon, mixing well between additions, and finally stir in the grated ginger and lemon zest.

3. Cut the peaches in half, remove the pits, and slice them into thick wedges. Arrange them in concentric circles in the skillet until the bottom is covered. Spoon the batter over the peaches and bake until a straw, toothpick, or cake tester inserted into the center comes out clean, about 45 to 50 minutes.

4. Cool the cake in the pan for 10 minutes, then invert a plate or cake plate over it, carefully turn them over, and remove the pan. Scrape any syrup that remains in the pan over the cake. Serve warm or at room temperature.

ICINGS, FROSTINGS, FILLINGS, AND TOPPINGS

Seven-Minute Frosting

MASTER RECIPE

This universal frosting is of course called Seven-Minute because that's how long it cooks. It's also artlessly called "boiled" icing in some old cookbooks, a name that's misleading, since, as is true of "boiled" custard or ham, it must never be allowed to actually boil. It's a good all-purpose frosting to have in your repertory, as its variations need only be limited by your imagination. My maternal grandmother taught me to make this frosting, and just as creaming butter and sugar brings her back, whipping up a batch of Seven-Minute Frosting is filled with good memories. Modern recipes often contain a pinch of cream of tartar and sometimes a tablespoon of corn syrup and both help stabilize the frosting, but since MaMa never used either, of course, neither do I.

Never make this frosting ahead, but only when you are ready to frost the cake, or its surface will harden and crust over.

Makes about 4 cups and ices three 9-inch layers

4 large egg whites
1 pound (2 cups) sugar
9 tablespoons water
Flavorings (see Variations, below)

1. Prepare the bottom pan of a large double boiler with 1 inch of water and bring it to a simmer over medium heat, then reduce the heat to a slow simmer. In the top pot, off heat, combine the egg whites, sugar, and water and beat until the sugar is dissolved.

2. Place the pan over the simmering water in the lower half of the double boiler, mak-

ing sure that it doesn't directly touch the water. Beat for 7 minutes with a whisk or hand-held mixer at medium speed, or until the frosting stands in soft peaks.

3. Remove it immediately from over the boiling water and beat in the flavoring. Continue beating until the frosting is thick enough to spread, and ice the cake at once.

NOTE: This frosting can also be used to make delicate decorations for cakes by coloring it and piping it into shapes with a pastry bag onto sheets of wax paper or a slab of marble. Using a thin, wide-bladed knife or spatula, let them dry and harden before trying to remove them.

VARIATIONS

VANILLA SEVEN-MINUTE FROSTING: Beat in 2 teaspoons of Homemade Bourbon Vanilla (see page 23) or 1 teaspoon commercial vanilla extract.

LEMON SEVEN-MINUTE FROSTING: Grate the zest of one lemon and substitute a tablespoon or so of its juice for an equal measure of the water. Beat the zest into the icing as directed in step 3. You can color it with a pinch of saffron or a drop or so of yellow food coloring, but I prefer to leave it snowy-white and garnish the top with Candied Citrus Threads (page 203), made from lemon zest.

ORANGE SEVEN-MINUTE FROSTING: Follow the same procedure as for lemon frosting, using the grated zest of half an orange and substituting all its juice for an equal volume of the water. (If you can get Seville oranges, their tart juice and bright rinds make an even better icing than regular juice oranges.) Beat the zest into the icing as directed in step 3. As with the lemon frosting, above, you may color it orange by mixing a drop of red and yellow food coloring, but I prefer a garnish of Candied Citrus Threads (page 203), made with orange zest.

PEPPERMINT SEVEN-MINUTE FROSTING: So it's hokey and retro-sixties—get over it: it also happens to be really good. Make the frosting as directed and fold in a cup of finely crushed peppermint stick candy.

Old-Fashioned Dark Fudge Frosting

The first chocolate cakes were not really chocolate at all, but yellow cake covered with simple chocolate icing, a confection that survives to this day in a towering, rich six- or eight-layered cake that is frosted with this icing. The earliest chocolate cakes had a much simpler topping— grated chocolate sprinkled over whipped cream or a meringue similar to Seven-Minute Frosting (page 195)—much as we would finish a cake today with powdered sugar. The next logical step was to fold the chocolate into the cream or meringue. All of these were rather fragile and not nearly as satisfying as rich, dense fudge frosting, so they disappeared almost as soon as fudge frosting came on the scene. This is the perfect frosting for Brown Velvet Cake (page 186), old-time Plain or 1, 2, 3, 4 Cake (page 176), or your favorite plain or chocolate cupcakes.

Makes about 6 cups, frosting one 2-layer cake

3 cups sugar

1 cup cocoa

1 teaspoon salt

1½ cups heavy cream

4 ounces (8 tablespoons or 1 stick) unsalted butter

4 ounces bittersweet chocolate, roughly chopped, or bittersweet chocolate chips (about 1 cup)

1 tablespoon Homemade Bourbon Vanilla (page 23) or 2 teaspoons vanilla extract

1. Combine the sugar, cocoa, and salt in a heavy-bottomed saucepan and whisk to mix. Slowly whisk in the cream and turn on the heat to medium. Bring it to a boil, stirring occasionally, and add the butter and chocolate, stirring until they are melted and smooth. Let it come back to boil and cook, stirring occasionally, until it reaches the soft-ball stage (234° to 240°F on a candy thermometer), about 2 to 3 minutes.

2. Remove from the heat and stir in the vanilla. Let it cool, undisturbed, until it is just warm (no more than 110°F). Beat the frosting with a mixer or wooden spoon until it is thick enough to spread, and spread it immediately onto the cake.

Real Buttercream Frosting

Rich yet ethereal, this sumptuous frosting lifts any cake from the mundane to the spectacular. This is a genuine French-style buttercream, in which softened and whipped butter is beaten into egg yolks that have been thickened and tempered with hot sugar syrup. The syrup should simmer long enough to reach the thread stage (235°F on a candy thermometer) and the custard must cool to room temperature or even slightly cooler or it will not set up properly. Any cake iced with this buttercream should be kept cold until it is served.

Makes about 4 cups, frosting one 2-layer cake

¾ cup sugar
¼ teaspoon cream of tartar
¼ teaspoon salt
⅓ cup water
5 large egg yolks
8 ounces (1 cup or 2 sticks) unsalted butter, softened to room temperature
Flavorings (see Variations, below)

1. Combine the sugar, cream of tartar, and salt in a small saucepan and whisk to mix. Stir in the water and place it over medium-high heat. Bring it to a boil, stirring occasionally, and reduce the heat to medium. Simmer 5 minutes, or until it reaches 235°F on a candy thermometer. Meanwhile, beat the egg yolks with an electric mixer fitted with rotary beaters at medium speed until they are light, thick, and almost doubled in volume, about 3 minutes.

2. Pour the boiling syrup into a heatproof measuring cup and immediately beat it into the egg yolks in a thin, steady stream. Continue beating at medium speed until it reaches room temperature and is no longer at all warm. You may want to refrigerate it for a few minutes.

3. Cream the butter in a separate bowl until light and fluffy, then beat it gradually into the syrup-custard a tablespoon at a time. It should begin to thicken suddenly as you add

the last ¼ cup of butter. Beat in the flavorings. If at this point it is not thick and holding peaks, chill it for about 30 minutes, or until it is very cool and quite thick, then beat it until it is thick enough to spread. Spread the frosting at once.

VARIATIONS

VANILLA BUTTERCREAM: Beat in 1 tablespoon of Homemade Bourbon Vanilla (page 23) or 1 teaspoon vanilla extract and 1 tablespoon bourbon.

LEMON OR ORANGE BUTTERCREAM: Beat in the grated zest of a lemon or orange and 2 to 3 tablespoons of lemon or orange juice or orange liqueur.

Mock Orange or Lemon Buttercream

Cruder and not nearly as delicate as true buttercream, the big drawback of this frosting is the cornstarch that is contained in American confectioners' sugar, which often lends a raw pasty aftertaste. It is a good quick fix for a strongly flavored cake, however, and flavorings like lemon or orange go a long way toward covering up its deficiencies. Like true buttercream, any cake frosted with this should be kept refrigerated.

Makes about 3½ cups frosting, enough for one 2-layer cake or 12 cupcakes

4 ounces (½ cup or 1 stick) unsalted butter, softened to room temperature
⅛ teaspoon salt
2¼ cups confectioners' sugar
Grated zest of 1 lemon or 1 orange
¼ cup lemon or orange juice or orange liqueur
3 to 4 tablespoons heavy cream

1. With a mixer at medium speed, cream the butter until light and fluffy. Add the salt and sift in the sugar. Beat the sugar into the butter at medium speed until it is thick and fluffy.

2. Beat in the zest and juice and then gradually beat in enough heavy cream, a tablespoon at a time, until the frosting is light and spreadable. Spread it at once.

Lemon Curd

The nicest and most traditional of fillings for lemon pies, tarts, and old-fashioned jelly cakes, Lemon Curd is singularly wonderful all on its own slathered over hot biscuits or toast. This amount is enough for one 9-inch pie shell, a dozen prebaked tartlet shells, or the filling for a 9-inch round Old-Fashioned Lemon Jelly Cake (page 182). It will keep, covered and refrigerated, for up to a month—or so I'm told: it has never lasted that long in my house.

Makes about 2½ cups

4 ounces (½ cup or 1 stick) unsalted butter
½ cup freshly squeezed lemon juice (about 4 to 5 lemons)
4 teaspoons grated lemon zest—or more, to taste
1 cup sugar
Salt
2 whole large eggs and 4 large egg yolks

1. Prepare the bottom pot of a double boiler with 1 inch of water and bring it to a boil over medium heat. Reduce the heat to a slow simmer. Put the top pot over direct, medium heat and put in the butter. Barely melt it, and then stir in the lemon juice, grated zest, sugar, and a small pinch of salt, stirring until the sugar and salt are dissolved, put it over—but not touching—the simmering water.

2. In a separate bowl, beat together the eggs and yolks until smooth. Slowly stir them into the butter, and cook, stirring constantly, until quite thick, about 8 minutes. The spoon should leave a distinct path in the curd. The custard continues to thicken as it cools, but won't reach the stiff consistency of a bottled lemon curd until it is cold, so don't overcook it. Remove it from the heat.

3. Keep stirring the curd until it has cooled somewhat and then pour it into another container and let it cool completely. Cover and refrigerate until thoroughly chilled before using.

NOTE: This is a simple recipe, but working with butter-and-egg custards can be a tricky business unless you pay attention to it every second. Take care not to allow the butter to get too hot before the eggs are added or they could curdle. If at any point it looks as if the mixture is getting too hot and is about to curdle, take it off the heat and beat in a little cold butter.

VARIATIONS

KEY LIME CURD: Substitute the juice and zest of Key limes for the lemon. If you can't get real Key limes, a plausible substitute can be made using equal amounts of juice from lemons and Persian limes.

ORANGE CURD: Substitute orange juice for all but a tablespoon of the lemon juice (for tartness), and use orange instead of lemon zest.

Candied Citrus Threads

This elegant, dainty candied peel is different from the kind that is used for fruitcakes and sweet buns. Thin, crisp, and delicate, these fine threads are a beautiful garnish for pies and cakes, especially those topped with a snowy Seven-Minute Frosting (page 195), meringue, or whipped cream. They are also delicious served as a last sweet bite after dinner—on their own or as a condiment for coffee. I learned to make it from Soul Food diva Joyce White, who likes to add a touch of vanilla.

Makes about 1 cup threads

3 large oranges or 4 large lemons
1¼ cups sugar
1 cup cold water
1 teaspoon Homemade Bourbon Vanilla (page 23) or ½ teaspoon commercial
     vanilla extract, optional

1. Wash the fruit and pat it dry. Remove the zest with a vegetable peeler in ½-inch-wide strips, avoiding any white pith. If there is any pith on the back of the zest, gently scrape it away with a sharp paring knife. Cut the zest into thin straw or matchstick strips, put them in a medium saucepan with enough cold water to cover them by an inch, and bring to a boil. Boil for 5 minutes, drain into a wire sieve, and rinse well with cold water.

2. Return the zest to the pan, cover with cold water, and bring to a boil. Reduce the heat to a slow simmer and cook until the peel is tender, about 20 to 25 minutes. Drain it and return to the pan. Add 1 cup of the sugar, the cold water, and optional vanilla (if you want a pure citrus flavor, you may want to omit it). Bring it to a simmer over low heat and simmer until the zest is translucent and the syrup is somewhat reduced and thickened, 20 to 30 minutes. Drain through a wire sieve, reserving the syrup—it's one of the best things about the whole recipe.

3. Spread the zest on wax or parchment paper and place it in a warm spot to dry for 1 hour. Toss the peel in the remaining ¼ cup sugar to coat, spread it on clean paper, and leave it to dry for several hours. When it is dry, store it in an airtight container. Keeps about 1 week or up to a month, refrigerated.

Brown Velvet Cake (page 186)

clockwise, from top: Spicy Cheese Straws (page 144),
Blue Cheese Straws (page 146), Lemon Pepper Benne Cocktail Bits (page 148)

Aunt Margaret's Fresh Apple Pound Cake (page 168)

Coconut Chess Pie (page 223), with Dark Chocolate Bourbon Sauce (page 251)

Sweet Potato Waffles (page 93)

Vidalia Sweet Onion and Country Ham Tart (page 261)

Top, Coconut Teacakes (page 130) and bottom, Bourbon Pecan Squares (page 118)

Creole Brioche (page 311)

Pies and Pastries

LIKE MOST OTHER AMERICAN baked goods, pie was not invented here. The pastries that we enjoy today were all born in Europe and the Middle East—precisely how, where, and when is a tangle that is beyond the scope of this book. And yet, "as American as apple pie" was not coined without reason; over the last four centuries, we have made this pastry indubitably our own. It is our symbol of ultimate comfort, our measure of national pride, and at least in popular song has even become a symbolic reminder of our complacency. The consternation among lovers of real French cooking over the thick, pielike quiches that have dominated American brunch menus since the seventies has always amused me: well, no, they are not authentic French quiche—they're American pie, and what, after all, is the matter with that?

Pie was and is my favorite baked sweet: as a boy, I'd choose it over cookies, cakes, or brownies any day, though I'd usually scrape the filling off the crust, leaving the pastry behind. Who knows why I didn't like piecrust—that's just how children are. Though I've long since grown out of that aversion, the habit is all too often still with me because, unhappily, so much of the pastry that lines a pie plate today is barely edible. I have a dear friend who makes the most heavenly sweet potato custard imaginable: the stuff is pure gold on your tongue. Yet if I had to rate the overall pie, I'd have to give it a B-, because she pours that ambrosial custard into a cheap store-bought pastry that is about as interesting to eat as stale graham crackers. Of all the things her mother taught her, pastry was not one of them, and she's always been too intimidated by it to try to make her own.

Don't let intimidation overshadow your own stellar pie filling with an indifferent pastry. Whether it's a luncheon quiche or potpie, a fancy dinner finale, or a special breakfast treat, a filling worth the trouble of making is worthy of a decent crust. Making a decent crust (especially if you own a food processor) is, pardon the cliché, easy as pie. Actually, most clichés become one because they are mostly true, and "easy as pie" is no exception. Making good pastry is not hard, and not nearly as complex and prone to failure as cakes, breads, or even cookies. The most complicated one to make is Puff Pastry (page 211), and that's because it's time consuming and a little tedious—not because it is at all difficult. All that a good hand at pastry requires is a little knowledge, a modicum of care, and practice.

EASY AS PIE: PASTRY-MAKING BASICS

With rare exception, keeping cool is the key to good pastry: not just your kitchen, but your temperament and everything else—especially the fat. If the fat warms enough to begin melting and turning oily, it won't suspend in the dough in the small, cohesive bits that flatten as the pastry is rolled out, creating the characteristic flakiness of a well-made piecrust. Instead of crisp, delicately flaky, and dry pastry, the results will be greasy, uneven, and heavy. That's why the chilled fat and liquid are kept ice cold, but it's also why everything else must stay cool, too: overhandling the dough with warm hands can be just as damaging. Old recipes, written when air-conditioning in the average kitchen consisted of opening a window or knocking the chinking out from between the logs in the wall, directed the baker to make up pastry in the cool of the morning, in a cold ceramic bowl, and on a cold work surface like marble, especially in warm weather. Some old cookbooks from the Deep South even went so far as to suggest that the housewife give up pastry making in summer. With air-conditioning practically universal, modern cooks rarely have to deal with extreme temperatures, but the caution in those old recipes remains a word to the wise. With them in mind, here are some key techniques and tips for making pastry like a pro:

* Have the fat and liquid ice cold. Chill the fat both before and after cutting it into smaller bits, and always use thoroughly chilled liquids.
* Use a cool or cold utensil to cut the fat into the flour. There are experienced pastry cooks who can work butter into a pastry with their fingers, but they are the exception that proves the rule: most of our hands and fingers are too warm, and handling the fat too much with them will make the pastry greasy and tough.
* Mix the dough in a cool ceramic or glass bowl and work it up on a cool (stone) or neutral (laminate or wood) surface to minimize warming.
* Chill the dough after mixing it, to give it a chance to cool, relax, and evenly absorb moisture, but always let it warm slightly to make it pliable enough to roll it out.
* Chill yourself out, too: get in a good mood, be patient, and handle the pastry lightly. Like most things in this life, pastry does not respond well to rough or careless handling.

ROLLING AND PLACING PASTRY IN THE PAN

Rolling pastry is not difficult, but it does require a light, quick hand. The only pitfalls at this point are overworking the dough by rolling it too vigorously or stretching it when you are both rolling and placing it in the pan. Stretched dough will try to return to its original shape when heated, causing it to shrink up and produce an uneven—and, often, unusable pie shell.

* Take the dough out of the refrigerator and let it sit at room temperature for 5 to 10 minutes before trying to roll it.

* Lightly flour a cool or neutral work surface (polished stone, wood, or plastic laminate all work fine, but the grout joints in tile surfaces make them impossible to use). Keep it lightly dusted with flour while you are working to prevent the pastry from sticking.

* Lightly flour the top of the pastry, and if the rolling pin begins sticking while you are rolling it out, give it another light dusting, but use no more flour than is absolutely necessary.

* Begin rolling from the center of the pastry outward with light pressure. The intention is to gradually flatten the dough by pressing—not stretching—it flat. Give it a quarter turn and roll again. Continue rolling, regularly giving the pastry quarter turns until it is the thickness needed for the individual recipe.

* There is no single "correct" thickness for a pastry shell: each recipe will indicate the thickness required, but for standard pies, a good rule of thumb is slightly less than ⅛ inch thick; for tarts and a few prebaked shells, it should be ⅛ inch or slightly more.

* To transfer the pastry to a pie plate or tart pan, fold it into quarters. Place the point dead center of the pan and unfold it gently, letting the pastry fall into the edges. Gently press (never stretch) it into the edges of the pie plate or into the edge and flutes of a tart pan.

* To trim the excess dough from a pie shell, gently hold it in place by laying your hand on the dough at the flat rim of the pan. Cut away the excess with a sharp knife held against the side rim of the pie plate. To trim a tart crust, roll it with a rolling pin until the sharp edges of the pan cut the crust away, taking care in the process not to stretch the dough. Don't hold a pie plate in the air and cut away the excess as you've seen models doing in those old nostalgic baking ads: that's a sure way to stretch the dough at the edge.

* When you trim the edges, save any scraps; you may need them for patches or for decorating the edges or top crust.

Prebaking a Pastry Blind (Without Filling)

Many recipes call for a pastry that is partially or even completely baked before filling it, which is why it is called baking the pastry "blind." Even pastries that will be filled and baked often benefit from prebaking to help ensure a light, delicate crust that doesn't get soggy.

FOR EACH CRUST:

1½ to 2 cups raw dried beans, rice, or metal pie weights

1 sheet aluminum foil large enough to cover the pastry plus 2-inch-wide strips foil
    for covering the edges (if fully baking the pastry)

1. Prepare Basic Pastry (page 210) or Puff Pastry (page 211) as directed in either recipe. Position a rack in the center of the oven (you may use a baking stone, if you like) and preheat it to 375°F.

2. Line the pie plate with the pastry and crimp the edges. Prick the bottom in several places with a fork. Butter a piece of foil and put over the pastry, buttered side down. Gently press it into the corners, being careful not to mash the edges of the pastry or tear it. Pour in the raw dried beans and gently shake it to level them. Bake on the center rack or stone for about 20 minutes. The exposed edges should be barely beginning to color.

3. Remove the pastry from the oven, carefully lift out the foil and beans, and return it to the oven. For a partially baked pastry, bake until it is beginning to color and the bottom looks dry, about 10 minutes longer. If the pastry bubbles up (as it will sometimes do), gently prick the bubbles with a fork. Cool it on a rack before filling it. For a fully baked shell, cover the edges with strips of foil to prevent overbrowning and bake until uniformly golden brown, about 5 to 10 minutes more. For prebaked individual tartlets, do them in exactly the same way. Put them on a large baking sheet, not touching, and bake exactly as you would a full-sized pie shell. They may take slightly less time, though in some ovens they may actually take a little longer.

Basic Pastry

This is a good all-purpose pie dough—flaky, tender, and buttery but not heavy. Its secret is lard, which helps to make any pastry tender. If you are not able to cook with lard, you may omit it and use vegetable shortening or an extra 2 tablespoons of butter. The food processor makes short work of this, and does a superior job if you don't overprocess it. The blade's speed can cause it to heat up quickly, in turn overheating the fat in the dough, so chill the blade in the freezer for a couple of minutes before using it.

Makes two 9-inch pie shells or one 9-inch pie with top crust

10 ounces (about 2 cups) Southern soft-wheat flour (see page 9) or pastry flour
½ teaspoon salt
4 ounces (8 tablespoons or 1 stick) unsalted butter, cut into ¼-inch chunks
1 ounce (2 tablespoons) lard, cut into small chunks
About ½ cup ice water

1. Put the flour and salt in a processor fitted with a chilled steel blade. Pulse it a few times to sift the flour, then add the butter and lard cut in bits. Pulse the machine until the flour resembles coarse meal—the texture of raw grits or polenta, the largest bits no bigger than small peas. If you are mixing by hand, put the flour and salt in a metal or ceramic bowl and whisk to blend them together. Add the butter and lard and cut them into the flour with a pastry blender, fork, or two knives.

2. Add ¼ cup of water and pulse to mix it in (or mix it in by hand with a fork). Pulse or mix in additional water by the spoonful until the dough just begins clumping together. It should be moist and no longer crumbly but not sticky or wet. Gather it into a ball, lightly dust it with flour, cover it well with plastic wrap, and flatten it into a ½-inch-thick disk. Chill for half an hour before rolling it out.

Puff Pastry

Light, delicate, and airy, this pastry used to be the standard for the best company piecrust. It is not difficult to make, if you keep everything as cold as possible and weigh all the ingredients carefully. The old instructions were to make up the pastry in a cool place, preferably early in the morning—still sound advice, even in our days of artificially cooled houses.

The recipe here is the usual one, for a pound of butter and 20 ounces of flour. If it's more than you need for the recipe you are making, it will keep, well wrapped, in the refrigerator for as long as a week. It also freezes well, and can be stored in the freezer for up to 3 months. If neither option is feasible, you can cut the recipe in half with care.

*Makes 2 pounds of dough, enough for 4 open-faced pies or 2 with top crust
9-inch pies*

1 pound (2 cups, 4 sticks) unsalted butter
20 ounces (about 4 cups) Southern soft-wheat flour (see page 9)
    or pastry flour
1 teaspoon salt
About ¾ cup ice water

1. If the butter is in one big block, cut it into quarters. Cut three of the quarters in half (into ⅛ pound, or 4-tablespoon chunks) and put them back into the refrigerator. Cut the remaining quarter into bits, working quickly, handling it as little as possible. Chill it briefly in the freezer until it is firm again.

2. Set aside ⅔ cup of the flour and whisk the remaining flour and salt together in a large, cool mixing bowl. Add the quarter-pound of butter cut into bits and cut it into the flour, using a pastry blender or two knives. The texture should be like raw grits or polenta.

3. Make a well in the center and add ½ cup of water. Stir it in lightly with a fork and keep adding water by tablespoons until the pastry is smooth and no longer crumbly, but not wet or sticky. Dust your hands and the pastry with some of the reserved flour and

gather it into a ball. Cover it well with plastic wrap and refrigerate it to let it rest for half an hour.

> NOTE: Steps 2 and 3 can be done in the food processor. Follow the method for Basic Pastry (page 210), using the ingredients given above.

4. Take the dough out and roll it out into a rectangle that is about ½ inch thick. Thinly slice one of the ⅛-pound chunks of butter and scatter the slices evenly over two-thirds of the pastry. Gently smooth it with a palette knife or pastry scraper, dust it lightly with a little of the reserved flour, and fold the blank, unbuttered third over the center, then fold the other side over it, like a letter. Dust the top with a little flour and roll it out until it is again ½ inch thick. Slice and spread over two-thirds of it another ⅛-pound chunk of the butter; flour and triple-fold it again, and roll it out ½ inch thick. Repeat until all the butter and flour are used.

5. Roll the pastry out ½ inch thick, fold it, and roll it out one last time. Fold the pastry, wrap it up, and put it in the refrigerator to rest for at least an hour before using it.

> NOTE: If at any time the dough starts to get too warm and soft, wrap it up, lay it on a cookie sheet and refrigerate it until it is firm again. This may seem overly cautious, but why go to all this trouble with your pastry and have it end up tough and oily? Ideally, this pastry should stay cold right up to the moment it goes into the oven. Classic French recipes call for the butter to be softened, and it is spread on each layer with a palate knife—a little easier to get even layers of butter but trickier to control temperature-wise. If you opt for that technique, chill the dough after each application of butter and rolling.

A Prebaked Puff-Pastry Top Crust

Sometimes all a pie filling needs is a showy top crust. When that is what is called for, there is nothing more showy and impressive than a tall, flaky puff pastry topping. Here is the basic method for prebaking that most elegant of lids.

Makes large or single-serving individual pies in any amount

1 recipe Puff Pastry (page 211) or 1 pound commercial puff pastry, or as much as is needed for the individual recipe
1 large egg white, beaten with 1 tablespoon water

1. Position a rack in the center of the oven (if you have a baking stone, put it on the rack—it makes a real difference with pastry), and preheat the oven to 400°F. Roll out the pastry to slightly under ¼ inch thick and cut it into the shape and size required by the recipe.

2. Lightly butter or line a baking sheet with cooking parchment and lay the pastry on it. If you like, cut the leftover scraps into decorative shapes, brush their bottoms with water, and arrange them on the top of the pastry. Brush the pastry with the egg white and water mixture and prick it through in several places with a fork. Bake until the pastry is puffed and golden, about 20 minutes for pies that will undergo further baking, 30 minutes for fillings that are fully cooked. Cool it on a rack before placing it on top of the pie unless the pie is to be served hot, in which case transfer the hot pastry to the pie and serve at once.

Prebaked Puff Pastry Shells

For fully cooked or cold fillings such as Lettice Bryan's Fresh Strawberry Tarts (page 264), these showy cases are easy to make, once you've mastered the Puff Pastry itself, and they make a big splash. Their big advantage is that, unlike baking regular pastry blind, they don't have to be weighted in the initial baking, since the whole point of them is to have a shell that is spectacularly puffed and delicate.

Makes 8 shells

1 recipe Puff Pastry (page 211) or 1 pound commercial puff pastry
1 large egg white, beaten with 1 tablespoon water

1. Position a rack in the upper third of the oven and preheat the oven to 400°F. Roll out the pastry to about a ¼-inch thickness. Cut it into sixteen circles about 3 inches in diameter (you may use either a fluted cutter or a regular round one). With a 2½-inch cutter of the same shape, cut out the center of eight of the rounds, setting aside the center bits for another use.

2. Brush the backs of the rings with water and place them over the remaining rounds, aligning any pattern in the cut edges. Brush the edges of the rings with the diluted egg white. Lightly butter a baking sheet or line it with parchment, lay the pastry shells on it, and bake them until they are puffed, a rich golden brown, and dry at the center, about 25 minutes.

Raised Pastry for Cobblers and Potpies

The leavening in this pastry produces a light, soft dough that is traditionally used for cobblers and potpies (pages 269–283). It also makes nice flat dumplings (called "slipperies" in many parts of the South) when rolled thin, cut into strips, and dropped into simmering, well-seasoned broth. Lard is the preferable fat in this pastry, as it contributes both lightness and tenderness, but butter will also work fine, and vegetable shortening will do if you prefer not to use lard. Though this pastry is easier to manage when made up by hand, with care it can be made with a food processor. The leavening makes for a light, airy, and delicate crust, but it also makes the pastry extremely brittle and difficult to work with. Keep it well dusted with flour when rolling it out and handle it carefully.

Makes enough pastry for one 9-inch deep-dish pie

10 ounces (about 2 cups) unbleached all-purpose, Southern soft-wheat flour
    (page 9), or pastry flour
½ teaspoon salt
1 teaspoon baking powder
½ teaspoon baking soda
6 ounces (¾ cup) chilled lard or butter, cut into bits
⅓ to ½ cup cold whole-milk buttermilk or plain whole-milk yogurt, thinned with
    milk to buttermilk consistency

1. Whisk together the flour, salt, baking powder, and soda in a metal or ceramic bowl. Add the fat to it, handling it as little as possible so it doesn't get oily. Work the fat into the flour, using a pastry blender or two knives until the mixture is the texture of coarse meal (raw grits or polenta), with lumps no bigger than small peas. If you are using the food processor, put the dry ingredients in the bowl fitted with the steel blade and pulse several times to mix. Add the fat and pulse until it resembles coarse meal with larger lumps no bigger than small peas.

2. Add ⅓ cup of the buttermilk, and lightly stir (or, with the food processor, pulse)

until the dough clumps together and is soft and smooth, but not sticky; add more by the spoonful as needed. (If you are doing it in the food processor, be careful not to over-process the dough as you add more buttermilk, but merely pulse until it just gathers into a ball.) This pastry will be softer—more like biscuit dough than pie pastry. Lightly dust the dough with flour and gather it into a ball. This pastry should be rolled and used right away.

THE CHESS PIE FAMILY

Chess pie, a venerable classic of the Southern baker's repertory, is a lingering legacy of a form of pastry that the English settlers brought into America during the early days of the seventeenth-century colonization. Its enigmatic name, also a part of that heritage, has been the subject of legends and tall tales that are as numerous and popular as they are false. Some of them—like the notion that it is derived from a modest baker's protest that, aw shucks, "it's jes' pie,"—are jes' plain silly. The confusion that has led to the popular legends and tales of the tall-tale-tellers can be laid at the door of the uneven and often uncodified spelling of Elizabethan and Jacobean English. As unromantic as the truth may be, "chess" is nothing more than a case of archaic spelling: a variant of cheese—which in those days often was used to mean "curd," even when it was not made from curdled milk or cream. Those early curds were the precursors not only of modern chess pie, but of all the butter and egg custards that survive on the modern Southern dessert board. The chess family has many branches, from the standard and now classic variations that carry the name, to rich, elegant relatives like Lemon Curd (page 201), to true cheesecakes (pages 245–250), and, of course, those transparent custards that are the foundation for those most celebrated of Southern pastries in the pecan pie branch of the family (page 231–234).

Lemon Buttermilk Chess Pie

Buttermilk pie is an old standby in Southern baking that had until recent years been neglected as old-fashioned and somewhat anachronistic, but it's happily making a comeback, both with home bakers and professional pastry chefs. Here, its tang is both intensified and gently mellowed with lemon in a handsome balance of sour and sweet that makes an ideal foil for just about any fresh seasonal fruit or fruit sauce.

Makes one 9-inch pie, serving 6 to 8

1 partially baked 9-inch pie shell (page 209) made with ½ recipe Basic Pastry (page 210)

1 large lemon

2 ounces (4 tablespoons) unsalted butter, softened

1½ cups sugar

4 large eggs

1 tablespoon unbleached all-purpose flour

2 tablespoons fine white stone-ground cornmeal

Salt

¾ cup whole-milk buttermilk or plain whole-milk yogurt thinned with milk to buttermilk consistency

Fresh Raspberry Bourbon Sauce (recipe follows), or lightly sweetened fresh seasonal fruit such as blueberries, blackberries, strawberries, or sliced peaches, nectarines, or plums

1. After the pie shell is partially baked, adjust the oven temperature to 350°F. and set the pastry aside to cool completely.

2. Grate the zest from the lemon, cut it in half, and juice it through a strainer. In a large mixing bowl, cream the butter, and gradually add the sugar, creaming until light and fluffy. Beat in the eggs one at a time and then the flour, meal, and a small pinch of salt. Finally, stir in the buttermilk, lemon juice, and zest.

3. Pour the custard into the prepared crust and bake it in the center of the oven for 10 minutes, then reduce the heat to 325°F. Bake until the pie is set, about 45 to 55 minutes. Cool it on a wire rack and serve at room temperature or slightly chilled, plain or with Fresh Raspberry Bourbon Sauce or seasonal fruit.

Fresh Raspberry Bourbon Sauce

This same recipe can be used to make a different sauce with blackberries, blueberries, pitted and halved cherries, or sliced peaches or mangoes. Refer to the Notes at the end of the recipe for each fruit.

Serves 4

½ pound fresh raspberries
2 tablespoons unsalted butter
3 to 4 tablespoons sugar, to taste
¼ cup warm bourbon

1. Gently rinse the berries under cold running water and drain well in a colander.
2. Melt the butter in a large sauté pan over medium-high heat. Add the berries and sprinkle them with sugar. Cook, shaking the pan constantly, until they are beginning to soften and break up, about a minute.
3. Add the bourbon, and—leaning well away from the pan—ignite it. Shake and stir the berries (with a long-handled utensil) until the flame dies out. Continue sautéing until the berries break down completely.
4. Strain the sauce to remove the seeds through a fine wire mesh sieve set over a warm serving bowl, pressing on the berries to extract as much of the juice and solids as possible. Stir the sauce well and serve warm or at room temperature.

NOTES ON USING OTHER FRUITS

BLACKBERRIES AND BLUEBERRIES: Allow ½ pound of washed and stemmed berries. After igniting the bourbon in step 3, sauté until the berries are tender but not breaking down completely, allowing them to stay whole, and omit the straining in step 4.

CHERRIES: Allow 10 ounces ripe cherries, halved and pitted. After igniting the bourbon, cook only until the fruit is tender in step 3 (it will not break down) and omit the straining step in step 4.

PEACHES OR MANGOES: Allow 1 heaping cup ripe, peeled, pitted, and diced fresh ripe peaches or mangoes. After igniting the bourbon, cook only until the fruit is tender in step 3 (it will not break down) and omit the straining step in step 4.

Brown Sugar or Butterscotch Chess Pie

Real butterscotch is made of sugar caramelized in butter; brown sugar merely blended with butter is a latter-day substitute that doesn't taste at all the same, but it's a rich, wonderful flavor on its own that has a long tradition in Southern baking, of which this old-fashioned standby is just one example. Delicious in pristine, ungarnished glory, it also makes a great foil for fresh fruit, either in a sauce like the previous recipe, or simply sweetened and spooned over the top. Try it with fresh slices of banana and Bourbon Whipped Cream (page 191) on the side. For a mellow lemon variation, substitute the grated zest and half the juice of a lemon for the bourbon.

Makes one 9-inch pie, serving 6 to 8

1 partially baked 9-inch pie shell (page 209) made with ½ recipe Basic Pastry (page 210)

4 ounces (½ cup or 1 stick) unsalted butter, softened

1½ cups firmly packed light brown sugar

4 large eggs

1 tablespoon unbleached all-purpose flour

2 tablespoons fine white stone-ground cornmeal

Salt

1 tablespoon bourbon

1. After the pie shell is partially baked, adjust the oven temperature to 350°F and set the pastry aside to cool completely.

2. In a large mixing bowl, cream the butter and sugar until light and fluffy. Beat in the eggs one at a time. Beat in the flour, cornmeal, a small pinch of salt, and bourbon. Pour the custard into the prepared crust and bake it in the center of the oven for 10 minutes, then reduce the heat to 325°F. Bake until the pie is set (a straw or toothpick inserted in the center will come out clean), about 35 to 40 minutes longer. Cool the pie on a wire rack. Serve it warm, at room temperature, or cold.

Chocolate Fudge Chess Pie

Nowadays this rich, chocolaty custard has been displaced by silky modern chiffon, cream, black-bottom, and the perennially popular chocolate pecan pie. But it is the granddaddy of all of them, with distinct charms of its own that are well worth rediscovering. If you'd like to try that modern favorite, chocolate pecan pie, just stir 1¼ cups of slivered Toasted Pecans (page 18) into the custard before pouring it into the pastry in step 3.

Makes one 9-inch pie, serving 6 to 8

1 partially baked 9-inch pie shell (page 209) made with ½ recipe Basic Pastry
    (page 210)
3 ounces bittersweet chocolate
4 ounces (½ cup or 1 stick) unsalted butter, softened
1 cup granulated sugar
½ cup firmly packed light brown sugar
2 tablespoons unbleached all-purpose flour
Salt
4 large eggs, lightly beaten
2 teaspoons Homemade Bourbon Vanilla (page 23)
    or 1 teaspoon vanilla extract
Bourbon Whipped Cream (page 191)

1. After the pie shell is partially baked, adjust the oven temperature to 350°F. and set the pastry aside to cool completely.

2. Prepare the bottom pot of a double boiler with 1 inch of water and bring it to a simmer over medium heat. Put the chocolate and butter in the top half and place it over the simmering water. Heat, stirring often, until the chocolate is melted and remove it from the heat. (This step can be done in the microwave at medium power until just melted.)

3. In a large mixing bowl, toss together the sugar, flour, and a small pinch of salt. Stir

in the eggs, and mix until smooth, then stir in the chocolate-butter and vanilla. Pour it into the prepared pastry and bake in the center of the oven for 10 minutes, then reduce the heat to 325°F and bake until set (a straw or toothpick inserted in the center will come out clean), about 35 to 40 minutes longer. Cool on a wire rack and serve at room temperature or cold, with a dollop of Bourbon Whipped Cream on each serving.

Coconut Chess Pie

Rich, chewy, and dense with coconut, there is nothing timid about this fine, satisfying pie. It's a real coconut lovers' confection, and as best I've been able to trace, the forerunner of the more delicate coconut custard and cream pies that have come into the American repertory in the last hundred or so years. Early versions were sometimes made only with the whites of the egg, but those had pretty much vanished by the middle of the nineteenth century. Though unorthodox by traditional standards, chocolate and coconut are just made for one another, and this pie really shines when it is served on a thin pool of Dark Chocolate Bourbon Sauce or is simply drizzled with melted bittersweet chocolate.

Makes one 9-inch pie, serving 6 to 8

1 partially baked 9-inch pie shell (page 209) made with ½ recipe Basic Pastry (page 210)

4 ounces (½ cup or 1 stick) unsalted butter

1 cup sugar

4 large eggs

¼ cup whole-milk buttermilk or plain whole-milk yogurt thinned with milk to buttermilk consistency

1 teaspoon Homemade Bourbon Vanilla (page 23) or ½ teaspoon vanilla extract

1 tablespoon light rum

Salt

1 cup freshly grated fresh coconut or unsweetened frozen coconut

Dark Chocolate Bourbon Sauce (page 251) or 2 ounces bittersweet chocolate

1. After the pie shell is partially baked, adjust the oven temperature to 350°F and set the pastry aside to cool completely.

2. Cream the butter and sugar until light and fluffy. Beat in the eggs, one at a time, and then the buttermilk, vanilla, rum, and a small pinch of salt. Fold in the coconut and pour it into the prepared pastry. Bake in the center of the oven for 10 minutes, then re-

duce the heat to 325°F and bake until just set and a straw inserted into the center comes out clean, about 35 to 40 minutes longer. When it begins to puff it is overdone, so check it after it has been baking for 40 minutes total. Cool it on a wire cooling rack and chill thoroughly before serving on plates lightly filmed with a pool of Dark Chocolate Bourbon Sauce or with bittersweet chocolate, melted in a double boiler over simmering water (or in the microwave at half power) and slightly cooled, drizzled over each serving.

Fresh Summer Fruit Kuchen or Custard Tart

This custard-bound fruit tart is almost as easy as it is versatile: it can change with the seasons, depending on what happens to be available. Like most simple things, it is only as good as its ingredients, so take care to use ripe, flavorful fruit. The custard is bland by itself: the first time I had it, made with tart raspberries, it was wonderful. But if the fruit is less assertive, the custard will need the boost of a little spice and acidity to bring out its flavor.

When you remove the rim of the tart pan and slide the tart off the pan bottom, follow the directions in step 4 with particular care: the shortbread pastry is very delicate and inclined to crumble.

Serves 8

FOR THE CRUST:

6 ounces (about 1¼ cups) unbleached all-purpose flour

1 tablespoon sugar

⅛ teaspoon salt

5 ounces (10 tablespoons) unsalted butter, softened

1½ tablespoons cider vinegar

FOR THE CUSTARD:

4 large eggs

1 cup light cream

1 cup sugar

1 teaspoon ground cinnamon (omit if using raspberries)

Salt

1 cup halved and pitted cherries or peeled, pitted, and diced peaches or mangoes,
   or stemmed, washed, and drained blackberries, blueberries, or raspberries

1 tablespoon bourbon (if using cherries or peaches or mangoes)
   or lemon juice

2 tablespoons unbleached all-purpose flour

1. Position a rack in the center of the oven and preheat the oven to 400°F. Whisk together the flour, sugar, and salt in a mixing bowl. Work in the butter with your fingers until the mixture resembles cookie dough. Work in the vinegar and press the dough evenly over the bottom and up the sides of a 10-inch round tart pan with a removable bottom. Bake until it begins to color, about 10 minutes. Remove it and set it aside on a wire rack to cool. Reduce the oven temperature to 375°F.

2. Prepare the bottom of a double boiler with 1 inch of water and bring it to a simmer over medium heat. Break the eggs into the top pot and beat until smooth. Whisk in the cream, sugar, cinnamon, and a small pinch of salt. Place it over the bottom half with the simmering water and cook, stirring constantly, until the custard is thick enough to coat the back of the spoon. Remove from the heat and stir until cooled slightly.

3. Toss the fruit with bourbon or lemon juice, if using, and then the flour and spread it evenly over the crust. Pour the custard evenly over the fruit and bake until the custard is set, about 40 minutes. Let cool for 15 minutes or so in the pan.

4. To remove the tart from the pan, place the pan on top of a large can or canister, making sure the pan is stable, and remove the rim. Move the bottom to a flat, stable surface and slip a thin, flexible metal spatula carefully under the crust and slide it around all sides to loosen it. This pastry is rather crumbly: you can just leave it on the pan bottom or very gently slide it onto a flat cake plate or platter. Serve warm or at room temperature.

Gingered Apple Custard Tart

Fruit custards are yet another old-fashioned variation on chess pie that go back to the early baking imported by English and French colonials. It shares much with clafoutis, the cakelike custard of France that became a staple along the Carolina and Georgia Lowcountry after French Huguenot planters, fleeing the slave revolts of Haiti, settled here in the late eighteenth century. Feel free to experiment with other fruit in this pie, especially pears, slightly under-ripe peaches, and plums.

Makes one 10-inch tart

1 recipe Basic Pastry (page 210)

4 small, tart apples such as Arkansas Black, Winesap, or Granny Smith

1 lemon, zest grated and reserved, halved

¼ cup firmly packed light brown sugar

3 tablespoons unbleached all-purpose flour

½ cup granulated sugar

¼ cup finely chopped crystallized ginger

1 large egg

Salt

½ cup heavy cream

1 tablespoon Homemade Bourbon Vanilla (page 23) or 1 teaspoon vanilla extract
mixed with 2 teaspoons bourbon

About 1 teaspoon ground cinnamon

1. Position a rack in the center of the oven and preheat the oven to 375°F. Roll out the pastry to a little more than ⅛ inch thick and line a 10-inch removable rim tart pan with it, pressing it into the fluted edges without stretching it. Cut off the excess by rolling the rolling pin over the edges, and prick well with a fork. Weight and partially bake it as directed on page 209.

2. Peel, core, and cut the apples into ½-inch-thick wedges (eighths is about right). Toss

them with the lemon zest, juice of half the lemon, brown sugar, and 1 tablespoon of the flour. Sprinkle the crust with a tablespoon of granulated sugar and arrange the apples on it in one layer of concentric circles. Scatter the ginger over them.

3. Lightly beat the egg and gradually beat in the remaining sugar and flour, a small pinch of salt, and cream. Stir in the vanilla and pour the custard evenly over the fruit. Liberally dust the top with ground cinnamon. Bake at 375°F for 10 minutes, reduce the temperature to 325°F, and bake until the fruit is tender and the custard is set and lightly browned, about 35 to 40 minutes longer. Let cool on a wire rack, and remove the side ring of the pan by placing the pan over a sturdy, flat round object (a 2-pound tomato can is perfect). Carefully slide the ring down off the sides, then carefully slide the tart onto a flat serving platter or a cutting board. Serve warm or at room temperature.

VARIATION

GINGERED PEAR CUSTARD TART: Use about 4 medium pears. If the fruit is especially juicy, add another tablespoon of flour when you are tossing the fruit with the brown sugar, lemon zest, and lemon juice.

Damson Custard Pie

While my father was pastor of Grassy Pond Baptist Church in Gaffney, South Carolina, we enjoyed the privilege of a previous pastor's passion for gardening. There was practically a grove of pecan trees, a sour cherry tree that was great for climbing (what other jungle gym has a built-in snack for the grabbing?) and, best of all, a damson plum tree, which every year produced plenty of lovely blue-black fruit for tart jam and for baking fresh in pies and cobblers. While we were there, this pie, richly flavored with damson jam, became one of my mother's specialties and my very favorite dessert. Though most of the time I have to make it with store-bought preserves, occasionally Cousin Dorothy shares her damson plum crop with my mother—and I get lucky. If you aren't so lucky, and cannot find commercial damson plum preserves, good-quality wild blueberry preserves make a fine substitute.

Makes one 9-inch pie

1 partially baked 9-inch pie shell (page 209) made with ½ recipe Basic Pastry
    (page 210)
4 large eggs
1 cup sugar
4 ounces (½ cup or 1 stick) unsalted butter, melted
Salt
1 teaspoon Homemade Bourbon Vanilla (page 23)
    or ½ teaspoon commercial extract
1 cup damson plum preserves, at room temperature
1 recipe Bourbon Whipped Cream (page 191), optional, for serving

1. After the pie shell is partially baked, adjust the oven temperature to 350°F and set the pastry aside to cool completely.

2. Break the eggs into a large mixing bowl and lightly beat them. Beat in the sugar and then the butter until light and smooth. Stir in a small pinch of salt and vanilla. Stir a little

of the custard into the preserves to soften them and then mix them into the remaining custard. Pour it into the prepared crust. Bake in the center of the oven until puffed, nicely browned, and set (a toothpick inserted into the center should come out clean), about 35 to 40 minutes. Cool it on a rack; it will deflate as it cools. Serve at room temperature or cold, plain or with Bourbon Whipped Cream.

Bourbon Pecan Pie

The family of pecan and other nut pies that are common throughout the South are direct descendants of almond and peanut chess pies—in which chopped or ground nuts are bound in a butter and egg custard, recipes for which go back at least into the early nineteenth century. The earliest recipes for pecan pie were made with sugar, butter, and eggs, but most modern pies contain large doses of corn syrup, which can be good, but for my taste are rather heavy and tooth-achingly sweet. This one hearkens back to those older pies, adding a suave splash of bourbon for mellowness.

Makes one 9-inch pie, serving 6 to 8

½ recipe Basic Pastry (page 210)
2 ounces (4 tablespoons or ½ stick) unsalted butter
3 large eggs
1½ cups firmly packed light brown sugar
Salt
1 tablespoon Homemade Bourbon Vanilla (page 23), or 1 teaspoon vanilla extract
2 tablespoons bourbon, plus 2 teaspoons if using vanilla extract
1¼ cups Toasted Pecans (page 18)

1. Position a rack in the center of the oven and preheat the oven to 375°F. Line a 9-inch pie plate with pastry, prick the bottom well with a fork, and decorate the edges with your fingers or the tines of the fork or cut bits of pastry. Weight and partially bake it as directed on page 209. Let it cool before filling it.

2. Put the butter in a saucepan and melt it over low heat. Turn off the heat and let it cool. Meanwhile, break the eggs into a mixing bowl and beat them until smooth. Stir in the sugar until dissolved. Stir in the butter, a small pinch of salt, vanilla, and bourbon, stirring (not beating) until smooth. Fold in the pecans and then pour it into the prepared pastry.

3. Bake for 10 minutes. Reduce the heat to 325°F, and bake until the filling is set (a sharp knife blade, toothpick, or straw should come out clean when inserted into the center). Cool on a wire rack and serve it cold or at room temperature.

Lemon Pecan Pie

Here the old chess pie tradition meets its modern pecan pie descendant head-on in a cross-generational collision that, in this case, can only be an especially happy one. The clean, tartness of lemon is a perfect balance for the buttery caramel richness of the butter, brown sugar, and pecan custard.

Makes one 9-inch pie, serving 8

½ recipe Basic Pastry (page 210)
4 large eggs
¾ cup granulated sugar
½ cup firmly packed brown sugar
Salt
Grated zest of 1 lemon
¼ cup freshly squeezed lemon juice (about 2 lemons)
1 tablespoon unbleached all-purpose flour
2 ounces (¼ cup or ½ stick) unsalted butter, melted and cooled
1½ cups roughly chopped Toasted Pecans (page 18)

1. Position a rack in the center of the oven and preheat the oven to 375°F. Line a 9-inch pie plate with pastry, prick the bottom well with a fork, and decorate the edges with your fingers or the tines of the fork or cut bits of pastry. Weight and partially bake it as directed on page 209. Let it cool before filling it.

2. Break the eggs into a mixing bowl and beat until the yolk and white are lightly mixed. Add both sugars and a small pinch salt and beat until the sugar and eggs are creamy. One at a time stir in the lemon zest and juice, flour, and then the melted butter, mixing until the custard is smooth. Stir in the pecans and pour the mixture into the pie shell.

3. Bake for 10 minutes. Reduce the heat to 325°F, and bake until the filling is set in the center (a sharp knife blade, toothpick, or straw should come out clean when inserted into the center). Cool on a wire rack and serve it cold or at room temperature.

Kentucky Chocolate Chip Bourbon Pie

An enormously popular dessert for Kentucky Derby fans on race day, both on-site in countless tailgate picnics and at thousands of derby parties throughout the country, is Derby Pie®, a specialty of Kern's Kitchen, the bakery in Louisville that has been making it since the 1960s. The recipe is a closely guarded secret and the name itself is trademarked, but that has not stopped variations of this unique chocolate chip and walnut confection from entering the culinary popular culture. Recipes claiming to be the authentic pie abound; says Louisville food journalist Sarah Fritschner, "just type 'derby pie' into your Internet search engine and see what happens." She also says none of these alleged recipes are close to authentic and some of them are alarmingly awful. The real thing is not to be missed, but to taste it, you'll have to go to Kern's Kitchen in Louisville or contact one of the outlets that distribute the pie nationwide (go to www.derbypie.com and click on "delivered to your door"). Off-line, one source is A Taste of Kentucky at (800) 444-0552.

While the imitations can't be called by the name and may not align with the Kern's secret recipe, they've earned a place in the home baker's repertory, and some of them are quite good in their own right. This version, similar to the one Sarah shared with me, includes bourbon and pecans, and a light finish of mint-scented whipped cream.

Makes one 9-inch pie

1 cup pecans, roughly chopped
½ recipe Basic Pastry (page 210)
½ cup firmly packed light brown sugar
½ cup granulated sugar
½ cup unbleached all-purpose flour
Salt
2 large eggs, lightly beaten
4 ounces (½ cup) unsalted butter, melted
3 tablespoons bourbon
1 teaspoon Homemade Bourbon Vanilla (page 23)
    or ½ teaspoon commercial vanilla extract

6 ounces (1 generous cup) semisweet chocolate chips
Mint Whipped Cream (page 192)

1. Position a rack in the center of the oven and preheat the oven to 325°F. Spread the pecans on a cookie sheet and toast them for about 10 minutes, until lightly colored. Remove them from the oven and let them cool. Increase the oven temperature to 350°F. Line a 9-inch pie plate with the pastry, flute or decorate the edges, prick the bottom well, and set it aside.

2. Whisk together both sugars, the flour, and a small pinch of salt. Stir in the eggs and then the butter, bourbon, and vanilla, mixing until smooth. Fold in the pecans and chocolate chips and pour them into the prepared pastry. Bake the pie until golden brown and set (a toothpick inserted in the center should come out clean), about 50 minutes. Serve warm with Mint Whipped Cream.

Golden Bourbon Pecan Tassies

These delicate, golden brown morsels are a standard for receptions all over the South. Though dainty and bite-sized, there's nothing timid about their flavor. Almost everyone has a special person and memory connected with pecan tassies—their wedding day, graduation, or just their mama's or grandmother's kitchen table on a cool autumn day after school. For me, they inevitably call to mind Southern cooking maven Nathalie Dupree, who wrote so warmly of them in her classic book Nathalie Dupree's Southern Memories, *and with whom I have been privileged to enjoy an enduring friendship. It is she who taught me to make them, and this recipe owes much to her.*

Makes 24 tassies

1 recipe Cream Cheese Pastry for Tassies and Tartlets
    (page 237), chilled
1 large egg
¾ cup light brown sugar
1 tablespoon bourbon
Salt
2 tablespoons unsalted butter, melted and cooled
½ cup roughly chopped Toasted Pecans (page 18)

1. Divide the pastry into twenty-four equal balls (about an inch in diameter). If the pastry begins to soften too much, lay the balls on a sheet of wax paper on a baking sheet and chill for a few minutes. Put a ball of pastry into each well of an ungreased mini (1¾-inch diameter) muffin tin. With flour-dusted fingers or a tart tamper dipped in flour, press the pastry into the bottom and sides of each well until it is level with the top. Refrigerate the shells while you make the filling.

2. Position a rack in the center of the oven and preheat the oven to 350°F. Lightly beat the egg and then beat in the brown sugar, bourbon, a small pinch of salt, and butter, beating until smooth.

3. Divide the pecans among the shells and spoon about 1½ teaspoons of the filling into each. Bake until golden brown and set, about 25 minutes.

VARIATIONS

CHOCOLATE PECAN TASSIES: Roughly chop ¼ cup of bittersweet chocolate chips until they are about one quarter of their original size, or chop a 1½-ounce-block of bittersweet chocolate to small bits. Toss the chocolate with the pecans, divide the mixture among the tart shells, then fill and bake as directed in step 3.

LEMON PECAN TASSIES: For a miniature variation of the Lemon Pecan Pie on page 232, add the grated zest of a lemon to the custard and substitute 2 tablespoons of its juice for the bourbon.

Cream Cheese Pastry for Tassies and Tartlets

This rich, delicate pastry is the classic one for pecan tassies but it is also good for any tartlet with a rich, very sweet filling. Try it filled with Lemon Curd (page 201).

Makes 24 tassie shells

One 3-ounce package cream cheese, softened
4 ounces (½ cup or 1 stick) unsalted butter, softened
¼ teaspoon salt
1 tablespoon sugar
1 cup unbleached all-purpose flour

1. With a mixer, cream the cheese and butter until light, fluffy, and smooth. Whisk together the salt, sugar, and flour, then work it into the cheese and butter until the pastry is smooth. This can be done in a food processor: process the cheese and butter until fluffy and light, then add the salt, sugar, and flour and pulse until the dough is smooth.

2. Scoop the dough onto a sheet of plastic wrap, form the dough into a ball, fold the wrap over it, and press it into a flat 1-inch-thick disk. Chill until the dough is firm, at least 2 hours. The dough can be made several hours or a day before you plan to use it.

Carolina Peanut Rum Pie

Peanut butter pie has become a popular dessert in many cafés and diners in Georgia and Virginia, where peanuts are a special part of the farming economy, but most of them are cream-style pies, usually served chilled or even frozen. The earliest peanut pies, however, were more like traditional pecan pie, with the nuts set in a transparent chess custard. In fact, one of the oldest recipes I've been able to find, from Sarah Rutledge's The Carolina Housewife *(1847), a fine, buttery custard enriched with nuts pounded to a paste with rum. It was called cheesecake, just as most early chess pies were. This pastry owes much to Miss Rutledge's recipe, but has the lively added richness and crunch of whole peanuts. Hard-core peanut lovers will love it plain, but it really begins to shine when finished with Dark Chocolate Bourbon Sauce, or a drizzle of melted bittersweet chocolate, or Bourbon Whipped Cream and freshly sliced bananas.*

Makes one 9-inch pie, serving 6 to 8

1 partially baked 9-inch pie shell (page 209)
    made from ½ recipe Basic Pastry (page 210)
2 ounces (4 tablespoons or ½ stick) unsalted butter
3 large eggs
½ cup granulated sugar
1 cup firmly packed light brown sugar
½ cup creamy all-natural peanut butter
Salt
1 teaspoon Homemade Bourbon Vanilla (page 23)
    or vanilla extract
¼ cup golden rum
1¼ cups unsalted roasted peanuts
Dark Chocolate Bourbon Sauce (page 251) or Bourbon Whipped Cream
    (page 191) and freshly sliced bananas, or *dulce di leche* ice cream,
    optional

1. After the pie shell is partially baked, adjust the oven temperature to 375°F and set the pastry aside to cool completely.

2. Put the butter in a saucepan and melt it over low heat. Turn off the heat and let it cool. Meanwhile, break the eggs into a mixing bowl and beat them until smooth. Whisk in both sugars and then the peanut butter, whisking until smooth. Stir (don't beat) in the melted butter, a small pinch of salt, vanilla, and rum, stirring until smooth. Fold in the peanuts and pour it into the prepared pastry.

3. Bake in the center of the oven for 10 minutes. Reduce the heat to 325°F, and bake until the filling is set in the center (a sharp knife blade, toothpick, or straw should come out clean when inserted into the center). Cool on a wire rack and serve it cold, at room temperature, or slightly warm, with any of the suggested accompaniments.

Marion's Key Lime Pie

Key lime pie became standard fare all over the Southeast during the twentieth century: almost every seafood restaurant from the Keys to the Outer Banks of North Carolina serves some version of it, usually the one popularized in the second half of the century—made with sweetened condensed milk clotted with highly acidic Key lime juice. That version is good, but frankly rather heavy and cloyingly sweet for my taste. Charleston-based food writer Marion Sullivan makes a subtler and altogether more satisfying one that is closer to the original pie, filled with buttery lime curd.

Makes one 9-inch pie, serving 6

FOR THE CRUST:
¾ cup graham cracker crumbs
¼ cup firmly packed light brown sugar
3 tablespoons unsalted butter, melted

FOR THE FILLING:
4 large eggs
1 cup granulated sugar
6 tablespoons freshly squeezed Key lime juice (not bottled) or 4 tablespoons
    Persian lime juice mixed with 2 tablespoons lemon juice
2 tablespoons finely chopped or grated Key lime or lemon zest
Salt
4 ounces (½ cup or 1 stick) unsalted butter, melted
1 cup lightly sweetened Whipped Cream (page 192)
1 lime, sliced, optional

1. Make the crumb crust by mixing together the crumbs and brown sugar and blending them with the butter until evenly moistened. Press the crust into a 9-inch pie pan and refrigerate for 30 minutes.

2. Position a rack in the center of the oven and preheat the oven to 300°F. Put 1 inch of water in the bottom half of a double boiler and bring it to a simmer over medium heat. Whisk together the eggs, granulated sugar, lime juice, chopped or grated zest, and a small pinch of salt in the top pot of the double boiler. Place it over the simmering water and cook, stirring constantly, until thickened. Slowly whisk in the butter and cook, stirring constantly, until thickened. Remove it from the heat and stir until cooled slightly.

3. Pour it into the prepared crumb crust and bake until it is set, about 20 minutes. Cool to room temperature, then refrigerate until chilled and firm. Just before serving, cover the pie with whipped cream or garnish each slice with a piped rosette of whipped cream and a slice of lime.

MaMa's Sweet Potato Custard Pies

For more than two centuries, sweet potato custard has been a defining standard for Southern baking. Virtually every regional cookbook from Mary Randolph's The Virginia House-Wife *(1824) right through to Bill Neal's modern classic* Biscuits, Spoonbread, and Sweet Potato Pie *has included some version of this dense, rich, and yet subtly mellow pie. For me, it will forever hold a peculiar and special place: my maternal grandmother's sweet potato custards have been a holiday standard in my family for at least four generations. Like sturdy bookends, her pies and coconut cake defined our Christmas dessert board, and while she often made pumpkin pie at Thanksgiving, she would not have let the day pass without at least one sweet potato custard, even when the turkey shared the table with candied yams. No matter the time of year that I taste it, every bite whispers of autumn leaves, frosted windowpanes, and mistletoe all at once.*

For more than a decade and through four cookbooks, I've tried to reproduce that special something that was MaMa's touch, both while she was at my side to coach me and in the years since she left us with only memories to guide. I don't know if I have completely succeeded, but if I had to try to describe her to you in a single taste, it would be this one, so I think it is pretty close.

Makes two 9-inch pies

3 pounds (5 to 6 medium) sweet potatoes
1 recipe Basic Pastry (page 210)
1 ounce (2 tablespoons) unsalted butter
1 cup sugar
4 large eggs, lightly beaten
Salt
1 teaspoon ground cinnamon, optional
½ teaspoon freshly grated nutmeg, optional
1 tablespoon Homemade Bourbon Vanilla (page 23) or 1 teaspoon vanilla extract
About ¼ cup heavy cream or evaporated milk
Bourbon Whipped Cream (page 191)

1. Scrub the potatoes well under cold running water. Put them in a large, heavy-bottomed pot and add enough cold water to cover by 1 inch. Bring to a boil over medium-high heat, reduce the heat to a steady simmer, loosely cover, and cook until the potatoes are tender (a fork or sharp knife should easily pass through). Drain and let cool enough to handle.

2. Meanwhile, position a rack in the center of the oven and preheat the oven to 375°F. Line two 9-inch pie plates with pastry and partially bake them (page 209).

3. While they're still hot, peel the sweet potatoes and puree them through a ricer or food mill into a large mixing bowl. Or, cut them in chunks, put them in the bowl, and mash them well with a fork or potato masher. Add the butter and sugar, mix until absorbed, then stir in the eggs, spices, and vanilla. Beat in enough cream to make the filling smooth and barely pourable—it should still be quite thick and not at all soupy. Pour the custard into the prepared pastry and smooth the top.

4. Bake the pies, without touching, until the filling is set at the center and the pastry is nicely browned, about 40 minutes. Cool on wire racks and serve at room temperature or cold with a healthy dollop of lightly sweetened whipped cream.

VARIATION

COCONUT-PECAN SWEET POTATO PIE: Myrtice Lewis, a retired caterer and great baker, makes a sweet potato soufflé topped with a streusel of butter, brown sugar, pecans, and coconut that will flat make you roll over and play dead, it's so good. Her topping sends MaMa's Sweet Potato Custard Pies right over the top.

Makes two 9-inch pies

1 recipe MaMa's Sweet Potato Custard Pies (page 242), not baked
   (see addition in step 1, below)
Grated zest of 1 orange
1 tablespoon freshly squeezed orange juice
4 ounces (1 stick) unsalted butter
1 cup firmly packed light brown sugar

1 cup roughly chopped pecans

1 cup grated unsweetened coconut

1. Prepare both pies as directed in the recipe (MaMa's Sweet Potato Custard Pies) up through step 3, adding the grated orange zest and juice to the custard with the spices and vanilla.

2. Melt the butter in a 2-quart saucepan over low heat. Turn off the heat and mix in the brown sugar, pecans, and coconut until all the ingredients are moistened with the butter. Spread the topping evenly over the custard filling of both pies. Bake at 375°F until the topping is nicely browned and the filling is set, about 40 minutes.

NOTE: The kind of sweet potato that you want for these pies and for Sweet Potato Cheesecake (page 245) has deep orange, almost carrot-colored, flesh and is sometimes sold in the South as a "yam" even though it is not related to a true yam botanically. They are rarely labeled by variety except in natural food grocers and farmer's markets, but such varieties as Louisiana Yam and Garnet are great for pies and cheesecake.

There are varying schools of thought on precooking sweet potatoes for pies, cakes, and breads. Some traditional cooks (like my grandmother) boil them in water to cover—either unpeeled and whole or peeled and cut into chunks; some wrap them in microwave-proof plastic wrap or wax paper and bake them in the microwave (on high for about 7 minutes, turning them halfway through); others bake them traditionally, wrapped in foil, in a 375°F oven (it will take about 45 minutes to an hour). I prefer the last method because it keeps them from absorbing more moisture and concentrates their flavor, but have followed my grandmother's method for her pie (pages 242–243). For a smooth puree, put the potatoes through a potato ricer or through a food mill. The ricer and food mill will catch the stringy bits that sweet potatoes sometimes have.

Sweet Potato Cheesecake

In the last decade of the twentieth century, pumpkin cheesecake made a big splash on Thanksgiving tables all across America, proving that even places that hold tradition dearer than life and breath itself are not immune to change. It was only a matter of time before some Southern baker substituted sweet potatoes for pumpkin. In this instance, however, the potatoes are no mere substitution: as anyone who has tasted them side by side knows, sweet potatoes are hands down more flavorful than the average American pumpkin pie.

This is so good that it seems a shame to confine it to the Thanksgiving table: autumn, winter, spring or summer, its silky richness is always satisfying.

Makes one 9-inch cake, serving about 12

1½ cups fine gingersnap crumbs (about 10 ounces of cookies)
3 ounces (6 tablespoons) unsalted butter, melted
8 ounces (1 cup) whole-milk ricotta cheese
Two 8-ounce packages cream cheese
1 cup firmly packed light brown sugar
3 tablespoons unbleached all-purpose flour
2 teaspoons ground cinnamon
1 teaspoon freshly grated nutmeg
Grated zest of 1 lemon
4 large eggs, at room temperature
2 cups mashed cooked sweet potatoes (see Note, page 244)

1. Position a rack in the center of the oven and preheat the oven to 300°F. Put the gingersnap crumbs in a mixing bowl and pour the melted butter over them. Stir until the crumbs are evenly moistened. Press the crumbs into the bottom and about a third of the way up the sides of a 9-inch springform pan. Refrigerate until needed.

2. In a food processor fitted with a steel blade, cream the ricotta, cream cheese, and brown sugar until smooth. Add the flour, spices, and lemon zest, and pulse until smooth.

Add in the eggs one at a time, pulsing after each addition until smooth; add the sweet potato puree, pulsing until evenly colored.

3. Pour the batter into the prepared pan. Bake 50 to 55 minutes, or until the center is almost set. Turn off the heat and let the cake cool in the oven for an hour. Remove it from the oven and let cool completely, then cover and chill at least 4 to 6 hours before serving.

Victoria's Cheesecake (Almond Raspberry Cheesecake)

In 1847, Sarah Rutledge anonymously published The Carolina Housewife, *the first printed cookbook to chronicle the unique cookery of the Carolina Lowcountry. Among its many recipes was a luscious almond custard pie with a thin layer of raspberry jam at the bottom called Victoria's Pudding, presumably named for Queen Victoria. Since custards like it were all very similar to—and often even called "cheese cake"—the trip from pie to cheesecake was a short one. Hold on to your willpower.*

Makes one 9-inch cake, serving about 12

1½ cups (10 ounces) fine Southern Shortbread (page 132) crumbs
    or other shortbread cookie crumbs
3 ounces (6 tablespoons) unsalted butter, melted
8 ounces almond paste
Two 8-ounce packages cream cheese
1 cup sugar, plus 2 tablespoons
3 tablespoons unbleached all-purpose flour
4 large eggs
1 tablespoon Amaretto
1 cup raspberry jam

FOR SERVING:
Dark Chocolate Bourbon Sauce (page 251)
2 cups Whipped Cream (page 192)
About ½ cup sliced almonds

1. Position a rack in the center of the oven and preheat the oven to 300°F. Combine the shortbread crumbs and melted butter in a mixing bowl. Stir until the crumbs are evenly moistened. Press the mixture into the bottom of a 9-inch springform pan and about a third of the way up the sides.

2. Break up the almond paste into small, even chunks. In a food processor fitted with the steel blade, put the cream cheese, 1 cup of the sugar, and the almond paste, and process until smooth. Beat in the flour and then the eggs, one at a time, pulsing the machine between each addition. Add the liqueur and pulse to mix it in.

3. Pour the batter into the prepared pan. Tap the pan several times on the counter to get any large air bubbles out of it. Bake until the center is almost set, about 50 to 55 minutes. Turn off the heat and let the cake cool in the oven for an hour.

4. Put the jam and the remaining 2 tablespoons of sugar into a small saucepan and melt it over medium heat. Bring it to a bubbling simmer and simmer 2 minutes, stirring occasionally to keep it smooth. Turn off the heat and strain the glaze through a fine wire mesh sieve. Spoon it over the top of the cake and evenly spread it over the entire top. Let the cake cool completely, cover, and chill for 4 to 8 hours before serving it.

5. To serve, float about 2 tablespoons of the chocolate sauce on the bottom of a dessert plate, tipping the plate to evenly coat it. Place a slice of the cake in the center, and garnish with a dollop of whipped cream, and a few sliced almonds.

Peanut Cheesecake

Dense, rich, and altogether irresistible for peanut lovers, this cheesecake only seems like a new idea. Sarah Rutledge included "groundnut cheesecakes" in The Carolina Housewife *in 1847—rich, buttery custards, thick with "groundnuts" (an old name for peanuts) beaten to a paste and baked in a puff pastry. It was part of the family of "cheese" or curded pastries that would become modern chess and pecan pie. While this one follows the lead of her idea, it departs in that it is a true cheesecake. It's very rich, so serve it in small portions. If your guests want more (which they will, of course), they can always indulge in a second helping.*

Makes one 9-inch cake, serving about 12 to 16

1½ cups fine Southern Shortbread (page 132) crumbs
    or other shortbread cookie crumbs
½ cup ground unsalted roasted peanuts (see Note, page 250)
3 ounces (6 tablespoons) unsalted butter, melted
Two 8-ounce packages cream cheese
1 cup granulated sugar
⅓ cup firmly packed light brown sugar
1½ cups all-natural creamy peanut butter
3 tablespoons unbleached all-purpose flour
4 large eggs
1 tablespoon golden rum

FOR SERVING:
Dark Chocolate Bourbon Sauce (page 251)
2 cups Whipped Cream (see page 192)
Chopped unsalted roasted peanuts

1. Position a rack in the center of the oven and preheat the oven to 300°F. Combine the shortbread crumbs, peanuts, and melted butter in a mixing bowl. Stir until the

crumbs are evenly moistened. Press the crumb mixture into the bottom of a 9-inch springform pan and about a third of the way up the sides.

2. In a food processor fitted with the steel blade, cream the cheese and both sugars together until smooth. Add the peanut butter and flour, and process until evenly colored, then beat in the eggs, one at a time, pulsing the machine between each addition. Finally, add the rum and pulse to mix it in.

3. Pour the batter into the prepared pan. Tap the pan several times on the counter to level the batter and get any large air bubbles out of it. Bake until the cake is almost set in the center, about 50 to 55 minutes. Turn off the heat and let the cake cool in the oven for an hour. Remove it from the oven and let it cool completely. Cover and chill in the refrigerator for 4 to 8 hours before cutting and serving.

4. To serve the cheesecake, float about 2 tablespoons of the chocolate sauce on the bottom of a dessert plate, tipping the plate to evenly coat it. Place a slice of the cake in the center, garnish with a dollop of whipped cream, and sprinkle a few chopped peanuts over all.

NOTE: Peanuts can be ground with a meat grinder, a manual chopper, or the food processor. If you use the latter, however, take care not to overprocess the nuts: they should be the texture of very coarse meal or raw grits.

Dark Chocolate Bourbon Sauce

This is a good, basic bittersweet chocolate sauce that's the perfect finishing accent for either Victoria's Cheesecake (page 247) or Peanut Cheesecake (page 249), and a pool of it on the plate underneath a slice of pound cake or custard pie lifts it from ordinary to special. It's also wonderful drizzled over ice cream or orange sherbet. Tailor it to a particular dessert by changing the flavoring, using any of the suggestions given at the end of the recipe.

Obviously, the better the chocolate, the better this sauce will be, but I first tested it with a national brand of semisweet baking chocolate and it was still pretty terrific.

Makes about 2 cups

⅓ cup sugar

1¼ cups water

8 ounces bittersweet chocolate, roughly chopped,
   or 8 ounces semisweet chocolate morsels

1 teaspoon Homemade Bourbon Vanilla (page 23)
   or 1 teaspoon bourbon and ¼ teaspoon vanilla extract

1. Put the sugar and water in a 2-quart saucepan and stir until the sugar is almost dissolved. Put the pan over medium-low heat and add the chocolate. Heat, stirring, until the chocolate is melted and smooth and almost simmering, about 5 minutes. Still stirring, simmer 2 to 3 minutes, until it is the smooth consistency of thin cream or custard. Don't overcook the chocolate or it will taste scorched and sharp. Remove it from the heat.

2. Stir in the flavoring, and keep stirring until it is cooled slightly. Strain it through a fine mesh strainer into a serving or storage bowl or jar and let it cool to room temperature before serving. It can be made as much as a week ahead; cover and store it in the refrigerator, but let it warm almost to room temperature before serving it. It will thicken considerably as it cools, so if you plan to float the sauce on the plate or pass it

separately for pouring, you'll want to thin it with room temperature water before serving it.

VARIATIONS: Try adding a pinch of cinnamon with the vanilla, or substitute raspberry or orange liqueur for the vanilla and add a little grated orange zest.

Bourbon Cherry Pie

Bourbon is a natural and incomparable paring for cherries: it is far superior to brandy or cognac in cherries jubilee, and lifts the simple flavors of a pie from good to sublime. It mellows out tart sour cherries and gives a kick to delicately sweet ones. Of course, cherries are the main event here, and bourbon cannot completely cover the taste of indifferent fruit, so use only the ripest and best that you can get. If they are very sweet and completely lacking tartness, the bourbon may need the help of a squeeze of lemon juice to give the pie the right balance.

Makes one 9-inch pie, serving 6

1 recipe Basic Pastry (page 210)
1 cup, plus 1 tablespoon sugar
4 cups pitted and halved dark cherries (about 2 pounds whole cherries)
Salt
2 tablespoons bourbon
3 tablespoons unsalted butter, cut into bits
3 tablespoons unbleached all-purpose flour

1. Position a rack in the center of the oven and preheat the oven to 450°F. Divide the pastry in half and roll out one half ⅛ inch thick. Line a 9-inch pie plate with it and prick the bottom well with a fork, but don't trim off the excess dough. Sprinkle the bottom with 1 tablespoon of the sugar. Roll out the remaining pastry and cut it with a sharp knife or fluted pastry wheel into ½-inch-wide strips.

2. Toss together the cherries, remaining sugar, a tiny pinch of salt, bourbon, and butter in a mixing bowl. Sprinkle in the flour and toss to mix. Pour the fruit into the prepared pastry and level it with a spatula.

3. Weave the lattice top as follows: lay strips of pastry ½ inch apart on top of the pie. Fold back every other strip and lay a strip crosswise along one edge over the strips that remain. Unfold the folded strips and fold back the ones that had not been folded before to the point where the crosswise strip covers them. Lay another strip of pastry ½ inch from

the other, unfold the folded strips, and repeat until the surface is covered with lattice. Trim off the excess at the edges of the strips, brush their undersides with water, and lightly press them into the bottom pastry to make them stick. Brush the edges of the pastry with a little water and fold the excess bottom pastry over the edges of the lattice. Press into place and flute the edges.

4. Put the pie in a large, rimmed cookie sheet and bake in the center of the oven for 15 minutes. Reduce the heat to 350F and bake until the top is golden brown and the filling is bubbly at the center and thickened, about 30 minutes more.

Gingered Peach Tart

My late aunt Alice Vermillion was a natural-born cook and baker with a keen instinct for flavor that rarely failed her. Unhappily, like so many cooks who worked by instinct rather than recipes, most of her knowledge went to her grave with her. Her sister (my mother) and I have spent hours talking about remembered meals and flavors, wistfully prodding one another's memories in the hope of recapturing some of those flavors. One thing that especially stood out in my memory was a fresh peach tart, the fruit laid in neat circles over a flaky, delicate shortbread crust, that once welcomed me home from a long and tiring business trip. Circumstances may have figured into it, but that was simply the best peach pie I have ever tasted, before or since. Later, she could never remember how she had made it, and I've been left with only my memory to guide me. Nonetheless, those memories are the inspiration for this luscious, gingery confection.

Serves 6

10 ounces (about 2 cups) Southern soft-wheat flour (see page 9)
    or unbleached all-purpose flour, plus 2 tablespoons
¼ cup white corn flour (superfine cornmeal, available at Latino markets
    and the ethnic food section of some supermarkets)
½ cup, plus about 2 tablespoons granulated sugar
Salt
1 teaspoon ground ginger
8 ounces (1 cup or 2 sticks) unsalted butter, cut into small bits
1 lemon
6 to 8 ripe peaches, preferably freestone
1 tablespoon freshly grated ginger
2 tablespoons bourbon
About 4 tablespoons turbinado ("raw") sugar
Whole nutmeg in a grater
Vanilla or *dulce de leche* ice cream, optional, for serving

1. Position a rack in the center of the oven and preheat the oven to 375°F. Whisk or sift together the flour (reserving 2 tablespoons), the corn flour, ½ cup of the sugar, a pinch of salt, and ground ginger. Add the butter and work it into the flour until it forms a smooth dough. If it is a little sticky, work in a little more flour. You may do the first part of this step in a food processor fitted with the steel blade. Put in the flours, sugar, salt, and ground ginger and pulse several times to sift. Add the butter and process until the mixture resembles coarse meal. Turn it out into a mixing bowl and finish blending the dough by hand, working in more flour as needed.

2. Turn the dough into a 12-inch round tart pan. Press it into a uniform layer over the entire surface and up the sides of the pan, pressing it into each flute. Prick it well with a fork and bake for 10 minutes, then remove it and let it cool while you prepare the peaches.

3. Bring a large pot half filled with water to a boil. Meanwhile, grate the zest from the lemon into a large glass or nonreactive metal bowl. Cut the lemon in half and juice it through a strainer into the bowl. When the water is boiling, slip the peaches into it and let them simmer for 1 minute. Immediately lift them out with a slotted spoon and rinse them under cold water. Drain and slip off the peel. Cut them in half, remove the pits, and slice them in thick wedges. As you cut them, put them in the bowl with the lemon juice, tossing to prevent discoloring.

4. Add the grated ginger and bourbon and toss. Sift the remaining 2 tablespoons of flour over the fruit and toss until smooth. Sprinkle the crust lightly with the remaining granulated sugar. Lift the peaches out of the juice, allowing the excess to flow back into the bowl, and arrange them on top of the crust, slightly overlapping in a single layer of concentric circles. Sprinkle well with the turbinado ("raw") sugar and generously grate nutmeg over the top.

5. Pour the remaining juices evenly over the tart and bake until the peaches are tender and the crust is golden brown, about 40 minutes. Serve warm or at room temperature with a scoop of ice cream on the side.

Green Tomato Pie

Thanks to Fanny Flagg and a movie that carries their name, fried green tomatoes hold a place of real honor on the Southern table. They're one Southern dish that almost everyone knows about. But green tomatoes see a lot more than a frying pan in Southern kitchens: the little ones are pickled whole, and the big ones are chopped into relish, stirred into the soup kettle, and even braised and broiled as a green vegetable. This very old-fashioned and unusual pie is less well known—in fact, it's rarely seen on modern tables—but that doesn't make it any less deserving of equal attention. The tart firmness of green tomatoes are an ideal pie filling that needs only a little sugar, lemon, and the barest trace of spice to make a delicious end to any late summer supper.

Makes one 9-inch pie, serving 6

4 to 6 medium green tomatoes
Salt
1 cup sugar, plus more, for sprinkling the tomatoes (see step 1)
1 recipe Basic Pastry (page 210)
2 tablespoons cornstarch
1 lemon
Whole nutmeg in a grater
Vanilla ice cream, optional, for serving

1. Thoroughly wash, core, and cut the tomatoes in half vertically. Thinly slice them crosswise into half rounds and layer them in a colander, sprinkling each layer lightly with salt and sugar. Set the colander in the sink and let them drain for at least 30 minutes. Meanwhile, divide the pastry into two pieces, one slightly larger than the other. Roll out the large piece ⅛ inch thick and line a 9-inch pie plate with it (page 207), pricking the bottom well with a fork. Don't trim off the edges. Chill it for half an hour.

2. Position a rack in the center of the oven and preheat the oven to 375°F. Whisk the remaining cup of sugar and the cornstarch together until well mixed. Grate the zest from

the lemon into the sugar mixture and whisk again to mix it. Cut the lemon in half and juice it through a strainer into a separate bowl.

3. Wipe the tomatoes dry with absorbent paper or towels. Sprinkle the prepared pastry shell generously with some of the sugar mixture and put a layer of the tomatoes over it, completely covering the pastry. Sprinkle the tomatoes with more of the sugar mixture, a generous grating of nutmeg, and a little of the lemon juice. Repeat with another layer of the tomatoes, sugar, and lemon juice until they are all used.

4. Roll out the remaining pastry ⅛ inch thick and place it over the pie, or cut it into ½-inch strips and weave a lattice top (see Bourbon Cherry Pie, page 253). Trim off the excess pastry, seal the edges by brushing them with cold water and then crimping or fluting them, and make several slashes in the top pastry. If you've made a solid pastry top crust, cut out decorative shapes from the excess pastry, brush the backs with water, and arrange them over the top crust. Bake until the pastry is evenly browned and the filling bubbly, about 45 to 50 minutes.

Let the pie cool and settle before cutting it, and serve it warm, at room temperature, or cold, with, if you like, a scoop of vanilla ice cream on the side.

Roasted Tomato and Onion Tart

A favorite summer luncheon dish all over my part of the South is tomato pie, a rich collaboration between fresh, ripe tomatoes, mayonnaise, cheese, and sometimes, a bit of crumbled bacon. They are delicious but often a bit on the soggy side. The Corpening Twins, Mary Barber and Sara Whiteford, a beautifully matched pair of chef-cookbook authors from North Carolina, solve the problem by roasting the tomatoes first. It is a little more trouble, but certainly worth it, for it not only cooks off some of the excess moisture, it also concentrates the ripe tomato flavor. Here, the tomatoes are spread in a single layer, tart-style, with roasted onions over a bed of soft bread crumbs. The result is a deeply traditional flavor without a soggy bottom crust.

Makes one 10-inch tart, serving 6 to 8

1¾ pounds ripe plum or medium slicing tomatoes, cored and sliced slightly less
    than ½ inch thick
Salt
About 2 tablespoons or more melted bacon drippings or olive oil
1 large yellow or red onion, trimmed, peeled, and thinly sliced
½ recipe Basic Pastry (page 210)
2 cups grated sharp white cheddar or Gruyère cheese (or both, mixed)
½ cup finely crumbled soft bread crumbs
2 large cloves garlic, lightly crushed, peeled, and minced
4 thick-cut slices bacon, cooked crisp and crumbled, optional
8 to 10 fresh basil leaves
Whole black pepper in a peppermill
1 cup mayonnaise

1. Position a rack in the upper third of the oven and preheat the oven to 400°F. Meanwhile, layer the tomatoes in a colander, sprinkling each layer with a little salt. Let them drain for at least 15 minutes, then pat them dry. Brush a large, rimmed baking sheet with drippings or oil and spread the tomatoes and onion over it in a single layer. Lightly brush

their tops with the fat and roast them until both are wilted and the onions are browned at the edges, about a half hour. Set aside to cool.

2. Roll out the pastry on a lightly floured work surface about ⅛ inch thick. Line a 10-inch fluted tart pan with it, pressing the pastry into the flutes without stretching it. Prick the bottom well, line it with parchment or buttered foil, weight it with pie weights or dried beans, and partially bake it as directed on page 209. Let it cool slightly. Reposition the oven rack to the center of the oven.

3. While the shell is still warm, scatter half the cheese evenly over it. Scatter the crumbs over the cheese and lay the tomatoes over them, overlapping slightly; scatter the onion, the garlic, and optional bacon. Tear the basil into small pieces and scatter them over the top. Season lightly with salt, if you're not using the bacon, and liberally grind pepper over all.

4. Stir the mayonnaise until it is smooth and drop it in evenly spaced dollops over the tomatoes. Spread it with a spatula (this is a little messy but get it as even as you can). Scatter the remaining cheese over the top, place the tart pan on a rimmed baking sheet, and bake until the top and crust are golden brown, about 25 to 30 minutes. Let it cool for about 10 minutes, then put the tart on a wide, flat canister or can, remove the side ring, and slide the tart off the bottom onto an unrimmed serving plate or cutting board. Serve warm or at room temperature.

Vidalia Sweet Onion and Country Ham Tart

Revered by many, dismissed as the twentieth century's greatest culinary hoax by others, sweet onions became big business for a sleepy farm town in south-central Georgia and put its name not only on the map but on nearly every chef's tongue in America. They also created something of a sweet onion war, with competitors popping up from Texas to the tiny South Carolina island of Wadmalaw, each claiming to be sweeter than any onion before it. Growing conditions and exact soil composition have a lot to do with just how sweet the onions really are, and fortunately, more level heads have quieted the claim that they can be eaten just like an apple, but they do tend to be milder than most other onions. Regardless of the variety, they all have one drawback in cooking: a very high moisture content. When used in recipes like this one, they benefit from a slow, gentle braising, which helps to get rid of some of that excess moisture and concentrates their sweetness. A touch of ham and sage gives them just the right savory counterpoint.

For a lot of people outside Georgia, including other Southerners and some pretty high-profile television chefs, pronouncing the name of this onion is a challenge that they fail to meet—not surprising since it's an Anglicized contraction of "via dahlia," Italian for the "way of the dahlias." Romance language origins notwithstanding, it's properly pronounced Vie-DAY-lee-yuh (or, by some locals, vie-DAY-yer, but never mind).

Makes one 10-inch tart, serving 6 as a luncheon main course,
8 as a first course

3 pounds (about 4 medium) Vidalia Sweet or other sweet onions
3 tablespoons unsalted butter
1 recipe Basic Pastry (page 210)
2 ounces (about ½ cup) thinly julienned country ham or prosciutto
1 large or 2 small cloves garlic
1 tablespoon chopped fresh sage or 2 teaspoons crumbled dried
½ cup dry white wine or dry sherry
Salt and whole black pepper in a peppermill

Whole nutmeg in a grater

½ cup soft bread crumbs

1 large egg white, beaten with 1 tablespoon water,
    optional (see step 5)

1. Peel and trim the onions and slice them thin. Put the onions and butter in a large, lidded, heavy-bottomed skillet, cover, and put it over low heat. Simmer slowly until they are very tender, almost falling apart—about 45 minutes.

2. Meanwhile, position a rack in the center of the oven and preheat the oven to 400°F. Divide the pastry into two parts, one slightly larger than the other; rewrap the smaller one, and return it to the refrigerator. Roll out the other portion, line a 10-inch fluted tart pan with it, pressing it carefully into the flutes without stretching it. Prick it well, line it with parchment or buttered foil, weight it, and partially bake it as directed on page 209. Set it aside on a wire rack to cool. If you are not finishing the tart right away, turn off the oven.

3. When the onions are very tender, uncover them and raise the heat to medium-high. There will be a lot of liquid in the pan. Bring it to a boil and completely evaporate it, stirring frequently to prevent scorching. Continue cooking, stirring almost constantly, until the onions are a rich golden color. Add the ham and cook until it loses its raw, red color, then add the garlic and sage and cook, tossing, until fragrant, about half a minute.

4. Pour in the wine, bring it to a boil, and let it almost evaporate, stirring frequently. The onions should still be quite moist but not soggy. Turn off the heat. Taste and season with salt as needed and a generous grinding of pepper and a grating of nutmeg. Sprinkle the crumbs over the onions, fold them in, and let the onions cool. The tart can be made up to several hours ahead through this step.

5. When you are ready to finish the tart reheat the oven to 400°F. Spread the onions evenly over the pastry shell. Roll out the remaining pastry and cut it into ½-inch-wide strips. Lay the strips lengthwise over the tart, spacing them about an inch apart. Tuck in the edge only on one side. Fold back every other strip and lay a strip crosswise over the strips that remain. Unfold the folded strips and fold back the ones that had not been folded back before to the crosswise strip. Lay another strip of pastry over them, unfold the folded strips, and repeat until the surface is covered with lattice. Tuck under the edges of

the strips. If you'd like a glossy finish on the pastry, brush it with the beaten egg white. Bake until the pastry is golden brown and the filling bubbly, about 30 to 35 minutes.

6. Let cool a few minutes, then put the tart on a wide, flat canister or can, slip off the side ring, and carefully slide the tart off the bottom onto an unrimmed serving plate or cutting board. Serve warm or at room temperature.

Lettice Bryan's Fresh Strawberry Tarts

We tend to think of fresh fruit tarts as something fairly modern, but they go back a very long way. This handsome old recipe from Lettice Bryan's The Kentucky Housewife, *published in 1839, is a fine example of how early such pastries appeared in the South, although the idea behind Mrs. Bryan's recipe is much older. These little tarts are particularly fresh tasting because none of the fruit ever sees the inside of a pan. Though Mrs. Bryan makes no mention of it, a garnish of sliced or small, whole berries, a sprig of fresh mint leaves, and a curl or two of finely julienned lemon zest would warm her old-fashioned heart.*

Makes 8 tarts

2 pounds small ripe strawberries
Sugar
½ lemon
2 cups heavy cream (minimum 36 percent milk fat)
1 recipe Prebaked Puff Pastry Shells (page 214)

1. Wash, stem, and mash to a pulp enough of the berries to make 1 cup of puree. Sweeten to taste with sugar. Add a squeeze or so of lemon juice to taste. In a stainless or glass bowl, beat the cream until it is just beginning to thicken, then add the puree and beat until it is thick and standing on its own. Refrigerate the cream until it is chilled.

2. When you are ready to serve the tarts, wash, dry, and stem the remaining berries, slicing the large ones but leaving the smaller ones whole. Sprinkle a teaspoon of sugar over the bottom of each pastry shell and stand as many berries in each, as will comfortably fit (pointed end up). Dust them with more sugar (how much will depend on the sweetness of the berries). Mound the thickened cream generously over the tops of each tart and serve at once.

NOTE: These tarts can be made several hours ahead through step 1. Don't put them together until you are ready to serve them, or the berries will start to throw off their juice and make the pastry soggy. The tarts can also be made with fresh raspberries or blackberries.

Sherry Cream Tarts

These old-fashioned tarts, delicate and refined, were originally served at teatime, and evoke images of dainty Victorian ladies' entertainments, but they also happen to be delicious, and no gentleman—then or now—would turn his nose up at them. They make a fine, elegant ending for just about any meal, whether that meal is a formal luncheon, dinner, or brunch, or a casual family supper.

Makes 6 tarts

5 tablespoons unbleached all-purpose flour
½ cup whole milk
½ cup sugar, plus 2 tablespoons
⅛ teaspoon salt
2½ cups heavy cream
4 large egg yolks
¼ cup dry sherry or Madeira
Grated zest of 1 large lemon
1 teaspoon orange flower water
Whole nutmeg in a grater
2 teaspoons lemon juice
6 prebaked small tart shells (see page 209), made from Basic Pastry (page 210)
Candied Citrus Threads (made with orange zest, page 203), for garnish
Mint sprigs, for garnish

1. Prepare the bottom pot of a double boiler with 1 inch of water and bring it to a simmer over medium heat. In a small bowl, lightly whisk the flour and then gradually whisk the milk into it until smooth. Combine ½ cup of the sugar, salt, and 1½ cups of the cream in the top of the double boiler and stir until the sugar dissolves. Scald the cream, stirring constantly, over direct medium-low heat. When it is almost boiling, put it over the simmering water.

2. Slowly stir the flour and milk solution into the hot cream, and cook, stirring constantly, until thick, about 5 minutes. Lightly beat the egg yolks in a separate bowl. Stir ½ cup of the hot cream into the yolks and then slowly stir them into the remaining hot cream and milk. Cook, stirring constantly, until it is quite thick. Stir in the wine a spoonful at a time, cooking until it is thick once again. Remove the top pot from the heat, stir in half the lemon zest and a generous grating of nutmeg, and continue stirring until the cream is cooled. Pour it into the prepared pastry shells and let it cool completely, then cover and chill thoroughly (about 2 hours).

3. When you are ready to serve the tarts, whip the remaining cream until frothy, then sprinkle the remaining sugar over it and whip it to stiff peaks. Fold in the remaining lemon zest, lemon juice, and the orange flower water. Pipe or spoon the cream onto the tarts and garnish them with Candied Citrus Threads and sprigs of mint.

Marmalade Meringue Tarts

Meringue-topped pies have a long history in American baking, and they remain a popular and common part of the home bakers repertory, but these tarts are not just topped with it—they are all meringue. Delicate and old-fashioned, these airy confections are rarely seen anymore, since, like Sherry Cream Tarts (page 266), they were mostly found at those all-but-vanished Victorian ladies' entertainments—teas, circle meetings, and afternoon receptions. They deserve a revival and need not be confined to that narrow, traditional role on the reception table, but also make a delicious ending to any luncheon, supper, or even dinner, particularly when the main course has been fish.

2 large egg whites
⅓ cup orange, lemon, or pink grapefruit marmalade
1 teaspoon freshly squeezed lemon juice
6 prebaked individual tart shells (page 209), made from Basic Pastry (page 210)

1. Position a rack in the upper third of the oven and preheat the oven to 375°F. In a metal or glass bowl, whip the egg whites until frothy, and then whip in the marmalade. Whip until the egg whites hold soft peaks and sprinkle in the lemon juice. Continue whipping until the meringue holds firm but not to the point where it forms dry peaks. This takes longer than a standard meringue, so be patient.

2. Mound the meringue into the prepared tart shells. Place them on a rimmed baking sheet and bake until the meringue is delicately browned and barely set, about 10 minutes. Don't let them get too brown or too set: they should still be moist in the center and slightly creamy. Cool on a wire rack and serve at room temperature, or chill and serve cold.

Cobblers and Other Deep-Dish Pies

No dessert evokes the season that inspires it better than a cobbler, that classic deep-dish fruit pie that is popular not only in the South, but all over America. Warm, juicy, and fragrant with the best and ripest fruit of the season, it's the distilled essence of a lazy summer day. There are hundreds of permutations: some crusted with a cakelike topping that rises to the surface from the bottom of the fruit during the baking, some topped with biscuits, some with standard pastry, and others with a classic raised pastry that is halfway between biscuit and piecrust. Some have pastry imbedded in the pie, like dumplings, while others barely have any crust at all.

How it came to be called "cobbler" is lost in time, but its antecedents are probably the deep-dish fruit pies that have been a part of the American baker's repertory from the beginning. Amelia Simmons included several such pies in *American Cookery,* the earliest cookbook known to have been penned by an American. The name seems to have come along in the last quarter of the nineteenth century. Before then, a "cobbler" in culinary usage was a drink—lemonade generously spiked with sherry or liquor. That's how Annabella P. Hill, one of Georgia's first printed cookery writers, understood it, and in her classic *Mrs. Hill's New Cook Book* (1867), she calls the pie a "cut-and-come-again" pie—a name that was strictly regional and was not to survive into the twentieth century. The original meaning of cobble was to roughly patch something together, and the most usual explanation for both pie and beverage is that they are rough, patched together affairs. It's as good an explanation as any.

Rough, cobblers may well be, and by all accounts they are considered homey, family desserts, served right from the dish in which they were baked, but that may not always have been so: Mrs. Hill directed a more elegant and old-fashioned presentation. She directed that the top crust of the pie be carefully lifted off, inverted on a serving dish, and filled with the cooked fruit. It was then garnished with broken bits of the side pastry laid all around the edges.

Deep-dish meat pies, the savory cousins of fruit cobblers, are equally ancient, and hearken back to the days when the pastry crust was a kind of preserving casement (indeed, in many ancient manuscripts the pastry was referred to as a "coffin"). As late as the nineteenth century, elaborately composed savory pies of meat and poultry were common in American cookbooks. Many of these pastries were meant to be served cold, that is, at room temperature, and their fillings were set with aspic instead of gravy. In some of them, especially those composed of game, the birds might even be left whole. Only a few of these pies have survived refrigeration, but those which do survive are counted as the best comfort food going.

Summer Fruit Cobbler

This is the version of cobbler that I grew up on—thick with fruit, almost soupy with juice, encased only on the top and sides with a raised pastry, and enriched with a dumplinglike layer of pastry at its center. I've never really warned to any of the others, especially those with the cakelike crust. The great thing about this one is that it's a kind of master recipe: you can make it with just about any seasonal fruit, from early cherries and berries to midsummer's plums, peaches, and nectarines, to the early apples and pears at summer's end. The seasonings can and should vary as you change the fruit with the season's progress, but the basic structure is the same.

Serves 4 to 6

1 recipe Raised Pastry for Cobblers and Potpies (page 215)
Sugar
5 cups ripe prepared fruit (see Notes, below)
1 tablespoon unbleached all-purpose flour
2 tablespoons bourbon
1 teaspoon ground spices (see Notes, below)
4 tablespoons unsalted butter, 3 tablespoons cut into bits
Vanilla or *dulce de leche* ice cream or 1 cup very cold heavy cream
    or Custard Sauce (page 274)

1. Position a rack in the center of the oven and preheat the oven to 375°F. Lightly flour a work surface and roll out two-thirds of the dough to a thickness of about ⅛ inch. Line the sides of a 9 × 2½-inch-deep ovenproof glass or pottery casserole with it and trim off and reserve the excess dough. Handle it carefully: the leavening makes raised pastry more brittle and prone to tearing than standard pastry.

2. Sprinkle the bottom with sugar and spread half the fruit over it. Sprinkle it generously with more sugar (how much will depend on the fruit), a tablespoon of flour, a tablespoon of bourbon, and half the spices. Scatter half the butter bits over all and lay the reserved strips of dough on top.

3. Roll out the remaining pastry to the same thickness as the bottom crust. If there are gaps in the middle layer of dough, trim enough from the edges of the remaining dough to fill them in. Sprinkle with sugar and put in the rest of the fruit. Sprinkle with more sugar and the remaining tablespoon of flour, bourbon, spices, and bits of butter. Lay the top crust over the fruit, and moisten the edges of the top and sides with a little water or milk, press them together, and crimp decoratively. Cut several gashes in the top crust. If there are any scraps of pastry left over, you may also cut decorative shapes from them, brush their backs with milk or water, and arrange them over the top. Put the dish on a rimmed cookie sheet to prevent dripping and bake for 20 minutes or until the crust is beginning to color.

4. Remove it from the oven, rub the top with the remaining butter, and dust it well with sugar. Return it to the oven and bake until the top is golden brown and the fruit is bubbly at the center, about 40 minutes more. Serve warm with ice cream, a pitcher of very cold heavy cream, or Custard Sauce passed separately.

NOTES ON PREPARING AND SPICING FRUITS FOR COBBLERS

APPLES: Peel, core, and thickly slice apples. For spice, cinnamon is the most usual in apple pies, but cardamom (instead, not with) is also wonderful. If the apples are not very tart, they also benefit from the zest and juice of a lemon.

BLACKBERRIES OR BLUEBERRIES: Wash and drain the berries, remove any stems and blemished fruit. Season with cinnamon or omit the spice altogether. If they aren't very tart, as with apples, the grated zest and a squeeze of lemon juice do wonders, but most of the time, they are *very* tart; and as a general rule, you'll need more sugar than acidity. Allow more than you think they'll need, at least a quarter cup per layer of fruit.

CHERRIES: Wash, halve, and pit them. For spice, sprinkle a teaspoon of Home-made Bourbon Vanilla (page 23) over each layer. A squeeze of lemon juice will give them a nice lift if they are very sweet and on the bland side.

PEACHES AND PLUMS: Wash the fruit under cold running water and drain. Peaches are usually peeled, but leave the skins on plums. To peel peaches, drop them in boiling water for 1 minute, lift them out, and immediately immerse in cold water. Pull away the skins. With either fruit, cut them in half, remove the pit, and thickly slice. For spice, cinnamon and nutmeg are classic with peaches, but so is a tablespoon or so of freshly grated gingerroot. By all means add the grated zest of a lemon or orange and a squeeze or so of juice.

Custard Sauce

Whether you call it by its elegant French name, "crème anglaise," or by its more prosaic and artlessly inaccurate Southern name "boiled custard," this standard transcends names and, with minor variations, is practically ubiquitous throughout the entire Western world. Not only is it delicious with cobbler, it adds suave richness to sliced fresh fruit and homey bread pudding, and cuts the intensity of rich chocolate or tart, acidic desserts. It's one sauce that every cook needs in his repertory.

Makes 2 cups

2 cups half-and-half
²/₃ cup sugar
6 large egg yolks, lightly beaten
2 tablespoons bourbon

1. Prepare the bottom of a double boiler with 1 inch of water, cover, and bring to a boil. Reduce the heat to medium. Stir together the half-and-half and sugar in the top half of the double boiler. Bring it almost to a boil, stirring constantly, over direct medium heat.

2. Place the pan over the simmering water. Beat half a cup of the hot half-and-half slowly into the egg yolks. Add this to the remaining half-and-half and cook, stirring constantly, until it coats the back of the spoon. It will be only lightly thickened; so take care not to overcook it. It will continue to thicken as it cools.

3. Remove the custard from the heat and stir until it is slightly cooled. Stir in the flavoring and keep stirring for another minute. Let it cool completely before serving or chill it in the refrigerator. Serve chilled or at room temperature.

Sweet Potato Cobbler

Sweet potato custard (page 242), close cousin to the All-American classic, pumpkin pie, is a standard in Southern baking. This homey cobbler is less well known, and not considered nearly so elegant as its sophisticated cousin, but it is probably older, having roots in those ancient deep-dish pies of English cookery. Some popular histories claim that Henry VIII favored a similar deep-dish pie of sliced sweet potatoes because he believed them, like so much New World produce, to have powerful aphrodisiacal qualities. It is a notion modern Southerners, who know that the main drawback to this tuber is its tendency to make one rather gaseous, inevitably find hysterically funny.

Southern author John Shelton Reed, famous for his quip that modern Atlanta is a living example of what a quarter of a million Southern men died to prevent, is especially partial to this pie and has long championed its return to every Southern table. John divides the versions between "Baptist" and "Episcopalian," the latter, of course, being well laced with bourbon. I give both my grandmother's (i.e., the Baptist) and John's way. Regardless of which way you make it, and whether you buy into the notion that it might be an aphrodisiac, I think you'll agree it's one of the most warming, welcome, and deeply satisfying things to curl up with at the end of a crisp autumn evening.

Makes one 9-inch deep-dish pie, serving 4 to 6

1¾ pounds (4 to 5 medium) sweet potatoes
1 recipe Raised Pastry for Cobblers and Potpies (page 215), not made ahead but
    where indicated in step 2
½ cup firmly packed light brown sugar
½ cup granulated sugar, plus about 2 tablespoons, for sprinkling on the top crust
    (see step 4)
1 teaspoon ground cinnamon, plus more, for dusting the top
Whole nutmeg in a grater
1 tablespoon Homemade Bourbon Vanilla (page 23) or 1 teaspoon vanilla extract
2 ounces (4 tablespoons or ½ stick) unsalted butter, cut into bits

½ cup bourbon, optional

Vanilla or cinnamon ice cream, optional

1. Peel and slice the sweet potatoes about ¼ inch thick; you should have five generous cups. If the potatoes are especially thick, cut them in half lengthwise before slicing. Put them in a heavy-bottomed saucepan and completely cover them with water. Bring them to a boil over medium-high heat, reduce the heat to medium, and simmer until about half done—beginning to give on the surface but still quite firm, about 8 minutes. Lift them out of the cooking water with a slotted spoon, reserving the cooking liquid.

2. Position a rack in the center of the oven and preheat the oven to 350°F. Make the pastry as directed and divide it into two balls, one a little larger than the other. Roll the larger piece out on a lightly floured work surface, rolled as thin as you can manage—about ⅛ inch thick. Line a 9-inch round deep casserole with the pastry and trim off and reserve any excess. It will probably tear: don't worry about it, just press it back together. Put in a layer of potatoes, dust them with both sugars and repeat. Dust them with half the cinnamon, a liberal grating of nutmeg, half the vanilla, and dot with a third of the bits of butter. Pour in half the bourbon, if using, and enough reserved cooking liquid to cover the potatoes. Lay the reserved pastry trimmings over the potatoes. Repeat the layers of potatoes and both sugars until the casserole is filled. Dust with the remaining cinnamon, a generous grating of nutmeg, the remaining vanilla, and dot with the other third of the butter. Add the rest of the bourbon and enough cooking liquid to completely cover the potatoes.

3. Roll out the remaining pastry and lay it on top of the casserole. Trim off the excess, crimp the edges together, and slash the pastry in several places to allow steam to escape.

4. Bake for about 40 to 45 minutes, until the pastry is golden and the filling is hot throughout and bubbly at the center. Dot the top well with the remaining butter. Sprinkle it with granulated sugar and dust generously with cinnamon. Bake until the top is golden brown, about 15 to 20 minutes longer. Let settle for 15 minutes before serving. It may be served hot, warm, or at room temperature, plain, with vanilla or cinnamon ice cream.

Oyster and Leek Pies

There is a popular legend, the subject of which varies from region to region, that a particular food that is nowadays elegant and expensive was once so plentiful that it was fed to workmen and prisoners and was roundly snubbed by moneyed society. Along the Eastern seaboard, the star of this unlikely legend was the oyster. But while plentiful these bivalves certainly were, historical records and period cookbooks do not bear out the legends. Oysters have always been elegant fare, and oyster pie, cased in ornamented puff pastry and rich with cream and sherry, was an especially well-loved supper and party dish in the eighteenth and nineteenth centuries. The drawback to these pastries was the main ingredient: oysters have a tendency to throw off tremendous amounts of liquor and shrink considerably as they cook, rendering the pastry soggy and the oysters hard and tasteless. A wise cook baked the pastry separately and filled it with creamed oysters just before sending it to table—a practice I've followed here.

Serves 6 as a first course

2 pints oysters, drained, reserving 1 cup of their liquor

2 tablespoons unsalted butter

1 medium leek, trimmed and washed (see Note, below),
   white and tender greens thinly sliced

2 large or 4 small scallions or other green onions,
   trimmed and thinly sliced

1 large or 2 small cloves garlic, lightly crushed and finely minced

2 quarter-sized slices fresh gingerroot, minced fine

1 tablespoon bourbon

1 tablespoon flour

1½ cups heavy cream (minimum 36 percent milkfat)

Whole nutmeg in a grater

Salt and whole white pepper in a peppermill

½ recipe Puff Pastry (page 211) or 1 pound thawed frozen puff pastry

½ cup soft bread crumbs

1. Put the reserved oyster liquor in a saucepan over medium heat and bring it to a simmer. Add the oysters, and as soon as they begin to plump, transfer them with a slotted spoon to a cool bowl, cover, and set aside. Bring the liquor to a full boil over medium heat and let it cook until it is reduced by half.

2. Meanwhile, put the butter in a sauté pan that will comfortably hold all the leeks in one layer. Turn on the heat to medium-high. When the butter is just melted, add the green onion and leeks and sauté, tossing frequently, until they are wilted, about 3 to 4 minutes. Add the garlic and ginger and continue sautéing until fragrant, about half a minute more. Add the bourbon and let it evaporate. Sprinkle in the flour and stir until smooth, then gradually stir in the reduced oyster liquor. Bring it to a simmer and stir in the cream. Bring the sauce to a simmer again and cook until thickened, about 5 minutes. It should be somewhat thicker than a cream sauce. Turn off the heat. Season liberally with a good grating of nutmeg, salt, if needed, and several grindings of white pepper. The oysters may be prepared up to this point several hours in advance. Cover and refrigerate the oysters and the sauce in separate containers if it is to be prepared more than an hour in advance.

3. Position a rack in the upper third of the oven and preheat the oven to 400°F. Roll out the puff pastry about three-sixteenth inch thick. Cut it into six circles using a ramekin as a guide, and place them on a lightly greased or parchment-lined baking sheet. Decorate and bake them as directed for A Prebaked Puff-Pastry Top Crust, page 213.

4. While the pastry bakes, reheat the cream sauce over medium heat. Just before the pastries are ready, fold the oysters and crumbs into the sauce and heat them through. Divide the filling among six ramekins. Top each with a circle of warm baked pastry and serve at once.

NOTE: To trim and clean a leek, cut away any dry or yellowed leaves, trim off the roots, and split it in half lengthwise. Holding the leek root end up, wash each half thoroughly under cold, running water, bending back the leaves and making sure to get all the dirt from between the layers. Drain well.

Creamy Chicken Potpies with Golden Cheddar Biscuit Crust

This well-loved standard of the American supper table may well be the ultimate comfort food, even among people who never had one that was not ready-made from the supermarket frozen-food case. It's also one of the few lingering reminders of those deep-dish meat pies that were so common in early American pantries and luncheon, tea, and supper tables.

Traditional versions of this pie usually take a couple of days to make: first, the chicken (usually a whole hen) is slowly simmered in aromatic broth, then cooled, skinned, and boned. The broth is used to make the gravy, or if the pie was meant to be served cold, it might be cooked down until it jellies when chilled. This version takes advantage of leftover roasted, baked, or poached chicken, or it can be made with fresh boneless cuts that are now widely available in the market. You can make it ahead, of course, but it can also be put together in minutes on the day you plan to serve it.

Serves 4

FOR THE FILLING:

3 cups skinned and diced cooked chicken or 1½ pounds raw boneless chicken meat (preferably both breast and thighs)

2 tablespoons unsalted butter

1 medium onion, trimmed, split lengthwise, peeled, and diced

1 large carrot, peeled and diced

2 large ribs celery, trimmed, strung, and diced

3 medium scallions, trimmed and sliced into ½-inch lengths

1 tablespoon chopped fresh sage or 1 teaspoon crumbled dried

1 tablespoon chopped fresh thyme or 1 teaspoon crumbled dried

¼ cup dry sherry

1 rounded tablespoon unbleached all-purpose flour

2 cups chicken broth

1 cup heavy cream (minimum 36 percent milkfat)

Salt and whole white pepper in a peppermill

Whole nutmeg in a grater
Ground cayenne pepper

FOR THE PASTRY:
1 cup Southern soft-wheat flour (see page 9), or unbleached all-purpose flour or
    pastry flour
1 teaspoon baking powder
½ teaspoon salt
2 tablespoons chilled lard or unsalted butter
½ cup (about 1½ ounces) grated sharp cheddar
⅓ to ½ cup whole-milk buttermilk or plain whole-milk yogurt thinned with milk to
    buttermilk consistency
1 large egg white, beaten together with 1 tablespoon of water

1. If you are using cooked chicken, skip to step 2. Skin and trim the chicken meat of excess fat and cut it into bite-sized chunks. Put the butter in a deep, lidded skillet and turn on the heat to medium-high. When the butter is melted and hot, add the chicken and sauté, tossing frequently, until it is beginning to brown. Remove it from the pan with a slotted spoon, leaving as much fat as possible in the pan.

2. Put the butter, onion, carrot, and celery in a deep, lidded skillet over medium-high heat; (if using fresh chicken meat, add the vegetables to the pan that the chicken was sautéed in). Sauté, tossing frequently, until the onion is translucent, about 5 minutes. Add the scallions and herbs and sauté until fragrant, about half a minute. Add the sherry and cook rapidly until it is evaporated.

3. Stir in the flour and cook until bubbly, then slowly whisk or stir in the broth, bring it to a simmer, and simmer until thick, about 4 minutes. Stir in the cream and bring it back to a simmer, seasoning with salt (if needed), a generous grinding of white pepper, a grating of nutmeg, and a small pinch of cayenne. Bring to a simmer and return the chicken to the pan. Reduce the heat to medium-low and simmer, stirring occasionally, until the cream is thick and the chicken is tender, about 15 to 20 minutes for fresh chicken, 5 minutes if precooked. Taste and adjust the seasonings, turn off the heat, and put it into a 9-inch casserole or divide the filling among 4 ramekins.

4. Meanwhile, position a rack in the center of the oven and preheat the oven to 375°F.

Make the pastry: sift the flour, baking powder, and salt into a mixing bowl. Add the lard and cut it in with a pastry blender until the mixture is the texture of coarse meal. Add the cheese and toss until it is well coated with flour.

5. Make a well in the center of the flour and pour in most of the buttermilk (you may not need quite all of it). Lightly mix until the dough clumps together, adding the remaining milk by spoonfuls until the dough is no longer crumbly.

6. Place the dough on a lightly floured work surface and pat flat to about 1 inch thick. Fold it in half and pat it flat again. Repeat twice more, then lightly flour the dough and roll or pat it out to ¼ inch thick. Cut the dough into a round or rounds a little larger than the casserole or ramekins that you are using and place the pastry over the filling. Excess pastry can be cut into decorative shapes for ornament; brush the bottoms with water before placing them. Brush the pastry with the beaten egg white and water. Bake until the pastry is risen and golden and the filling is hot through, about 30 minutes.

Virginia Ham Turnovers

Real, slow-smoked, and dry-cured hams are one of the South's great treasures, on a par with the finest hams in the world, and of those, Virginia hams are among the best of the best—on par with German Westphalian and Italy's Parma hams as synonymous with the best you can get. Dry-curing intensifies the flavor of these hams, and a little goes a long way. In the Deep South, we shave them wafer thin and stuff them into biscuits—both the fluffy breakfast variety and dense, old-fashioned beaten biscuits. These delicate pastries are another classic way of serving that ham that takes the almost prosaic pairing of ham and cheese to a whole new dimension.

Makes 36 turnovers, serving 12 to 18

2 recipes Puff Pastry (page 211), or 2 pounds (2 packages) frozen puff pastry, thawed but chilled

About ¼ cup Dijon mustard

2 tablespoons chopped fresh sage or 2 teaspoons crumbled dried

2 tablespoons chopped fresh thyme or 2 teaspoons crumbled dried

5 ounces Gruyère or extra-sharp cheddar, grated

10 ounces (about 2 cups) thinly shaved cooked Virginia dry-cured ("country") ham

1. Roll the pastry out to about ⅛ inch thick (frozen pastry does not need additional rolling—just unfold it). Cut it into thirty-six equal 3-inch squares (you'll get nine squares per sheet of commercial pastry). Spread a little mustard over the center of each square, leaving the edges clear. Top with a sprinkling of herbs and cheese and mound a little ham in the center. Brush the edges with water, fold the pastry over on a diagonal, forming a triangle, and seal it by pressing the edge with the tines of a fork. Prick the top of each once with a fork. Lay the pastries on a lightly buttered cookie sheet, loosely cover, and refrigerate until ready to cook them. The pastry can be made up to a day ahead to this point.

2. Position a rack in upper third of the oven and preheat the oven to 375°F. Bake the pastries until puffed and golden brown, about 20 to 25 minutes.

NOTE: The recipe can be increased or decreased depending on how many or how few you need. For an elegant first course at dinner or as a luncheon main course, you may increase the size of each turnover to a 6-inch square. The baking time won't vary more than a minute or two.

Yeast Baking—
The Ancient Loaf

BISCUITS AND CORNBREAD have become such icons of the Southern table, that they overshadow an even older tradition that was once equally rich and justly famous: the fine, ancient art of yeast baking. As the allure of quickbread took hold of the Southern imagination, many of the old yeast-leavened breads fell by the way-side, neglected and half-forgotten, at best treated as anachronistic relics of a dim, overromanticized past. The nostalgic magic of Mama's bread first blossomed on those memories, and reached its fullest flower as each generation became farther removed from the actuality. Not all of those breads disappeared, of course, and happily, a renewed interest in America's real culinary heritage has helped stir an interest in that rich tradition of regional yeast breads—a good thing, for that neglected past is worth revisiting if we're to fully appreciate those traditions and bring them forward to the present.

The most useful thing to know about yeast baking in colonial and early republican America is that it continued to follow northern European practice, taking little from the New World and, ironically, almost nothing directly from Africa, where many historians believe it to have been born in the Nile River valley. Understanding that European underpinning is the key to understanding so much of Southern and, indeed, all of American cooking, for the yeast breads of those early Americans (at least, in the upper classes) differed very little from the daily bread of England and western Europe. Cast in round loaves or rolls directly on the floor of a wood-fired domed brick oven, they very much resemble the crusty "Continental" breads that are being discovered—or, more accurately, rediscovered—by artisan bakers all over our country today.

Just as was true of Europe, that basic bread eventually developed distinctively regional character from one part of the South to another. In the Carolina and Georgia Lowcountry, where rice ruled supreme, moisture-rich boiled rice was worked into the dough for a loaf that would stay fresh and sweet in the humid and sometimes fetid marshy air of the coastal cities and plantations. In Creole New Orleans, it was rolled into long, narrow baguettes like the professionally baked loaves of France. In Virginia, it was molded into top-knotted manchets, the large round rolls that the Cavaliers had known in their native England. In various places, breads for tea and breakfast were enriched with potatoes and sweet potatoes, and in rural areas where homemade yeast was the only kind a baker could count on, the crumb had a distinctive tang due to a soupy homemade leavening of potato fermented with wild yeast that came to be known as "salt-rising" and "sourdough." In refined homes, company bread might be enriched with milk, eggs, and butter or lard. The elemental daily yeast bread, however, was very basic, consisting of wheat flour, water, yeast, and a little salt, much as it had been in precolonial Europe and, indeed, still is to this day.

All that changed with the advent of commercial baking powder and yeast, steel-roller mills, and mechanized bakeries. It does not take a logistics genius to figure out that a hardworking, overextended housekeeper is no longer going to knead bread regularly if she doesn't have to, even when the bread that replaced her homemade loaf was inferior to it in just about every way possible. She had to make choices about how her time was used, and while baking bread can be immensely satisfying, it is still hard work, especially when it has to be done regularly amid an endless cycle of household and barnyard chores. For someone whose responsibilities are already stretched to the limit, a job that doesn't have to be done is the most likely thing to be neglected.

At any rate, homemade yeast bread slipped into a secondary role, reserved for special occasions and company dinners, and as people became accustomed to the soft, puffy insubstantial bread of commercial bakeries—and indeed, even to prefer it—homemade rolls and loaves became increasingly insubstantial. Carolina rice bread completely vanished; the crusty, substantial rolls that the founding fathers of Old Virginia took for granted gave way to soft, airy clouds of enriched dough that had charms of their own, but a delicacy that can never be quite as satisfying; Sally Lunn became more like coffeecake than bread. The bread of Creole New Orleans probably suffered the least, but it, too, inevitably changed.

Well, whether we like it or not, the only constant in any society is change, and not all the changes have been bad. Many handsome new breads have sprouted from those old branches; professional artisan bakers are reintroducing very fine breads; and while home bakers may no longer bake daily or even weekly, the quality bar has been raised and there's a better understanding of how to get the most from modern yeast and flour. The recipes that follow, from forgotten treasures to fresh new classics, tell a story of an ever-evolving breadbasket. As you take them into your own hands and ovens, know that you are sharing in that heritage, and, whether you are Southern or not, making it your own.

YEAST BREAD BASICS

Unlike baking powder breads, in which a chemical compound leavens dough by way of a chemical reaction, yeast bread begins as a living thing. All yeast, even the active dry variety, is a live organism, a fungus that is all around us. This organism infiltrates the moist bread dough, feeding on its natural sugars and starches. The gas it produces as it feeds and multiplies is trapped in the elastic strands of gluten that have been activated and locked together by kneading. These resulting pockets of gas are what make the dough expand and rise. The yeast eventually dies in the oven, but it needs to stay alive until its last wild burst of growth as it begins to overheat, so the dough must be given proper care. If you are an experienced yeast bread baker, you probably don't need any instruction, but for novices and occasional bakers, here are a few helpful notes on yeast-based baking.

THE INGREDIENTS

Yeast

There are three types of yeast leavening used in modern baking—active dry yeast, compressed fresh yeast, and homemade sourdough starter. All have unique properties of their own, but before we review them, a few words about using modern yeast in general.

After the introduction of active dry yeast in the last century, it became almost axiomatic that most American yeast bread recipes contained way too much of the stuff. Why is open to speculation: our general impatience as a culture, a misreading of the old recipes using homemade yeast cakes that were weaker and less stable than modern dry yeast, or, more likely, nothing more than a failure to understand just how powerful and active this form of yeast actually is.

The homemade "patent" yeast of early America was made by fermenting a brew of water, hops, flour, cornmeal, and brewer's yeast. The resulting paste was then spread out, dried slowly in a shady spot, and cut into small, even cakes. When the baker was ready to make bread, she dissolved a cake in water or scalded and cooled milk, and used the liquid to make up the dough, which is why the recipes often called for "a tumbler of yeast." It was fairly stable and reliable, but not nearly as powerful as modern yeast and so larger doses of it were necessary.

Just remember: while the first rising of any yeast dough may be slow, it does occur on its own time; it requires nothing of the baker other than a warm, draft-free spot and protection from drying out, and can mostly be left unattended while it does its business— while you are asleep, at work, or puttering around in your garden. Once the dough has been through its first rise, the yeast will have multiplied on its own, and the final rise after the shaping will go more quickly.

Here are a few pertinent notes on the yeast varieties used in this book.

ACTIVE DRY YEAST: as compressed fresh yeast—the kind used by professional bakers—becomes less widely available, this is the kind of yeast that most home bakers will have to be content with, the kind most commonly found in every supermarket. It works just fine as long as it isn't overused. Fortunately, modern bakers have a better understanding of dry yeast, and are using much smaller doses; the result is much finer bread. A scant quarter of a teaspoon of active dry yeast (roughly equal in strength to a modern half-ounce cake of fresh compressed yeast) is ample to leaven dough made with up to 40 ounces (8 cups) of flour. Its first rise will be slower, but the bread will be more stable, finer in texture, and will not have the sour aftertaste that over-yeasting produces.

Look for preservative free dry yeast, make sure the expiration date is at least six months ahead of when you plan to use it, and only buy as much as you will use within that length of time. When I first started baking, I would stock up when it was on sale; what a waste of money! Some of it would inevitably go stale and die before I could use it up. Make sure that the yeast has been stored properly in the market: preferably on a lower shelf (where it is usually a little cooler) and away from direct sunlight (which could over-heat it even in an air-conditioned space). That's exactly how you'll want to store it at home, too. It won't hurt anything to store it in the refrigerator, and once you open a packet, it should always be refrigerated. Be wary of dry yeast sold in bulk in jars: it often contains preservatives, and rarely will you be able to use it all before it goes bad.

RAPID-RISE OR INSTANT DRY YEAST: this type of active dry yeast has been engineered to grow like mad during the first rise so that it takes much less time without the sour bite of over-yeasting. Many good home bakers—my mother included—have used it successfully but I rarely care how long the first rise takes, and still adhere to the belief that a slow fermentation makes better bread in the long run, so I've never really used the stuff.

COMPRESSED FRESH YEAST: this form of yeast is superior to active dry yeast, but is not always easy for home bakers to come by. A few specialty markets sell it and it's available through some baker's mail order catalogs, but it's highly perishable and so few stores carry it nowadays. Once professional bakers could be persuaded to sell you a little, but nowadays obliging professionals are hard to find. If you try that route, I'd advise you to buy it from a bakery whose bread you like, because they're hardly going to sell yeast to someone who isn't buying *their* bread. Buy only as much yeast as you can use within a couple of weeks and keep it refrigerated. If you're buying it off the shelf, you'll find it in a refrigerated case; look for an even creamy tan color and a clean yeasty smell. Avoid any that is dry, crumbly, gray, and stale or sour smelling.

SOURDOUGH: this is a form of homemade yeast, a soupy batter made with potato and sometimes flour in which wild yeast flourish. Because it is fermented, it lends a mild tanginess to the finished loaf, hence the name. It's discussed in some detail in the section on breads that are made with it.

Flour

Contrary to popular belief, bread flour is not always the "best" flour for yeast baking. While it is true that its high-gluten content makes for well-risen bread, volume is not the only mark of a well-made loaf. Each type of flour has its own advantages: soft-wheat flour gives bread a fine texture and superior flavor; hard wheat's high moisture absorption increases the bread's shelf life; for some breads, a blend of both (i.e., all-purpose flour) strikes the best balance between volume, texture, and flavor. Each recipe will tell you which type of flour to use. But what matters more than the type of wheat is quality and freshness. Flour is, of course, an organic substance and, like all other natural things, eventually decays and goes rancid. Make sure that it is sweet and wheaty smelling: if it smells sharp and a little sour, it's gone rancid: throw it out.

Water

The most elemental ingredient in all cooking, water is often taken too much for granted. Yet the quality of the water you use can affect—sometimes drastically—your yeast baking. If you use treated city water (and nowadays, most Americans do), it is a good idea to filter it or use bottled spring or distilled water for your bread making, since some of the lingering chemicals in treated water can be detrimental to yeast growth. Many American recipes specify heated water, or worse, warm tap water, which may contain traces of the anticorrosive chemicals that domestic water heaters usually contain. Yeast seems to be healthiest when dissolved in water that is at room temperature (for most of us that's between 70° and 75°F) and no higher than 110°F. If you are making bread in the winter and the water is actually cold, or you want to give the yeast an early boost, warm the water briefly and let it cool to less than 110°F.

Milk

Milk is often used in enriched breads, making a lighter, softer crumb that keeps fresh longer than bread made with water; it also adds subtle flavor. All the old recipes called for the milk to be scalded because it contained enzymes and other organisms that inhibit yeast growth. Pasteurization has taken care of that, but I still find that the dough performs better if even pasteurized milk is warmed first. Always let the milk cool to less than 110°F before adding it to the yeast.

Salt

Salt adds flavor to bread, and a certain amount of it in the mix helps control the fermentation, but too much of it can damage yeast, so take care not to overuse salt in the dough, particularly if you are using the sponge method. Use a pure sea or kosher salt, and remember that flaked salt does not measure the same as small-grained salt like the kind usually used at the table. In these recipes, I used refined sea salt. You will want to round the spoon measure of kosher salt to get the same amount.

Sugar and Other Sweeteners

The proper job of sugar and other sweeteners in yeast bread is to lend the dough sweetness. It is neither necessary nor desirable as food for the yeast growth. In part because of the lower natural sugar content of modern milled flour, many bakers in the last century began adding small doses of sugar to boost the initial rise, but the yeast does not need it, and I find the artificial stimulation does the bread no good in the long run, and it doesn't really do much to boost the first rising. Unless the bread is meant to be sweet, sugar is unnecessary.

THE PROCESS

Measuring

Most of the recipes in this and the cake chapter use weight measures, by far and away the more dependable method of measuring flour. Even that is not absolutely foolproof: moisture content (which affects weight), and absorbency (which affects the ratio of liquid to flour), can vary a bit, even within the same bag of flour. A lot depends on how well sealed the storage container is and on the ambient humidity of the day. In the end, however, the best and only truly reliable measure is the feel of the dough. That is one reason I am not fond of bread machines and always recommend a brief hand kneading for any dough that is made in a mixer or food processor. No machine will be able to tell you when the dough is too slack or too stiff, but an experienced pair of hands will detect it without fail. Take the time to learn not only how the dough should look, but how it should feel under your fingers.

For more on weight and volume measuring, see page 33.

Sifting and Whisking Dry Ingredients

The object in yeast bread making is almost always to mix dry ingredients evenly and not to aerate the flour (as sifting before volume measuring is intended to do). A fine wire whisk does equally as good a job of mixing as a sifter, and is a lot less messy.

The Sponge

In many classic French, English, and early American bread making, the yeast is activated in a thin batter or sponge. Within that moist, warm environment, the yeast thrives and multiplies naturally, making for a stronger, more active yeast growth all around. The sponge also makes it possible to leaven dough with far less processed yeast. You can make acceptable bread by omitting the sponge process, and not all the recipes in this chapter call for it, but almost any bread is the better for having been started with one. I often mix the sponge in the food processor and put the flour on top of it, but also use the more traditional method of burying it within the bowl of flour: put about a third of the flour on the bottom of the bowl, pour the sponge into it, and then cover it with most of the remaining flour, holding back a little flour to mix in while you are kneading. This prevents it from crusting on the surface and makes the final mixing a little easier.

Mixing and Kneading the Dough

Food processors and mixers are fine gadgets, saving a lot of labor and making the modern cook's job easier. Few of us make breads and cakes often enough to have the strength and stamina in our hands to cream butter, beat cake batter, or stir flour into a dough that is too slack to knead by hand. However, they do have their drawbacks, especially in bread making. They cannot tell you when the dough is too loose or too stiff (unless, of course, the dough is so stiff that it stops the motor) and it is possible (though not very) to actually overwork dough in a machine. Using the machine to mix a soupy sponge, a batter, or a sticky dough such as Sally Lunn or challah sure saves a lot of elbow and wrist fatigue, but even with those, the machine doesn't make the process carefree. You still need to pay attention and sometimes get your hands a little sticky by feeling the dough or batter to be sure of its consistency. Food processors especially can make overworking the dough more likely, overheating and damaging the glutens. Even when I've used it to mix the dough, I still turn it out of the bowl to finish the kneading by hand. The mixer is a little more flexible: its dough hook will do a good job of kneading, but you should still give it a few turns by hand.

Contrary to what you have been told, kneading is no time to have a temper fit or take out your aggressions. If you are angry or are using the dough as a whipping boy, you are more likely to beat the heck out of it than knead it. I've quoted this bit of wisdom from John Taylor's classic *Hoppin' John's Lowcountry Cooking* in other books before, but it bears repeating: "You will get out of a loaf of bread only what you put into it . . . get into a good mood while you knead the loaf. If you try instead to take out your anger on the dough, you will end up with a knotty, uneven bread." Amen, Bubba.

I put on music that will get me in a good mood if I'm not already in one, that will help me set a good rhythm in the kneading. Renée Fleming singing just about anything does it for me, and I can't imagine trying to knead to anything really aggressive like acid rock or hip-hop, but that's my taste: choose music that you like. Next find a rhythm and motion that is comfortable for you and your hands. There's really no one right movement: the object is to evenly distribute the moisture, activate the glutens, and lock them together into the strong chains that make the dough elastic. This is how I do it: I put the ball of dough on a lightly floured surface, take the heels of both hands and push it away from me. This stretches and flattens the ball. Then I double back the end that is farthest from me, like folding a sheet of paper or a towel, press it down with the heel of my hand, and give it a quarter turn. Then I repeat this motion until the dough is elastic and smooth, meaning that it settles into a smooth ball and the surface springs back into shape when pressed with a finger.

Preparing the Oven

While it offers real advantages to all baking, a ceramic baking stone (or terra-cotta tiles) is all but essential to good yeast baking, making the difference between merely good and great bread. Even pan-molded loaves and rolls bake more evenly and handsomely on the stone's even, radiant heat. To equip the oven with a stone and provide the supplemental steam for that last wild burst of growth before the yeast gives up the ghost, see pages 26–28.

Classical Southern Wheat Bread

MASTER DOUGH RECIPE

This bread has very old European roots: when America was colonized, it had long been the daily bread of the European upper classes—at least since the fourteenth century—and naturally, the colonists brought it with them. Until the mid- to late-nineteenth century, it became our daily bread as well, but as the old brick wood-fired ovens gave way to cast-iron ranges and mechanized bakeries, this bread also gave way to pan-molded loaves of increasing puffiness and decreasing character.

Today, artisan bakers are bringing many wonderful breads to America's tables, and this lovely, crusty loaf deserves its place among them. The dough was fairly standard in all the old cookbooks, and was used for all the early hand-molded loaves, from Mary Randolph's topknotted hard rolls to the French loaves of Creole New Orleans. This is the recipe for the basic dough. Following it are directions for molding and baking a few of the more common shapes. Though I prefer to bake this bread directly on a baking stone, it can also be baked in loaf pans if you want a more regular, compact loaf to slice for sandwiches and breakfast toast.

Wheat, in this case, means only wheat flour: Southerners have long distinguished yeast-leavened white bread from our ubiquitous biscuits and cornbread by variously calling it "white," "light," or "wheat" bread. That last is especially confusing for modern Americans, since I have included a little whole-wheat flour in the dough—but that is only to approximate the character that it would have had when made up with the kind of stone-milled white flour that early American cooks would have had: it's still "white" bread.

Makes 1 round loaf or 2 baguettes or about 12 large rolls

¼ teaspoon active dry yeast or ½-ounce cake compressed fresh yeast

1½ cups water, at room temperature

20 ounces (about 4 cups) unbleached all-purpose flour, including
    ¼ cup whole-wheat pastry flour

1 rounded teaspoon salt

1. In a heatproof glass or ceramic bowl that will hold at least 3 quarts, dissolve the yeast in the water and let it proof for 10 minutes. Stir in 1½ cups of the flour, beating until smooth, and cover it with the remaining flour. Sprinkle the salt over the top and cover the bowl with a damp, double-folded linen towel or plastic wrap. Let it rise in a warm draft-free spot until the starter has doubled and made deep fissures in the dry flour, about 4 hours.

2. Work in most of the remaining flour, holding back a little for kneading, then turn the dough out onto a lightly floured work surface and knead it until it is elastic and smooth, about 8 to 10 minutes. It should readily spring back when you press it with a finger. These first two steps can be done in a food processor fitted with a plastic blade. Refer to the Note below.

3. Gather the dough into a ball, lightly flour it, and put it back into the bowl. Cover with a damp double-folded towel or plastic wrap. Let it rise until doubled, about 4 to 6 hours. The rise will be slower than you are accustomed to, but be patient: the bread will be stronger and better tasting. In a cool spot, it can be left to rise overnight.

4. When the dough has doubled, turn it out onto a lightly floured surface and knead it lightly for a minute or two, until it is smooth again, but don't work it too much at this stage. It is now ready for shaping and baking as directed in any of the recipes that follow.

NOTE: The mixing and initial kneading can be done in the food processor. The dough does not, perhaps, have as nice a texture as hand-mixed dough, because the hand method offers more control, but it does the job well enough. Fit the food processor bowl with the plastic blade and put in the yeast and water. Pulse to mix and dissolve the yeast and let it proof for 10 minutes. Add 1½ cups of the flour. Turn on the machine and let it run for about half a minute, to thoroughly mix the starter. Scrape down the sides, add the remaining flour, sprinkle the salt on top, and replace the cover. Let it stand until the starter is doubled. Turn on the machine again and run it until the dough forms into a ball. Let it knead for a minute in the machine, then turn the dough out onto a floured surface and finish the kneading by hand.

The Round Cast Loaf

This is the simplest loaf made with the dough for Classical Southern Wheat Bread. It makes a lovely, crusty round that is very satisfying to eat as is, but it also makes wonderful toast and croutons.

You'll need a baking stone to make this bread. If you don't have or want to buy a baker's peel, you can use a rimless baking sheet instead.

Makes 1 round loaf

1 recipe Classical Southern Wheat Bread dough (page 294)
¼ cup water

1. After the second kneading in step 4 of the Master Dough Recipe, shape the dough into a ball, pinching the bottom to seal it where it is gathered, and lightly dust all sides with flour. Place it on a baker's peel (see Headnote, above) that is lightly dusted with corn-meal, rice flour, or semolina flour, cover with a damp towel, and let it rise until doubled. (I do this on top of the range while my oven heats and it takes about an hour. It will take longer if your oven isn't under the cooktop.)

2. Meanwhile, prepare the oven with a baking stone and pan as directed on pages 26–28. Preheat it to 450°F while the bread does its final rise, but for no less than half an hour.

3. Uncover and slash the dough in a tick-tack-toe pattern with a single-edged razor or sharp knife. Slide the peel onto the baking stone and with a quick, sure jerk, pull it out, leaving the dough on the stone. Using a clean spray bottle, lightly spray the oven floor with the water, being careful not to spray it on the heating element or the stone.

4. Bake the bread for 15 minutes. Reduce the heat to 400°F and bake another 15 minutes, then check to make sure that the bread is not browning unevenly. If you find that it is, put on a pair of oven mitts and turn the loaf carefully. If it's browning too quickly, reduce the temperature to 350°F. Bake until it gives off a hollow thump when you tap the bottom, about 15 minutes more. Cool the loaf on a wire rack.

Old Virginia Hard Rolls

This is the way bread came to the table in the upper-class households of old England, where the rolls were called manchets, and later, in colonial Virginia, where Mrs. Randolph recorded the method in The Virginia House-Wife *(1824). The top of the dough was slashed in a circle, so that the finished loaf had a topknot like a rough cottage loaf.*

In order to re-create the rolls as they were first made, they must be baked directly on the baking stone. It takes a little finesse and a quick sure hand to do it successfully, so it's a good idea to practice the maneuver with a cold oven first. You may, of course, opt to bake the rolls on a baking or cookie sheet.

Makes about 1 dozen large rolls

1 recipe Classical Southern Wheat Bread dough (page 294)
¼ cup water

1. After the dough has been kneaded the second time in step 4 of the master recipe, pull off small handfuls and make them into balls about 2 inches round. Place them on a baker's peel lightly dusted with cornmeal, rice flour, or semolina flour, or onto a lightly greased baking sheet. Cover it with a damp linen towel and let it rise until it is doubled once again.

2. Prepare the oven with a baking stone and pan as directed on pages 26–28. Preheat it at 450°F. for at least half an hour while the shaped rolls go through the final rise.

3. Be ready to work quickly, in order not to let the oven lose too much heat. After the stone is thoroughly preheated and the rolls are ready to go in, proceed as follows:

* Quickly slash the center of each roll in a deep circle (this will form a topknot) or simply slash them in an X pattern.
* Open the oven and slide the rack containing the stone carefully out as far as it will go without tipping the rack.
* With a quick jerk of the peel, deposit the rolls on the baking stone, or place them

quickly, one at a time, onto the baking stone, allowing enough space around each to accommodate the final rising. Quickly slide the stone back into the oven; using a clean bottle, spray the floor of the oven with water, being careful not to spray the heating element, and close the door. If you are baking the rolls on a baking sheet, simply place the sheet directly on the stone.

4. Bake until the rolls are well browned and give off a hollow thump when tapped, about 20 minutes. If you feel they are browning too quickly, turn the heat down to 400°F.

French Creole Baguettes

In the Creole communities of New Orleans, it isn't just the cooking that mirrors old France; the daily bread reflects French practice as well. Under the surface it is the same basic dough as was baked into the round loaves of England and early Virginia, except that it was shaped instead into the classic long, thin loaves that their ancestors had known in France.

Makes 2 baguettes

1 recipe Classical Southern Wheat Bread (page 294)
¼ cup water
1 large egg white, beaten with 1 tablespoon water, optional (see step 3)

1. After the last kneading in step 4 of the master recipe, divide the dough in half. Lightly flour a work surface and pat each half into a long rectangle about 12 inches long and ½ inch thick. Roll the two long sides inward to the middle, then gently pinch them together at the seam. Lightly roll each into a sausage shape 14 inches long and a little thicker than an inch in diameter. Lay them on a baker's peel lightly dusted with cornmeal, rice flour, or semolina flour, cover with a damp linen towel, and let rise until doubled.

2. Prepare the oven with a baking stone as directed on pages 26–28. Preheat at 450°F for at least half an hour. Check the loaves to be sure they are not sticking to the peel. With a single-edged razor or sharp knife held almost parallel to the surface of the loaf, make three or four quick, sure diagonal slashes in each baguette. Deposit them onto the stone with a quick jerk of the peel; using a clean bottle, spray the floor of the oven with water, being careful not to spray the heating element, and close the door.

3. Bake for 15 minutes, then lower the heat to 400°F. If you want a glossy finish to the baguettes, brush them with the egg white and water solution. Bake until the loaves are nicely browned and hollow sounding when thumped on the bottom, about 15 or 20 minutes more.

NOTE: Baguettes can, of course, be baked on a baking sheet or in one of the trough-shaped pans specifically made for baguettes, but I prefer the character that baking directly on the stone achieves.

Carolina Rice Bread

This is one of the world's finest regional breads. Lowcountry cooking authority John Martin Taylor—at whose table I first tasted it and who taught me to make it—says it was once the daily bread of Charleston, and he has crusaded for years to restore it to its place. Almost every Charlestonian who tastes this handsome bread can't imagine how a city that lives on traditions could let one this delicious slip away virtually unnoticed.

The practice of supplementing expensive wheat flour with other, less costly, grains (or even potatoes, nuts, and peas) is an ancient one. Historian Karen Hess, who wrote a thorough, loving history of this bread in The Carolina Rice Kitchen, *believes that the practice of adding rice to yeast bread originated in colonial Carolina. But here the rice does much more than just stretch the dough; its inherent moisture makes a remarkably moist, tender loaf that keeps fresh and sweet for at least a week—no small feat in a hot, humid climate like that of the Lowcountry. The recipe I give here is from Sarah Rutledge's classic* The Carolina Housewife, *published in 1847. The only change I've made is to cut the original quantities in half, which I find makes for easier handling, and, anyway, it is about as much bread as my small household can eat in a week.*

Makes one large round or two 9-inch-pan loaves

1 quart water
½ pound raw long-grain white rice, washed and drained (see Note, below)
2 teaspoons salt
½ teaspoon active dry yeast or ½-ounce cake compressed fresh yeast
32 ounces (about 7 cups) unbleached all-purpose flour,
    including ¼ cup whole-wheat pastry flour

1. Put the quart of water in a large, stainless-steel pot that will later hold all the ingredients and bring it to a boil over medium-high heat. Stir in the rice and salt. Let it come back to a boil and reduce the heat to a slow simmer. Cook, uncovered, until the rice is soft and most (if not all) of the liquid is absorbed, about 18 to 20 minutes. Remove it from the

heat and let it cool to less than 110°F. (The center should be warm but not hot when you stick your finger into it.)

2. Gently stir the yeast into the rice and let it stand for about 10 minutes. Add about half the flour and work it in. You'll think something is terribly wrong, that you'll never get it all worked in, but keep at it: the rice will be sticky and soft again in no time. Keep adding flour by the handfuls until the dough is too stiff to stir.

3. Sprinkle a work surface with flour and turn the dough out onto it. Gradually knead in the rest of the flour. Again, at first you will feel as if something is terribly wrong, that you'll never get that much flour worked in, but keep at it.

4. When all the flour is worked in, knead the dough for 8 to 10 minutes. It will still be slightly sticky, so don't add more flour than is necessary to keep it from sticking to the work surface. When the dough is elastic and smooth, gather it into a ball, dust with flour, and put it into a bowl that will hold at least twice its volume. Cover it with a damp, double-folded linen towel (or plastic wrap) and set it aside until doubled, about 4 to 6 hours.

5. Lightly flour a work surface and turn the dough out onto it. Punch it down and give it a light kneading, about a minute. Shape it, either into a single ball (for a cast loaf) or two oval loaves (for pan loaves), and dust all sides with flour. Place the single loaf on a baker's peel lightly dusted with rice flour or semolina flour, or put the divided dough into two lightly greased 9-inch loaf pans. Cover it with a damp towel and set it in a warm place until it is doubled once again, 1 to 1½ hours (I do this on top of the range while the oven preheats). Meanwhile, prepare the oven with a baking stone as directed on pages 26–28 and preheat it to 450°F for at least 30 minutes.

7. When the dough has doubled, slash the top—a tic-tac-toe pattern for the round, down the center of the pan loaves. Slide the round loaf onto the baking stone with a sharp jerk of the peel or place the pans directly onto it. Using a clean bottle, spray the floor of the oven with water, being careful not to spray the heating element, and close the door.

8. Bake at 450°F for 15 minutes and reduce the heat to 400°F. Bake for about 15 more minutes. If the bread seems to be browning too quickly, turn the heat down to 350°F. If you are baking in pans, Taylor suggests removing the loaves from the pans at this point and returning them "naked" to the oven, which will make them crustier. Bake until golden brown and hollow sounding when thumped on the bottom, about half an hour more. Let the bread cool on a wire rack before cutting it.

NOTE: With Carolina Gold at a premium and only available regionally, I prefer an aromatic Southeast Asian long-grain rice for this bread, such as basmati or Jasmine rice, both of which have a fairly consistent absorption rate and lend a delicious hint of nuttiness to the bread. Commercial long-grain rice will work, but it has less character. Its absorption can vary, so it may need a little more water. Keep a teakettle of simmering water on hand until you know the absorptive properties of your rice. The bread keeps remarkably well—up to 8 days in cool weather—but keep it loosely wrapped; sealed plastic or foil will trap the abundant moisture that remains in the crumb and make the bread mold faster.

"Irish" Potato Bread

Rub half a dozen Irish potatoes, peeled, through a coarse sieve; mix them thoroughly with twice the quantity of flour; add one egg, a tablespoonful of butter, a teaspoonful of salt, a tumbler of tepid water or fresh sweet milk, in which has been dissolved a tablespoonful of leaven; make a smooth dough, and, after being well risen, mould into loaves or long rolls; bake in a rather quick oven. This bread keeps well. —Annabella P. Hill, *Mrs. Hill's New Cook Book,* 1867

The bread that Mrs. Hill so lucidly described did not, of course, have anything to do with Ireland. Throughout the Deep South, sweet potatoes have been a staple for more than three centuries, so much so that, well into my living memory, they were simply called "potatoes" (see, for example, the recipe that follows this one). White potatoes were called "Irish" potatoes to distinguish them—a linguistic quirk that survives in parts of the South to this day. Mrs. Hill took for granted that anyone would know that, just as she took for granted that you'd have sense enough to cook the potatoes before trying to press them through a sieve. Potato bread is still popular in the South: the dough is easy to manage, it makes a light but very satisfying loaf, and as Mrs. Hill aptly observed, it does keep well.

Makes two 9-inch loaves or about 24 rolls

14 ounces baking potatoes (about 1 large or 2 medium)
1 cup whole milk
¼ teaspoon active dry yeast or ½-ounce cake compressed
    fresh yeast
20 ounces (about 4 cups) unbleached all-purpose flour or bread flour,
    including ¼ cup of whole-wheat pastry flour
1 teaspoon salt
2 tablespoons unsalted butter, softened
1 large egg, lightly beaten

1. Scrub the potatoes under cold running water. Put them in small, heavy-bottomed pot and completely cover them with water. Bring to a boil over medium-high heat, reduce the heat to medium, and cook until tender and easily pierced with a fork or paring knife blade. Drain and let cool enough to handle.

2. Scald the milk in a small saucepan over medium heat, remove it from the stove, and cool it to about 110°F. Dissolve the yeast in it and proof for 10 minutes. Reserve a cup of flour for kneading and in a mixing bowl whisk together the remaining flour and salt. Peel the potatoes and put them through a ricer. You should have 2 cups. Work the butter into the potatoes until smooth. Beat the egg into the milk and yeast, and then gradually beat it into the potato.

3. Make a well in the center of the flour and salt and pour the liquids into it. Work them together into a smooth, soft dough. Lightly sprinkle a work surface with some of the reserved flour and turn the dough out onto it. Knead until it is elastic and smooth, about 8 minutes, working in all the remaining flour. Clean the mixing bowl and return the dough to it, cover it with plastic wrap or a damp, double-folded linen towel, and let it rise until doubled, about 4 hours.

4. Lightly butter two 9-inch loaf pans or a large baking sheet. Punch down the dough and knead it for a minute. This dough is soft and a little sticky: you may need to sprinkle it with a little more flour. Divide it in half, shape it into ovals, and put it into the two loaf pans. To make rolls, the dough is a little easier to handle if you chill it before punching it down and shaping it. You may roll it out ½ inch thick and cut it into rounds with a 1½-inch biscuit cutter. Make a crease down the center of each, fold the rounds in half, and place them on the baking sheet, leaving about an inch between them. You can also shape the dough into cloverleaf rolls (page 323) in buttered muffin tins or in a round cluster (see French Rolls, page 308). Loosely cover the loaves or rolls with a damp towel and let them rise until doubled again, about 1 to 1½ hours.

5. Position a rack in the upper third of the oven and preheat the oven to 450°F. If you are baking the bread in loaves, slash each quickly down the center with a sharp knife or single-edged razor blade. In either shape, brush the bread lightly with butter.

6. For loaves, bake for 10 minutes, reduce the heat to 375°F, and bake until risen and golden brown, about 20 to 25 minutes longer. Turn the loaves out onto a wire cooling rack and let cool before cutting. Bake the rolls at 450°F until golden brown, about 16 to 18 minutes. Serve warm.

Sweet Potato Tea Buns

Boil and mash a potato, rub into it as much flour as will make it like bread, add spice and sugar to your taste, with a spoonful of yeast; when it is risen well, work in a piece of butter; bake it in small rolls, to be eaten hot with butter, either for breakfast or tea. —Mary Randolph, *The Virginia House-wife*, 1824

I seldom have reason to disagree with my mentor and teacher, historian Karen Hess, but here I do. Mrs. Hess, noting that Mrs. Randolph always specified "sweet potato" when that was her intent, maintains that this recipe, following European tradition, was for a sweet roll made with white potatoes. I believe she was letting the title carry her intent and using cook's short-hand in the recipe, especially since sweet potato bread later became a Virginia specialty. Like so many other Southern breads and griddlecakes, these handsome rolls were eventually replaced by baking powder–leavened biscuits, which, while good, just don't compare. These handsome buns deserve to be restored to the repertory of all American bakers.

Makes 1 dozen small buns

1 generous cup hot cooked mashed sweet potatoes (about 2 medium potatoes)
½ cup sugar
½ cup whole milk
¼ teaspoon active dry yeast or ½-ounce cake compressed fresh yeast
14 ounces (about 3 light cups) unbleached all-purpose flour
¼ teaspoon salt
1 teaspoon ground cinnamon
½ teaspoon freshly grated nutmeg
3 tablespoons unsalted butter, softened

1. Mix the potatoes well with sugar until it is incorporated and let them cool slightly. Scald the milk in a heavy-bottomed saucepan over medium-low heat, let it cool to just

under 110°F, and dissolve the yeast in it. Let it proof for 10 minutes and stir it into the potatoes until smooth.

2. In a separate bowl, whisk together 2 cups of the flour, the salt, and the spices. Add the potatoes and milk and stir it into a smooth dough. It will be somewhat sticky. Dust a work surface with some of the remaining flour, turn the dough out onto it, and knead in enough of the remaining flour until it is soft but no longer sticky. Continue kneading for 5 to 6 minutes, until the dough is elastic and smooth. Clean the bowl and return the dough to it, cover it with plastic wrap or a damp, double-folded linen towel, and let it rise until doubled, about 4 hours, or in a cool place overnight if you want the rolls for breakfast or brunch.

3. Lightly grease a 9-inch round cake pan. Turn out the dough onto a lightly floured work surface and work 2 tablespoons of the butter into it until it is incorporated and the dough is smooth again. Lightly flour it just enough to keep it from sticking and roll it into a long sausage shape about 1½ inches in diameter; divide it into twelve equal pieces. Butter your hands and roll each piece into a ball, pinching it together in the place where the dough is gathered, and place them, lightly touching, in the prepared pan. Loosely cover with a damp towel and let rise until almost doubled again, about 1 to 1½ hours.

4. Position a rack in the upper third of the oven and preheat the oven to 450°F. Melt the remaining butter and brush it generously over the tops of the rolls. Bake until golden brown, about 20 to 25 minutes. Serve hot with additional butter passed separately.

French Rolls

A recurring theme in old Southern cookbooks, from Mary Randolph right into the twentieth century, were rich, delicate rolls, enriched with eggs, milk, and often a little sugar, and called, enigmatically, "French" rolls. Aside from a vague resemblance to brioche, however, they have little or nothing in common with the daily bread of France. The name actually speaks, not of French, but of a lingering English influence on the language and substance of American baking: bread enriched with eggs, milk, and added fat was often called "French" bread in England, a practice English colonials continued on our side of the Atlantic. Such enrichments add to the delicacy and keeping qualities of bread, and in the days when the housewife made all her family's bread, one that lasted beyond a couple of days was always prized.

Makes 3 dozen rolls

¼ teaspoon active dry yeast or ½-ounce cake compressed fresh yeast

1 cup water

1 cup whole milk

½ cup sugar

40 ounces (about 8 cups) or unbleached all-purpose flour,
    including ¼ cup whole-wheat pastry flour

2 teaspoons salt

4 large eggs, lightly beaten

8 ounces (½ pound or 2 sticks), plus 4 tablespoons unsalted butter, melted

1. Dissolve the yeast in the water and let it proof for 10 minutes. Meanwhile, scald the milk in a heavy-bottomed saucepan over medium heat. Remove it from the heat and stir in the sugar until it is dissolved. Let it cool to 100°F and stir in the dissolved yeast.

2. Whisk together the flour and salt in a large mixing bowl and make a well in the center. Lightly beat the eggs into the milk and yeast and pour it into the center of the flour. By hand or with a mixer fitted with a paddle, gradually stir the flour into it until it be-

comes almost too stiff to stir, then work in most of the rest of the flour by hand. The dough will be very soft—almost too soft to handle.

3. Work a cup of the butter into the dough by hand or with the mixer fitted with a dough hook and work it until the dough is elastic and smooth, about 8 minutes. Rub a clean bowl with 2 tablespoons melted butter and put in the dough, turning it until it is coated on the outside, cover it with plastic wrap and leave it in a warmish spot to rise until it is doubled, about 4 to 6 hours, then refrigerate the dough until it is chilled.

4. Lightly flour your hands and a work surface. Roll the chilled dough out into a long sausage shape about 1½ inches round. Pinch off lumps from the dough of equal size and lightly roll them into a ball. Lightly butter three 9-inch round cake pans. Put in the balls of dough in concentric circles, slightly touching one another, and loosely cover with damp linen towels. Let them rise until doubled—about an hour. Alternatively, the bread can be baked as individual rolls in muffin tins. Lightly butter three twelve-well standard muffin tins. Pinch off lumps of the dough and roll them out into ½-inch diameter by 6-inch-long sausage shapes. Coil them into the cups of the muffin tin, forming a spiral with the center sticking up slightly. Cover with damp linen towels and let rise as directed above.

5. Position a rack in the center of the oven and preheat the oven to 350°F. Uncover the rolls and lightly brush the tops with the remaining melted butter. Bake until they are risen and golden brown on top, about 18 to 20 minutes.

Bailee's Challah

Ever since Savannah matron Leila Habersham opened what may have been Georgia's first cooking school just after the War Between the States, Savannah has enjoyed a legacy of fine cooking teachers. Roughly a hundred years later, Bailee Tenenbaum Kronowitz, a master cooking teacher and baker, carried that legacy forward to several generations of Savannah cooks. Though she has retired from teaching and is no longer baking, her challah—the egg bread that is traditional for Jewish Sabbath dinners and bar/bat mitzvahs—is still celebrated in the memory of her family and of her students of all religious persuasions, and in the kitchens of those generations of home bakers who learned the technique under her patient, guiding hand.

Makes 1 large braided loaf or 24 small brioche rolls

½ teaspoon active dry yeast or ½-ounce cake compressed fresh yeast
¼ cup water
½ cup whole milk
4 ounces (1 stick or ½ cup) unsalted butter
⅓ cup sugar, plus 1 tablespoon
½ teaspoon salt
3¼ cups (about 1 pound) unbleached all-purpose flour
4 large eggs

1. Dissolve the yeast in the water and let proof 10 minutes. Scald the milk over medium heat in a heavy-bottomed pan, and let it cool to lukewarm. With a mixer fitted with a paddle or a wooden spoon, cream the butter, ⅓ cup sugar, and salt. Add the milk and a cup of the flour and mix well. Separate one egg, setting the white aside, covered and refrigerated, in a metal or glass bowl. Beat the yeast into the dough and then add the yolk and three remaining eggs, one at a time, beating well between each addition. Add the remaining flour and beat 5 to 8 minutes. The dough should be quite soft.

2. Cover with a double-folded damp linen towel and let it rise until doubled, about

2 hours. Beat the dough down by stirring vigorously with the mixer or a spoon. Cover tightly with plastic wrap and refrigerate for 8 hours or overnight.

3. Working while the dough is quite cold, punch it down and turn it out onto a floured work surface. Divide the dough into six even pieces and roll each out in a long sausagelike cylinder about 1 inch in diameter and 12 to 13 inches long. Braid three of the lengths together (the outside pieces alternate, always crossing them to the middle) and place them on a buttered baking sheet. Braid the remaining three lengths together and put it directly on top of the first braid. Cover loosely with a damp cloth and let it double, about an hour.

4. Position a rack in the center of the oven and preheat the oven to 350°F. Beat the reserved egg white with the remaining tablespoon of sugar and brush it generously over the loaf. Bake until golden brown and hollow sounding when tapped, about 30 minutes.

5. To make brioche with their characteristic topknot, butter a twenty-four-well standard muffin tin or fluted brioche tins. Cut the cold dough into quarters, setting aside one quarter. Cut the remaining three quarters into twenty-four equal pieces and shape them into smooth balls, tucking the cut edges underneath. Place them in the prepared tins and divide the remaining quarter of dough into twenty-four small balls. Gently indent the top of the larger balls of dough, brush them with water, and top them with the smaller balls. Loosely cover with a damp linen cloth and let it rise until it is doubled, about an hour.

6. Position a rack in the center of the oven and preheat the oven to 375°F. Beat the reserved egg white and remaining tablespoon of sugar together and brush it over the rolls. Bake until golden brown and done, about 15 minutes.

VARIATION

CREOLE BRIOCHE: Traditional Creole Brioche dough is for all intents and purposes like Bailee's, the proportions so near as to make no real appreciable difference. Unlike classic French brioche, baked in their fluted cups and crowned with a jaunty little topknot as in Bailee's recipe, Creole Brioche was originally baked in a cluster, with a single large roll in the center and rings of smaller rolls surrounding it to form a round cake—suggesting that it actually shares a lot more in common with the "French Rolls" of the Anglo-American Eastern seaboard (see page 308) than with actual French baking. Make Bailee's dough up through step 2, and when you are ready to shape it, butter two 9-inch-round cake pans, punch down the cold dough, and divide it into balls about the size of an egg, making two balls twice the size of the others. Put the large balls in the center of each pan and arrange the others around it, barely touching one another, in concentric rings. Cover with a damp towel and let it double, about an hour. Position a rack in the center of the oven and preheat it to 400°F. Brush it with the beaten egg white and sugar and bake until the brioche are a glossy golden brown, about 30 minutes.

From the New Orleans *Picayune's* 1901 classic, the *Creole Cook Book,* comes another variation on brioche colloquially known as "bullfrogs." Probably derived from the French loaf known as an *epi,* a baguette shaped to resemble a head of wheat grain, the dough is shaped into egg-sized rounds that are placed, slightly touching, in an eight-inch-long chain about three-inches wide (two rolls abreast and about six rolls long) on a lightly greased baking sheet. Though the dough for bullfrogs was not quite as rich as brioche (it contained about half the quantity of butter), brioche dough can be shaped the same way.

Mama's Buttermilk Bread

This is my mother's all-purpose yeast dough, which she uses for practically all her bread—loaves, rolls, and whole-wheat bread (see variations, page 314). It's standard fare for Thanksgiving and Christmas at home, and Mama frequently makes it to give away to a shut-in, ailing, or grieving neighbor. Buttermilk makes a tender, sweet-tasting bread that keeps well, freezes (and thaws) well, and even after it has begun to go a little stale, still makes terrific toast. Mama bakes her bread both in small loaf pans and cut into biscuit-like rolls, but it is her small, neat loaves that say home and love best for me. If you want larger loaves, divide the dough into thirds and bake it in 9-inch loaf pans.

Makes four small (7-inch) loaves or three 9-inch loaves or about 3 dozen rolls

32 ounces (about 7 cups) unbleached all-purpose flour or bread flour,
    including ¼ cup whole-wheat pastry flour
2 tablespoons sugar
1 teaspoon baking soda
1 teaspoon salt
2 cups whole-milk buttermilk, or plain whole-milk yogurt thinned with milk
    to buttermilk consistency
½ cup water
4 tablespoons unsalted butter or oil
¼ teaspoon active dry yeast or ½-ounce cake compressed fresh yeast

1. Reserve 1 cup of flour to use during the kneading. Whisk or sift together the remaining flour, sugar, soda, and salt.

2. Heat the milk, water, and butter until just warm (to about 110°F) and stir until the butter is melted. Let it cool slightly and dissolve the yeast in it. Proof for 10 minutes, then make a well in the center of the dry ingredients and pour in the liquid. Work it together into a soft, cohesive dough. Lightly sprinkle a work surface with some of the reserved

flour and turn the dough out onto it. Knead about 8 minutes, adding the reserved flour as needed, until the dough is elastic and smooth.

3. Clean the mixing bowl and return the dough to it, cover with a double-folded damp towel or plastic wrap, and let rise in a draft-free spot until doubled, about 4 hours, or lightly oil the bowl before putting the dough in, cover with plastic wrap, let it rise in the refrigerator overnight or for at least 8 hours, keeping it refrigerated until you are ready for the final shaping and rising.

4. Lightly grease four small (7½ × 2¼-inch) loaf pans with butter or olive oil. Punch the dough down and lightly knead for about 1 minute. Divide it into quarters, shape each one into an oblong loaf, and put them into the greased pans. Cover with a double-folded damp towel and let rise in a warm spot until the loaves have doubled and clear the tops of the pans, about 1 to 1½ hours.

5. Meanwhile, position a rack in the center of the oven and preheat the oven to 375°F. Uncover the bread and bake for 20 minutes, then increase the oven temperature to 400°F and continue baking until the loaves are well browned and hollow sounding when tapped on the bottom, about 15 minutes longer. Turn the bread out of the pans and cool it on wire racks.

VARIATIONS

BUTTERMILK ROLLS OR YEAST BISCUITS: This dough can be cut or shaped into rolls using any shape you like. Mama cuts them into simple yeast biscuits: Roll the dough out about ¼ inch thick and cut with a biscuit cutter. Place the biscuits on a greased baking sheet, spacing them a little apart for separate rolls or put them into a round pan, slightly touching one another. Cover with a damp linen towel and let rise until doubled, then bake at 450°F until browned, about 12 to 15 minutes. For pocketbook rolls, press the rounds firmly down the center with a knife, fold over, and place on a lightly greased baking sheet, not touching; cover, let rise, and then bake as above. For cloverleaf rolls, flour your hands, pinch off 1-inch lumps of dough, and roll them into tight smooth balls. Lightly butter twelve-well standard muffin tins and put in three balls per well. Cover, let rise, and bake as above.

WHOLE-WHEAT BUTTERMILK BREAD: Substitute from 1 to 3 cups of whole-wheat flour for the regular flour. Mama varies the amount depending on whether she is making it for herself or for a neighbor whose tastes will determine how mild or intensely wheaty the bread needs to be. Most whole-wheat flour tends to be a little on the thirsty side: you may need a little more liquid for the dough, so have about a quarter of a cup of room temperature water close at hand as you mix the dough, so that you can add a little at a time as the dough needs it.

Mama Edith's Bread

An interesting aspect of bread making is the way a loaf will often take on some of the character and personality of its baker. Edith Wakefield was all country gingham and lace, sentimental and tenderhearted to a fault, and yet tough and wise in ways that defy the usual preconception of sentimentality. She came into my life by way of her exquisitely beautiful daughter, Kathy, one of my lifelong closest friends. Edith in turn became a dear friend, one of the "Mamas" in every Southern man's life who is as important as she is impossible to explain, and we remained close until she died.

Edith's bread is a distillation of her essence: warm and earthy as whole wheat and molasses, simple and old-fashioned and yet wise and forward-looking, always meeting and embracing the world as she found it. Neither Kathy nor I remember lecithin or canola oil in her earlier bread—both found their way into the mix later on—but that, too, was typical of her adaptable nature. As age challenged her, making her more conscious of health issues, she met the challenge head on.

Makes two 9-inch loaves

FOR THE SPONGE:

¼ teaspoon active dry yeast or ½-ounce cake compressed fresh yeast

1½ cups lukewarm water

1 tablespoon granulated lecithin (available at natural food grocers; see Note, below), optional

1 tablespoon salt

2 tablespoons unsulfured molasses

10 ounces (about 2 cups) unbleached all-purpose flour

FOR THE DOUGH:

½ cup water

3 tablespoons canola oil

½ cup unsulfured molasses

20 ounces (about 4 cups) whole-wheat flour, preferably organic
About 2 tablespoons unsalted butter, melted

1. To make the sponge, dissolve the yeast in the water and let it proof 10 minutes. Stir in the lecithin, if you are using it, salt, and molasses, then gradually whisk in the all-purpose flour until it forms a smooth, thick batter. Cover with plastic wrap and let rise in a warm place until doubled.

2. When you are ready to make the dough, bring ½ cup water to a boil and remove it from the heat. Stir in the oil and molasses, let it cool to lukewarm, and then mix it into the sponge. Gradually stir in the whole-wheat flour until it is too stiff to stir and then sprinkle some of the flour onto a work surface, turn the dough out onto it, and work in the remaining flour by hand until the dough is no longer sticky but still fairly soft. Knead it until it is elastic and smooth, about 8 minutes.

3. Clean and dry the mixing bowl and rub it liberally with oil. Put in the dough and turn it several times to lightly grease all sides. Cover with plastic wrap or a damp, double-folded linen towel and let it rise until doubled, about 4 to 6 hours.

4. Lightly oil two 9-inch loaf pans. Punch the dough down, cut it in half, and lightly knead each half until smooth again—about 2 minutes. Shape into loaves and invert the prepared pans over them. Let rest for 15 minutes, then turn the pans face up and put the loaves into the pans, cover with a damp cloth, and let rise until the top of the loaf clears the top of the pan.

5. Position a rack in the center of the oven and preheat the oven to 350°F. Uncover the bread, place the pans in the oven, and bake until the tops are uniformly brown, about 40 to 45 minutes. Remove the bread from the pans and put them right side up on a cooling rack. Brush the tops with melted butter while still quite warm.

ABOUT LECITHIN: Lecithin is a natural emulsifier found in foods such as egg yolks. It helps suspend fat in liquid emulsions like oil and vinegar salad dressing. Studies have found that it also may be beneficial in helping to lower serum cholesterol levels, and Edith may have been using it partly for that reason, but its main job in this bread is to help amalgamate the oil into the dough, making it smoother and more manageable. It also slightly improves the finished loaf's keeping qualities. If you are not able to find granulated lecithin, liquid lecithin or a large egg yolk may be substituted or the lecithin can just be omitted altogether. The bread is a little more even and smooth with it, and does stay fresh a day or so longer, but the recipe will still work without the enrichment.

Sourdough Starter and Sourdough Starter II

People who make sourdough bread are usually glad to give away a cup or so of starter, especially if they don't make bread every week; feeding the starter without taking some away makes for huge volumes of the stuff. That's why a variation of this bread is often called "Friendship Loaf"—the starter thrives on being spread around. If you don't know someone who makes sourdough, however, and are wary of depending solely on such wild yeasts as inhabit the air of your kitchen, you can create a starter using packaged yeast. It will take a few weeks for any starter to hit its prime, so be patient with it. Eventually, the natural wild yeast in the air will begin to impregnate even a starter begun with commercial yeast, giving it a character unique to your kitchen.

Some of the recipes in this section are designed with starter that does not contain flour, and the ingredients list will call for Sourdough Starter II if that is the case, but either starter can be used. To substitute one for the other, see page 320.

Makes about 5 cups starter

½ cup sugar
2 cups warm (110°F) water
¼ teaspoon active dry yeast or ½-ounce cake compressed fresh yeast
1 medium potato, boiled soft, peeled, and mashed,
    or 6 tablespoons instant potato flakes
10 ounces (about 2 cups) unbleached all-purpose or bread flour, optional

1. Stir the sugar into the water until it is dissolved. Sprinkle in the yeast and let stand a few minutes, until the yeast is dissolved into the liquid and creamy. Stir in the mashed potato or potato flakes. Sprinkle in the flour if you are using it and stir until it is smooth. Some bakers prefer a thin, flourless starter, and some prefer the thicker batterlike starter. The latter is thought to be more durable and forgiving of uneven feeding.

2. Loosely cover the starter (use loose foil with holes punched into it with a carving fork, a damp linen towel, or plastic wrap stretched tight and punctured with a carving

fork—the starter must be able to breathe) and let it stand at room temperature for 24 hours. Cover and refrigerate the starter until ready to use it.

FEEDING THE STARTER

To keep the starter healthy and vigorous, feed it once a week, especially when it is still quite young. After a few months, it'll get more forgiving, and will tolerate longer intervals between feedings, but try to maintain a regular schedule, and feed it no less than every two weeks if you don't make bread regularly.

1 cup warm (110°F) water
½ cup sugar
3 tablespoons instant potato flakes, or cooked mashed potato
5 ounces (about 1 cup) unbleached all-purpose or bread flour, optional

1. Remove the starter from the refrigerator. Stir the water and sugar together until the sugar dissolves, and stir in the potato flakes. Sprinkle the flour over, if you are using it, and stir until it forms a smooth batter. Stir this into the starter, loosely cover it (I used a glass casserole with a glass lid, but punctured foil or a towel will work), and let it stand 8 to 10 hours.

2. Take up 1 cup of the starter to make bread, or to give away to a friend if you are not making bread right away. Cover and refrigerate the remaining starter (or all of it if you are not making bread or giving any away).

SUBSTITUTING SOURDOUGH STARTERS IN BREAD RECIPES

Whether or not you feed your starter with flour (which makes a starter the consistency of thin pancake batter), it can be used in any sourdough bread recipe. To substitute one starter for the other, here are some basic rules of thumb. If your starter is flour-based and the recipe calls for the thinner starter without flour, just hold back ½ cup of the flour called for. If your starter doesn't contain flour and the recipe calls for a starter with flour, just allow an extra half a cup of flour.

Almost any conventional bread recipe can become sourdough by substituting starter for the conventional yeast and some of the liquid: allow a cup of starter for 4 to 8 cups of flour. Omit the yeast and proofing liquid and hold back ½ cup of the liquid called for in the recipe (for a starter with flour), or a cup of liquid if the starter does not contain flour.

Basic Sourdough Bread

This basic dough is a real kitchen workhorse: its uses need be limited only by your imagination. It makes wonderful dinner rolls, a fine, compact loaf for sandwiches and toast, a satisfyingly crusty round cottage loaf, and can even be put to use in sweet breads for breakfast or brunch. Adding oil to the dough helps to increase its keeping qualities: well wrapped in both wax paper and foil, the loaves last up to a week, and are still good for toasting for a few days after that.

Makes 2 loaves

1 cup Sourdough Starter (page 319)
1½ cups warm (no more than 110°F) water
¼ cup oil (olive, canola, or another vegetable oil)
28 ounces (about 6 cups) unbleached bread flour or all-purpose flour,
    including ¼ cup whole-wheat pastry flour
1 tablespoon salt

1. Combine the starter, water, and oil in large work bowl that will allow the volume of the dough to double without overflowing. Gradually stir in the flour until the dough is too stiff to stir, then turn it out onto a lightly floured work surface and work in the salt and remaining flour until the dough is no longer sticky but smooth and still fairly soft. Knead it until it is elastic and smooth—at least 8 to 10 minutes. Put the dough back into the mixing bowl and loosely cover the bowl with a damp, double-folded towel or plastic wrap and let it rise in a draft-free spot 8 to 10 hours or overnight.

2. Punch down the dough and let it rest for 10 minutes. Lightly flour a work surface and turn the dough out onto it and lightly knead it for about 2 minutes, until smooth again. Cut it into two equal portions and shape them into oval or round loaves. Lightly oil a large baking sheet and place the two loaves on it, leaving at least 3 inches between them and 2 inches on the other sides, or put them into two lightly greased 9-inch bread pans. Cover once more with a double-folded damp towel or plastic wrap and let them rise in a

warm, draft-free spot, until doubled (about 3 to 5 hours; let the pan loaves rise until they clear the tops of the pans).

3. Position the rack in the center of the oven and preheat the oven to 350°F. Make three diagonal slashes across the top of each free-form oval loaf, or lengthwise down the center of the pan loaves, with a single-edge razor blade or sharp knife. Place the pans in the oven and bake about 35 to 40 minutes, or until the bread sounds hollow when thumped. Remove the loaves from the pans and cool them on a wire rack.

VARIATION

SOURDOUGH CLOVERLEAF ROLLS: Make the dough as directed in step 1 of the previous recipe for Basic Sourdough Bread. After the initial rising, turn it out onto a floured work surface, punch it down, and knead for a minute. Butter two standard twelve-well muffin pans. Lightly flour your hands and pinch off walnut-sized lumps (about 1 inch) of the dough and shape them into uniform balls, placing them three to each well of the pans as you go. Cover the pans with a double-folded damp cloth and let them rise in a warm, draft-free spot until the dough is doubled and is clearing the top of the pans. Position the rack in the center of the oven and preheat the oven to 350°F. Lightly brush the rolls with melted butter and bake for about 30 minutes. If you need fewer rolls, you may divide the dough in half and make a single loaf and a dozen rolls.

SOURDOUGH CAST COTTAGE LOAVES: Sourdough makes a terrifically good cast loaf (a whole round loaf baked on the stone—see page 296). Make the dough as directed in step 1 of the recipe for Basic Sourdough Bread (page 322). You may want to work a little more flour into the dough so that it holds its shape without a pan. After a couple of times, you will know how it should feel under your hands. After it has gone through the initial rise, punch it down and divide it in half, lightly knead each half, and shape it into a ball. Lightly flour each ball and place it on a baker's peel or rimless baking sheet dusted with a little semolina flour. Cover with a damp towel. Let it rise until it is doubled, then slash and bake it as directed in step 3, above.

Lyn's Rosemary Sourdough Bread

Sourdough starter can almost become a member of the family. My own starter was given to me by my friend Lyn McDonald, who, when her family moved to Savannah a few years ago, had carefully nursed it all the way from Alabama in its own cooler. Lyn's starter had been given to her by her next-door neighbor, and was an important link back to that friendship. When Lyn recently became ill, she was almost as worried about who would look after her starter as she was her sons and husband.

True to her generous nature, when she gave me the starter, it was accompanied by a loaf of this, her favorite bread, delicately flavored with honey and fragrant with rosemary.

Makes 2 oval loaves

1 cup Sourdough Starter (page 319)
1½ cups warm (no more than 110°F) water
¼ cup olive oil
¼ cup honey
28 ounces (about 6 cups) unbleached bread flour
   or unbleached all-purpose flour
1 tablespoon salt
1 rounded tablespoon chopped fresh rosemary

1. Combine the starter, water, oil, and honey in a large work bowl that will allow the volume of the dough to double without overflowing. Add the flour and salt and work it in until the dough is smooth. Loosely cover the bowl with punctured foil or a damp cloth and let it rise overnight (8 to 10 hours).

2. Punch it down and let it rest for 10 minutes. Lightly flour a work surface and turn the dough out onto it. Knead for about 5 minutes. Sprinkle the rosemary over it and knead until the herb is incorporated and the dough is elastic and smooth, about 2 minutes longer. Cut into two equal portions, and shape each into oval loaves. Lightly oil a large baking sheet and place the two loaves on it, leaving at least 2 inches clear on all sides.

Cover with a damp cloth and let rise 3 to 5 hours in a warm, draft-free spot, until doubled in bulk.

3. Position the rack in the center of the oven and preheat the oven to 350°F. Make three diagonal slashes across the top of each loaf with a single-edge razor blade or sharp knife. Place the pan in the oven and bake about 35 to 40 minutes, or until the bread sounds hollow when thumped on the bottom. Remove the loaves to a wire rack to cool.

Mary Lizzie's Whole-Wheat Sourdough

Mary Lizzie Kitchengs came into my life when she moved to Savannah from Bainbridge, Georgia, to live with her daughter, Maryan, and granddaughter, Mary Margaret. Very shortly, they were known to all of us as "The Three Mary's," the wonderfully biblical tone of which tickled Mary Lizzie's rich sense of humor. One of the distinct privileges of my life was to know this lovely lady, share her love and wisdom, and, when her life had come full circle, to be at her bedside with the other two Mary's as she died. While she was able to bake, the daily bread of Mary Lizzie's household (and of several others) was this tangy-sweet whole-wheat loaf that she made at least once a week. Whenever its warm, sweet smell fills my kitchen, I can almost feel Mary Lizzie near at hand, laughing at me, at herself, at all the quirks of the world we live in, and handing out advice that can only come from one who has lived well.

If Mary Lizzie had a fault, it was a raging sweet tooth, and this recipe makes a very sweet loaf. Feel free to adjust the sugar to suit your taste. Once you've made it a few times, you'll know how you like it.

Makes three 9-inch loaves

1½ cups Sourdough Starter II (without flour, page 319)
½ cup sugar
½ cup oil (olive, canola, or peanut)
1¼ teaspoons salt
1½ cups water
20 ounces (about 4 cups) unbleached bread flour
10 ounces (about 2 cups) whole-wheat flour
About 3 tablespoons unsalted butter

1. Mix the starter together with the sugar, oil, salt, and water. Whisk together the flours in a large mixing bowl that will hold double the volume of the flour, make a well in the center, and pour the liquid into it. Gradually work it into a smooth, stiff dough. Knead it lightly until it is elastic and smooth, about 6 minutes. Clean the bowl, return the

dough to it, and cover with a double folded damp towel or plastic wrap. Let it rise until doubled, about 6 to 8 hours or overnight.

2. Lightly grease three 9-inch loaf pans. Punch the dough down and divide it into three equal portions. Knead each portion separately until it is elastic and smooth, about 5 minutes. Put the dough into the prepared pans, cover with double-folded damp towels, and let them rise until doubled, about 6 hours.

3. Position a rack in the center of the oven and preheat the oven to 350°F. Uncover the loaves and bake until golden brown and hollow-sounding when tapped on the bottom, about 35 minutes. While the bread is baking, melt the butter over low heat and turn off the heat. When the loaves are done, remove them from the pans and brush the tops generously with butter. Let them cool before slicing.

Cinnamon Raisin and Pecan Sourdough Bread

This quintessential American breakfast bread is good hot from the oven, but when it really shines is later, toasted and slathered with butter or cream cheese. Sourdough gives it a subtle bite that counterpoints the sweet spiral of brown sugar and raisins, but if the slow rise is longer than you would wish, the loaf can be made with almost any enriched bread dough—Mama's Buttermilk Bread (page 313) or Lee Smith's Mama's Loaf Bread (page xvii) are two especially suitable candidates.

Makes two 9-inch loaves

1 cup Sourdough Starter (page 319)
1½ cups whole milk, warmed to 110°F
6 tablespoons unsalted butter, melted and cooled
½ cup honey
28 ounces (about 6 cups) unbleached bread flour or unbleached all-purpose flour,
    including ¼ cup whole-wheat pastry flour
2 teaspoons salt
½ cup raisins
1 cup water
1 cup firmly packed light brown sugar
2 teaspoons powdered cinnamon
½ cup roughly chopped Toasted Pecans (page 18)

1. Combine the starter, milk, 4 tablespoons of butter, and the honey. Whisk together the flour and salt in a large work bowl that will comfortably hold twice the dough's volume. Make a well in the center, pour in the liquids, and work them in until the dough is cohesive. If the dough seems dry sprinkle in a little water. Turn the dough out onto a lightly floured work surface and knead until it is elastic and smooth, about 8 minutes. Clean the bowl and return the dough to it. Loosely cover with a damp, double-folded

linen cloth, set it in a draft-free spot, and let it rise until doubled, about 8 hours or overnight.

2. When ready to shape the bread, put the raisins in a heatproof bowl. Bring 1 cup of water to a boil, pour it over them, let them plump for 10 minutes, and drain thoroughly. Lightly butter two 9-inch pans and have them ready. Lightly flour a work surface. Punch the dough down and turn it out onto it. Lightly knead for about 2 to 3 minutes, or until elastic and smooth once again. Divide the dough in half. Flatten and stretch each into a rectangle about almost as thin as a pizza crust. Sprinkle them evenly with the sugar, cinnamon, raisins, and pecans. Roll each into a cylinder from the short side, carefully pinching them together at the seam and ends. Put the dough into the prepared pans, cover with a damp cloth and let them rise in a warm, draft-free spot until the dough clears the top of the pans, about 2 to 4 hours.

3. Position the rack in the center of oven and preheat the oven to 350°F. Make a longitudinal slash down the center of each loaf with a single-edge razor blade or sharp knife and brush them with the remaining 2 tablespoons melted butter. Bake for about 35 to 40 minutes, or until the bread sounds hollow when thumped on the bottom. Turn the loaves out of the pans onto wire racks to cool.

Apple-Pecan Sticky Buns

You can certainly make sticky buns with any yeast dough, but the slow-rising characteristics of sourdough make it ideal for making them ahead; well covered, they go through a slow 24-hour rise in the refrigerator before baking. This calls for half the amount of Basic Sourdough Bread; I always make a full recipe, using half for a regular loaf of bread and the remaining half for these buns. If you are cooking for a crowd, of course, you can also double the recipe and use a full recipe of bread dough.

Makes 9 to 12 buns

¾ cup firmly packed light brown sugar

½ cup honey

2 ounces (¼ cup or ½ stick) unsalted butter

½ cup broken pecans

1 lemon

1 small, or ½ large, tart apple such as Winesap, Arkansas Black, or Granny Smith

Granulated sugar

2 pounds (½ recipe; about a 6-inch round lump) Basic Sourdough Bread dough (page 322)

1 teaspoon ground cinnamon

¼ cup finely chopped crystallized ginger

1. Butter a 9 × 9 × 2-inch baking pan or the wells of two six-well jumbo muffin pans. Combine the brown sugar, honey, and butter in a small saucepan over medium heat. Simmer 2 minutes and pour the mixture into the pan or divide it equally among the wells of the muffin pans. Sprinkle the nuts evenly over the syrup. Grate the zest from the lemon and then cut it in half. Peel, core, and cut the apple into quite small (¼-inch) dice. Put it into a bowl and squeeze the juice from half the lemon over it. Sprinkle with sugar and lightly toss until the apple dice are evenly coated.

2. Roll and stretch the dough on a lightly floured work surface into a 15 × 8-inch rec-

tangle. Sprinkle it with the cinnamon and lemon zest, then scatter the ginger and apple over it. Roll it up from one of the long sides like a jelly roll and with a sharp knife cut it into nine (or twelve, if making it in the muffin tins) equal slices. Put them spiral up into the prepared pan. Cover them with plastic wrap and let them rise until doubled, about 3 to 5 hours, depending on the warmth of the room, or cover well and refrigerate for up to 24 hours.

3. Position a rack in the center of the oven and preheat the oven to 375°F. Bake for about 25 minutes if using muffin tins or up to 35 minutes if making them in a square pan, until risen and golden brown. Remove the buns from the oven, carefully loosen any edges of the buns that may be sticking to the sides, and invert the pan over a flat platter, or baking sheet. Carefully lift the pan away from the buns. Spoon any pecan syrup mixture that runs to the sides back on top of the buns to evenly distribute it. Let stand until just warm and the syrup is set. Serve warm or at room temperature.

Postscript: The Art of Toasting

The magic of homemade bread is at its peak, of course, as it comes hot from the oven, its rich, heady fragrance filling the house and spilling outside, irresistibly drawing the family home. But that kind of magic can last for only a few minutes, and, while the bread may continue to deliciously satisfy for several days to come, it remains at optimum freshness for, at best, a week—most loaves, less than that. Fortunately, it is only when bread passes its prime that it becomes ideal for one of the most satisfying things in all of home baking and the best argument for the benefits of good homemade bread: toast.

Real toast is an event, a transcending moment when old bread is elevated into something that is equally as magical and satisfying as it had been when it was fresh from the oven. The art of making it well was once taken more seriously than it is today. Made by suspending the sliced bread on a toasting fork or rack before a blazing open fire, it took practiced skill and real finesse to get an even golden brown without scorching the edges or drying out the center. Moreover, toasting added the subtle yet enriching hint of hardwood smoke. Slathered with butter after the fact, or half-toasted, buttered, and then finished until the buttered side was a burnished gold, there could not be anything more satisfying at breakfast or teatime—or, for that matter, any time at all.

Automatic toasters often do the job adequately, but barely: they can be uneven, producing under-browned spots and scorched edges, and they have distinct limits. It is not possible, for example, to make that old-fashioned golden-crisp buttered toast just described, or that deeply satisfying childhood treat, cinnamon toast. And besides, it is the dull artlessness of popping regular slices of commercial bread into a machine that has made us lose that sense of wonder in a piece of perfectly toasted bread.

While it does not have the romance of an open-hearth and toasting fork, the oven broiler does a very good job of toasting. It will take more attention and skill than an automatic toaster, but its results are far more rewarding, and are well worth the extra effort you will put into rediscovering this almost forgotten art.

Position a rack about 6 inches below the oven broiler and preheat the broiling element for about 5 minutes. Slice any bread that is at least a day old to the thickness that you like (but not less than ⅜-inch) and arrange it on a baking sheet. Toast, watching it carefully, until the top is golden brown, about 2 to 3 minutes, depending on the heat of your broiler. Turn and toast until the second side is beginning to color.

There are now three ways of finishing the toast from here:

For dry toast, continue toasting until the top is evenly golden and serve piping hot with softened unsalted or lightly salted butter passed separately.

For old-fashioned buttered toast, remove it from the oven as the second side is just beginning to color, and spread softened unsalted butter thinly but evenly over the top surface (about half to one tablespoon per slice), or scatter the same amount of thinly sliced cold butter over the surface and broil until the butter begins to melt, then remove it and spread the butter evenly. Return it to the oven, buttered side up, and broil until the toast is colored a deep, rich gold—or to your taste—about 1 to 2 minutes longer.

To make that favorite childhood treat, cinnamon toast, spread the bread with butter as for buttered toast and, before returning it to the broiler, sprinkle it generously with cinnamon sugar (recipe follows) and broil until the sugar is caramelized and the edges of the toast are almost beginning to scorch.

Broiler toasting need not be confined to yeast loaf bread. All three variations spectacularly recycle day old biscuits and rolls (split them in half and toast only the split side) and restore new life to any pound cake that is beginning to go stale.

Still another wonderful and yet nearly forgotten way of toasting bread is in a skillet. Cast iron is ideal but heavy-bottomed coated aluminum will do the job. Preheat the pan over medium heat until it is evenly hot. Lightly spread the sliced bread on both sides with softened butter, and pan-broil, turning it occasionally, until it is uniformly golden and crisp on the surface, about 3 to 4 minutes per side.

Regardless of how you finish it, enjoy toast immediately, while it is still piping hot, and be warned: once you get used to having proper toast, your automatic toaster is likely to end up in a yard sale.

Cinnamon Sugar

Makes about 1 cup

About 1 cup granulated or superfine sugar
About 1 tablespoon ground cinnamon

1. Put 1 cup of sugar and 1 scant tablespoon of cinnamon in a clear glass jar or zipper-locking plastic bag. Seal and shake until the color is uniform. Taste and adjust the cinnamon, adding a little more cinnamon or cutting it with a tablespoon or so of sugar, depending on your taste. After a couple of batches, you'll know exactly how you like it.

2. Store the sugar in a dark cupboard either in the mixing jar or bag or, for convenient seasoning of toast, sweet fritters, pancakes, and even waffles, in a lidded shaker.

Bibliography and Reading List

Acton, Eliza. *Modern Cookery for Private Families.* London: Longman, Brown, Green and Longmans, 1845 and 1855. (Reprint, Lewis, England: Southover Press, 1993.)

Andrews, Mrs. Lewis R., and Mrs. J. Reanney Kelly, eds. *Maryland's Way: The Hammond-Harwood House Cook Book* (14th Edition, 1995). Annapolis, Md.: Hammond-Harwood House Association, 1963.

Aunt Julia's Cook Book. Esso Corporation, n.d., c. 1936.

Barker, Ben, and Karen Barker. *Not Afraid of Flavor.* Chapel Hill, N.C.: University of North Carolina Press, 1999.

Barker, Karen. *Sweet Stuff: Karen Barker's American Desserts.* Chapel Hill, N.C.: University of North Carolina Press, 2004.

Bremer, Mary Moore. *New Orleans Recipes.* New Orleans: General Printing, 1932. Referenced: 8th (1942) printing.

Bronz, Ruth Adams. *Miss Ruby's American Cooking.* New York: HarperCollins, 1989.

Brown, Marion, *Marion Brown's Southern Cook Book,* Chapel Hill, N.C.: University of North Carolina Press, 1951 (revised edition, 1968).

Brown, Theresa C. *Theresa C. Brown's Modern Domestic Cookery,* Edward Perry, Printer, Charleston, S.C., 1871. Facsimile Reprint, Williamston, S.C.: Pendleton District Historical and Recreational Commission, 1985.

Bryan, Lettice. *The Kentucky Housewife.* Cincinnati, Ohio: Shepard and Sterns, 1839. Facsimile reprint with introduction by Bill Neal, Columbia, S.C.: University of South Carolina Press, 1991.

Child, Julia. *From Julia Child's Kitchen.* New York: Alfred A. Knopf, 1982.

Child, Lydia Maria. *The American Frugal Housewife.* Boston: American Stationers' Company, 1836 (originally published 1829).

Christ Church Cook Book. Savannah: Women of Christ Episcopal Church, 1956.

Clark, Libby, ed., with Janet Cheatham Bell (food writer), and Jessica B. Harris (food consultant). *The Black Family Reunion Cook Book.* Tradey House, publishers, for the National Council of Negro Women, 1991.

Colquitt, Harriett Ross. *The Savannah Cook Book.* Charleston: Walker Evans & Cogswell, 1933.

The Congressional Cook Book. Washington, D.C.: Congressional Club, 1927, revised edition, 1933.

Corriher, Shirley. *Cookwise: The Hows & Whys of Successful Cooking.* New York: William Morrow, 1997.

Country Cooking from Tri-Cities. Hickory Grove, S.C.: Tri-City Jaycee-ettes, 1976.

Cox, Eugenia Barrs, ed. *Low Country Cooking: A Collection of Recipes from Liberty County and the Georgia Low Country.* Hinesville, Ga.: Liberty County Historical Society, 1988.

The Creole Cook Book. New Orleans: The New Orleans Picayune, 1900. Reprint, 2nd Edition, *The Picayune's Creole Cook Book,* with introduction and notes by Marcelle Bienvenu, New York: Random House, 1987.

Crump, Nancy Carter. "Foodways of the Albemarle Region." *Journal of Early Southern Decorative Arts,* Vol. XIX, No. 1, May 1993.

Darden, Norma Jean, and Carole Darden. *Spoonbread and Strawberry Wine.* New York: Fawcett Crest, 1978.

David, Elizabeth, American edition with Karen Hess, ed. *English Bread and Yeast Cookery.* New York: Viking Press, 1980.

DeBolt, Margaret Wayt, and Emma Rylander Law. *Savannah Sampler Cookbook.* West Chester, Pa.: Whitford Press, 1978.

———, Emma Rylander Law, and Carter Olive. *Georgia Entertains.* Nashville, Tenn.: Rutledge Hill Press, 1988 (originally published as *Georgia Sampler Cookbook,* 1983).

Deen, Paula H. *The Lady & Sons Just Desserts.* New York: Simon & Schuster, 2002.

Dull, Henrietta Stanley. *Southern Cooking.* Atlanta: Ruralist Press, 1928. Facsimile reprint, Atlanta: Cherokee Press, 1989.

Dupree, Nathalie. *Cooking of the South.* New York: Irena Chalmers Cookbooks, 1982.

————. *Nathalie Dupree's Southern Memories.* New York: Clarkson-Potter, 1993.

————. *New Southern Cooking.* New York: Alfred A. Knopf, 1986.

Edge, John T. *A Gracious Plenty.* New York: G. P. Putnam's Sons, 1999.

Edminston, Mrs. Jack R., and Mrs. James W. Heacock, Jr., eds. *When Dinnerbells Ring.* Talladega, Ala.: Talladega Junior Welfare League, 1978.

Edwards, Yvonne B. *Celebrating Our 70th Year: A Memorable Collection of Treasured Recipes.* Surry, Va.: S. Wallace Edwards and Sons, 1996.

Egerton, John, *Southern Food.* New York: Alfred A. Knopf, 1987.

The Ever Ready Cook Book. Savannah: Rector's Aid Society of St. John's Episcopal Church, N.D., but before 1915.

Favorite Recipes from Savannah Homes, Many Before Unpublished: A Collection of Well Tested and Practical Recipes. Savannah: Ladies of the Bishop Beckwith Society, 1904.

First Come, First Served . . . in Savannah. Savannah: Parent Teachers Organization of St. Andrew's School, 1999.

Fisher, Mrs. Abby. *What Mrs. Fisher Knows About Old Southern Cooking.* San Francisco: Women's Co-coperative Printing Office, 1881. Facsimile Reprint, Karen Hess, ed., Bedford, Mass.: Applewood Books, 1995.

Flexnor, Marion W. *Dixie Dishes.* Boston: Hale, Cushman & Flint, 1941.

Fox, Minnie C. *The Bluegrass Cook Book.* New York: Fox, Duffield, 1904.

From Savannah Kitchens. Savannah: Women of Christ Episcopal Church, 1959.

Garmey, Jane. *Great British Cooking: A Well Kept Secret.* New York: Random House, 1981.

Glenn, Camille. *The Heritage of Southern Cooking.* New York: Workman, 1986.

Gordon, Eleanor Kinzie (Mrs. William W.). Household Notebook, c. 1858–1910 (Collection of the Juliette Gordon Low Birthplace, Girl Scouts of America).

Hale, Sarah Josepha. *The Good Housekeeper.* 6th Edition. Boston: Otis, Broaders, 1841. Facsimile Reprint, with introduction by Jan B. Longone, New York: Dover Publications, 1996.

Harper, Pat, ed., with Elaine Simmons. *Savannah Style.* Savannah: Junior League of Savannah, 1980.

Harris, Jessica B. *Iron Pots and Wooden Spoons.* New York: Athenaeum, 1989.

————. *The Welcome Table.* New York: Simon & Schuster, 1995.

Hartley, Grace. *Grace Hartley's Southern Cookbook.* New York: Galahad Books, 1985.

Harvey, Ann H., executive ed., *Southern Living. The Southern Heritage Cook Book Library.* Birmingham, Ala.: Oxmoor House, 1985.

Heritage Receipts from St. John's. Savannah: Episcopal Church Women, St. John's Church, n.d. (c. 1978).

Hess, Karen. *The Carolina Rice Kitchen.* Columbia, S.C.: University of South Carolina Press, 1992, including in facsimile the *Carolina Rice Cook Book.*

Hickory Grove Centennial Favorites. Hickory Grove, S.C.: Tri-City Women's League, 1988.

Hill, Annabella P. *Mrs. Hill's New Cook Book.* New York: James O'Kane, 1867. Facsimile Reprint, Damon L. Fowler, ed., *Mrs. Hill's Southern Practical Cookery and Receipt Book.* Columbia, S.C.: University of South Carolina Press, 1995.

Horry, Harriott Pinckney. Household notebook, 1770–1819. Transcription with historical notes by Richard J. Hooker, *A Colonial Plantation Cookbook: The Receipt Book of Harriott Pinckney Horry, 1770.* Columbia, S.C.: University of South Carolina Press, 1984.

The Housekeeper's Friend. Fincastle, Virginia: Ladies' Aid Society of the First Presbyterian Church of Fincastle, 1896.

The Housewife's Friend. Knoxville, Tenn.: Ladies Aid Society of Trinity Methodist Episcopal Church, 1926.

Huguenin, Mary Vereen, and Anne Montague Stoney, eds. *Charleston Receipts.* Charleston: Walker, Evans & Cogswell, Junior League of Charleston, 1950.

Hunter, Ethel Farmer. *Secrets of Southern Cooking.* New York: Tudor, 1956.

Jamison, Cheryl Alters, and Bill Jamison. *American Home Cooking.* New York: Broadway Books, 1999.

Leslie, Eliza. *Miss Leslie's New Cookery Book.* Philadelphia: T. B. Peterson and Brothers, 1857.

———. *Seventy-Five Receipts for Pastry, Cakes, and Sweetmeats By A Lady of Philadelphia.* Boston: Monroe and Francis, 1828.

Lewis, Edna. *In Pursuit of Flavor.* New York: Alfred A. Knopf, 1988.

———. *The Taste of Country Cooking.* New York: Alfred A. Knopf, 1978.

———, and Scott Peacock. *The Gift of Southern Cooking.* New York: Alfred A. Knopf, 2003.

Lincoln, Mrs. D. A. (Mary J.). *Mrs. Lincoln's Boston Cook Book.* Boston: Roberts Brothers,

1887. Reprint, as *The Boston Cooking School Cook Book,* New York: Dover Publications, 1996.

Lundy, Ronni. *Shuck Beans, Stack Cakes, and Honest Fried Chicken.* New York: Atlantic Monthly Press, 1991.

Lustig, Lillie S., ed., with S. Claire Sondheim and Sarah Russel. *The Southern Cook Book of Fine Old Recipes.* Asheville, N.C.: Three Mountaineers, 1938.

Manning, Mrs. Stephen C. Manuscript receipt book. Private collection. New Orleans: C. 1890–1910.

McCoin, Choice, ed. *300 Years of Carolina Cooking.* Greenville, S.C.: Junior League of Greenville, 1970.

McColloch-Williams, Martha. *Dishes and Beverages of the Old South.* McBride, Nast New York, 1913. Facsimile with introduction by John Egerton, Nashville, Tenn.: University of Tennessee Press, 1988.

McRee, Patsy. *The Kitchen and the Cotton Patch.* Anniston, Ala.: Higginbotham, 1982 (10th printing; First Edition, 1948).

Meldrim, Frances Casey (Mrs. Peter W.), and Sophie Meldrim Shonnard. Household notebook, private collection, Savannah, Georgia, 1890–1945.

Metter, Maude. *A Virginia Ham Cookbook.* Williamsburg, Va.: Old Chickahominy House Restaurant, n.d.

Mitchell, Patricia B. *Soul on Rice: African Influences on American cooking.* Macon, Ga.: Tubman African American Museum, 1993.

Mountain Elegance. Asheville, N.C.: Junior League of Asheville, 1982.

Neal, Moreton. *Remembering Bill Neal.* Chapel Hill, N.C.: University of North Carolina Press, 2004.

Neal, William F. *Bill Neal's Southern Cooking.* Revised Edition. Chapel Hill, N.C.: University of North Carolina Press, 1989.

Neal, William F. (Bill). *Biscuits, Spoonbread, and Sweet Potato Pie.* New York: Alfred A. Knopf, 1990.

Nesbit, Martha Giddens. *Savannah Collection.* Orlando, Fla.: Noran Printing, 1986.
———. *Savannah Entertains.* Charleston, S.C.: Wyrick, 1996.

Osteen, Louis. *Louis Osteen's Charleston Cuisine.* Chapel Hill: Algonquin Books, 1999.

Parloa, Maria. *Miss Parloa's New Cook Book.* Boston: Estes & Lauriat, 1885 (First Edition: 1880).

Patent, Greg. *Baking in America.* New York: Houghton Mifflin, 2002.

Prudhomme, Paul. *Chef Paul Prudhomme's Louisiana Kitchen.* New York: William Morrow, 1984.

The Quaker Cook Book. High Point, N.C.: Women's Auxiliary of High Point Friends Meeting, 1954.

The Queen of the Kitchen: A Collection of Old Maryland Receipts for Cooking, from a Receipt Book Used for Many Years. Baltimore, Md.: Lucas Brothers, 1870.

Ragan, Bill. *The Georgia Cookbook.* 3rd edition, Milledgeville, Ga.: Prestwood Graphics, 1993.

Randolph, Mary. *The Virginia House-wife.* Washington, D.C.: Davis and Forth, 1824. Revised and enlarged editions, 1825 and 1828; facsimile reprint, Karen Hess, ed. Columbia, S.C.: University of South Carolina Press, 1984.

Rankin, Jane Lee. *Cookin' Up a Storm: The Life and Recipes of Annie Johnson.* New York: Grace, 1998.

Ravenel, Rose P., and Elizabeth Ravenel Harrigan, ed. *Charleston Recollections and Receipts: Rose P. Ravenel's Cookbook.* Columbia, S.C.: University of South Carolina Press, 1983.

Rawlings, Marjorie Kinnan. *Cross Creek Cookery.* New York: Charles Scribner's Sons, 1942.

Reid, Catha W., and Joseph T. Bruce, Jr. *The Sandlapper Cookbook.* Lexington, S.C.: Sandlapper Press, 1973.

Rhett, Blanche S., with Lettie Gay and Helen Woodward. *Two Hundred Years of Charleston Cooking.* Facsimile, Columbia, S.C.: University of South Carolina Press, 1976 (First Edition, 1930).

Rudisill, Marie. *Sook's Cookbook.* Atlanta: Longstreet Press, 1989.

Rutledge, Sarah. *The Carolina Housewife, or House and Home.* Charleston, S.C.: W. R. Babcock, 1847. Facsimile reprint, with introduction by Anna Welles Rutledge, Columbia, S.C.: University of South Carolina Press, 1979.

Sanders, Dori. *Dori Sanders' Country Cooking.* Chapel Hill, N.C.: Algonquin Books, 1995.

The Savannah Cook Book. Savannah: Ladies of Westminster Presbyterian Church, 1909. (Not to be confused with the Colquitt book of 1933.)

The Shadows-on-The-Teche Cookbook. Huntsville, Ala.: Shadows Service League, 1982.

Simmons, Amelia. *American Cookery.* Hartford, Conn.: Hudson and Goodwin, 1796. Facsimile, with Foreword by Mary Tolford Wilson, by Oxford University Press, 1958; Facsimile reprint, as *The First American Cookbook.* Boston: Dover Publications, 1984.

Smart-Grosvenor, Vertamae. ‡*Vibration Cooking, Or Travel Notes of a Geechee Girl,* 3rd edition. New York: Ballantine Books, 1992.

Smith, E[liza ?]. *The Compleat Housewife: or, Accomplsh'd Gentlewoman's Companion.* London: R. Ware, et al., 1727. Referenced: 15th (1753) Edition.

Smokey Mountain Magic. Johnson City, Tenn.: Junior League of Johnson City, 1960.

Stamps, Martha Phelps. *The New Southern Basics.* Nashville, Tenn.: Cumberland House/Hearthside Books, 1997.

Starr, Kathy. *The Soul of Southern Cooking.* Oxford, Miss.: University Press of Mississippi, 1989. Reprint, Montgomery: NewSouth Books, 2001.

Stoney, Louisa Cheves Smythe, ed. *Carolina Rice Cook Book.* Charleston, S.C.: Lucas-Richardson, 1901. Facsimile by University of South Carolina Press: *see* Hess, Karen.

Taylor, John Martin. *Hoppin' John's Charleston, Beaufort and Savannah: Dining at Home in the Lowcountry.* New York: Clarkson-Potter, 1997.

———. *Hoppin' John's Lowcountry Cooking.* New York: Bantam Books, 1993.

———. *The New Southern Cook.* New York: Bantam, 1995.

Taylor, (Hoppin') John Martin. *The Fearless Frying Cookbook.* New York: Workman, 1997.

Terry, Elizabeth. *Savannah Seasons.* New York: Doubleday, 1996.

Texas Cook Book. Houston: Ladies Association of First Presbyterian Church, 1883. Facsimile reprint, with introduction by David Wade and Mary Faulk Kooch. *The First Texas Cook Book.* Austin, Tex.: Eakin Publications, 1986.

Thompson, Lois, and V. V. (Pete) Thompson, eds. *Authentic Southern Recipes from the Colonial Inn.* Hillsborough, N.C.: Colonial Inn, 1972.

Thornton, Phineas. *The Southern Gardener and Receipt Book.* 2nd Edition. Newark: A. L. Dennis, 1845. First Edition, 1840.

Tucker, Martha Goode. Household notebook, c. 1855–68. Transcription, *Housekeeping Diary of an Antebellum Lady.* Milledgeville, Ga.: Milledgeville Town Committee, National Society of the Colonial Dames of America, 1990.

Tyree, Marion Cabell, ed. *Housekeeping in Old Virginia.* Louisville: John P. Morton, 1879.

Verstille, Mrs. Ellen J. *Verstille's Southern Cookery.* New York: Owens & Agar, 1866.

Villas, James, and Martha Pearl Villas. *My Mother's Southern Kitchen.* New York: William Morrow, 1994.

———. *My Mother's Southern Desserts.* New York: William Morrow, 1998.

Voltz, Jeanne, and Caroline Stuart. *The Florida Cookbook.* New York: Alfred A. Knopf, 1995.

Walter, Eugene. *Delectable Dishes from Termite Hall.* New York: Madaloni Press, 1982. Reprint, Townsend, Ga.: Books on the Bluff/The Book Shop, 2001.

Waring, Mary Joseph. *The Centennial Receipt Book.* Anonymously published as "by a Southern Lady" (Charleston ?), 1876.

Warren, Mildred Evans. *The Art of Southern Cooking.* Garden City, N.Y.: Doubleday, 1967.

Wilkes, Sema Americus, with Introduction by John T. Edge. *Mrs. Wilkes' Boardinghouse Cookbook.* Berkeley, Calif.: Ten Speed Press/Design Press, 2001.

Wilson, Mrs. Henry Lumnpkin Wilson, ed. *Tested Recipe Cook Book.* Atlanta: Foote and Davies, 1895. Facsimile, with introduction by Darlene Roth, *Atlanta Exposition Cookbook.* Athens, Ga.: Brown Thrasher Books, 1984.

Wilson, Justin. *Louisiana Home Grown.* New York: MacMillan, 1990.

———. *The Justin Wilson Cook Book.* Gretna, La.: Pelican, 1976 (originally published 1965).

Ye Old Time Salzburger Cook Book. Ebenezer, Ga.: Georgia Salzburger Society, n.d.

Metric Equivalencies

LIQUID AND DRY MEASURE EQUIVALENCIES

Customary	Metric
¼ teaspoon	1.25 milliliters
½ teaspoon	2.5 milliliters
1 teaspoon	5 milliliters
1 tablespoon	15 milliliters
1 fluid ounce	30 milliliters
¼ cup	60 milliliters
⅓ cup	80 milliliters
½ cup	120 milliliters
1 cup	240 milliliters
1 pint (2 cups)	480 milliliters
1 quart (4 cups)	960 milliliters (.96 liter)
1 gallon (4 quarts)	3.84 liters
1 ounce (by weight)	28 grams
¼ pound (4 ounces)	114 grams
1 pound (16 ounces)	454 grams
2.2 pounds	1 kilogram (1000 grams)

OVEN-TEMPERATURE EQUIVALENCIES

Description	°Fahrenheit	°Celcius
Cool	200	90
Very slow	250	120
Slow	300–325	150–160
Moderately slow	325–350	160–180
Moderate	350–375	180–190
Moderately hot	375–400	190–200
Hot	400–450	200–230
Very hot	450–500	230–260

Index

folding, technique for, 154–55

food processor, kneading in, 295

Fowler, Granny, 180

French baking, influence of, 3

French Creole baguettes, 299–300

French rolls, 308–9

fresh raspberry bourbon sauce, 218–19

fresh summer fruit kuchen or custard tart, 225–26

fresh yeast, compressed, 288–89

fried breads, *see* griddled and fried baking

Fritschner, Sarah, 233

fritters:

    bell (beignets), 108

    Carolina rice jam, 105–6

    savory rice (rice pups), 99–100

    souffléed (Creole *pets-de-nonne*), 107–8

frostings, *see* icings

fruitcakes:

    applesauce raisin pound cake, 166–67

    Aunt Margaret's fresh apple pound cake, 168–69

fruit custards, 227

fruit pies, fried, 109–10

fruits:

    in chess pies, 219

    dried, 189

    fresh summer, kuchen or custard tart, 225–26

    summer cobbler, 271–73

frying thermometer, 69

fudge:

    brown velvet cake with dark frosting, 186–87

    chocolate chess pie, 221–22

    old-fashioned dark frosting, 197

German baking, influence of, 3

Gift of Southern Cooking, The (Lewis and Peacock), 95

ginger:

    apple custard tart, 227–28

    -lemon-scented benne wafers, 140–41

    peach tart, 255–56

    peach upside-down cake, 193–94

    pear custard tart, 228

    and rosemary-scented fried apple pies, 109–10

gingerroot, 24

glaze, lemon sugar, 172–73

gluten, 32

golden bourbon pecan tassies, 235–36

golden cheddar biscuit crust, with creamy chicken potpies, 279–81

goose and duck fat, 23

grains, sources, 11–12

granulated sugar, 13

Greek baking, influence of, 3

green tomato pie, 257–58

griddled and fried baking, 68–112

    batty or corn griddlecakes, 81–82

    beignets (bell fritters), 108

Carolina rice jam fritters, 105–6

chicken (or skillet) biscuits, 97–98

chicken mushroom puffs, 111–12

classic Creole calas, 101–2

Creole *pets-de-nonne* (souffléed fritters), 107–8

equipment for, 69

flannel cakes, 77–78

fried peach pies with orange, 110

hominy griddles, 87–88

hot water cornbread, 83

hush puppies, 95–96

Joan's water cornbread, 84

Mrs. Hill's crumpets, 75–76

Mrs. Randolph's "quire of paper pancakes," 79–80

muffins, 71–72

muffin tips, 74

quick calas, 103–4

rice griddles, 89–90

rice pups, or savory rice fritters, 99–100

rosemary- and ginger-scented fried apple pies, 109–10

Savannah rice waffles, 91–92

sourdough muffins, 73–74

sweet potato griddlecakes, 85–86

sweet potato waffles, 93–94

waffle wisdom, 92

yeast-raised waffles, 78

grits:

    how to cook, 66

    leftover, in hominy griddles, 87–88